W9-CUK-080

To my husband Paul and his parents
Rose & Ted Hirschberg for their inspiration
and encouragement

TABLE OF CONTENTS

INTRODUCTION

The publication of this, the Fourth Edition, culminates
four years of additions and improvements to the text. It is
also very gratifying to us to have received so much positive
response from Editions 1 thru 3.

The original idea of this book developed from a course
Rita was giving in San Francisco on Chinese characters. Her
students of the written language, after mastering their first
characters, soon found a need for a reference book that
serves the purpose of a dictionary. However, as you may have
already found, the Chinese dictionary contains too much
information for the beginning and intermediate student. A
good Chinese dictionary will contain 10,000 or more characters whereas only about 3000 are commonly used. In fact, in
a study done by Chen Hegin, it was found that if you were to
learn the 1400 characters which appear most frequently in
Chinese publications, you would know about 94% of the characters you will ever see in these publications. Learning 2800
characters would give you about 98% comprehension, with the
remaining 2% provided by the other 7000 characters in the
dictionary. What happens is that it is difficult to find
anything in the dictionary. It is the purpose of this book
to provide a handy reference by limiting the contents to the
approximately 2900 most popular words. In addition, by
grouping them by radicals, the learning of new words becomes
much easier; it is reduced to a matter of putting familiar
pieces together, that is, combining radicals already known
to form new characters.

Another feature of the book is that it is practically
unique in giving both Mandarin and Cantonese pronounciations.
In the fourth edition we have adopted the Yale romanization

for Cantonese for the benefit of those familiar with this
popular Cantonese romanization system. The Mandarin pronounciation is given in both Yale and Pinyin systems. We have
caught and corrected hopefully all of the errors of Edition
3; the index and radical chart have also been improved.

With that aside, we want to convey a more important
thought. It is that Chinese is the richest and possibly
most beautiful language in the world. In pursuing your
interest in the language, you will begin to discover the
wisdom of centuries, the heritage of many generations. If
this book can help you on your way, then we have all the
satisfaction we need. Good Luck!

Rita Choy Hirschberg
Paul Hirschberg

San Francisco   1981

CHINESE CHARACTERS

Development of the Characters

Unlike Western languages, Chinese does not have an alphabet, per se. Each "letter", or character, represents a whole word. Very often two or three characters are used together for non-basic words. Actually, each character is really a picture; many characters have been traced back to very basic picture forms. The primitive shapes of these characters have evolved over a long period of time. Their forms have changed due to technical developments in writing implements. But basically they are just drawings of objects, animals, nature, and the human experience. For example, let us look at some characters:

Early Form	Meaning	Modern Form
	eye	目
	sun	日
	water	水
	hill	山
	door	門
	car	車
	moon	月

Some of these characters still resemble their meanings; others have changed beyond recognition. Most characters are composed of combinations of basic characters like these.

The Chinese language has over forty thousand characters. Many of these are formal, literary words that are seldom used and are only found in operas, ancient books, poems, and on paintings. A Chinese typewriter will usually carry about seven thousand, of which about twenty-five hundred are sufficient for everyday communication. This book contains approximately twenty-nine hundred of the most commonly used characters.

Radicals - The Roots of Chinese

We mentioned earlier that most characters are composed of combinations of basic characters. For example, the word for "good" is written"

好   hóu   hǎu

But really, the two halves of this word are actually words by themselves:

女   means woman   néui   nyǔ
子   means son, male   jí   dz

Another example is the word for "clear":

明   mìhng   míng

The two halves mean:

日   sun   yaht   r̀
月   moon   yuht   ywè

These halves are elements called radicals. Strictly

- 8 -

speaking, there is only one radical per word, which is the
element which is the most important, and by which the word
may be found in a dictionary. Characters that have the radical 亻, which means man, will have something to do with
humans. Characters with 木 radicals (wood) will be in some
way related to wood, and so forth. Sometimes a radical will
be present in a word for its sound; that is, the meaning of
the character may have nothing to do with the meaning of the
radical; however, the pronounciation of the character might
be the same or similar to that of the radical.

When two or more radicals are combined to form a word
they are reduced in size to form a character of equal size,
i.e.

| 人 | man | yàhn | rén |
| 你 | you | néih | nǐ |

Sometimes the radicals change shape when they appear in
certain positions in a character. For example, "man" is
normally written 人 . When it appears on the left side of
a character it is written 亻 . "Heart" is normally written
心 . When appearing on the left side in a word it is
written 忄 . Here are some more examples:

Original Radical	Alternate Form	Definition
人	亻	man
刀	刂	knife
已	卩	seal
土	土	earth
女	女	female
子	孑	son

- 9 -

Original Radical	Alternate Form	Definition
巛	川	stream
心	忄	heart
手	扌	hand
木	木	wood
水	氵	water
火	灬	fire*
爪	爫	claws
牛	牜	ox
犬	犭	dog
玉	王	jade
目	罒	eye
示	礻	reveal
禾	禾	grain
竹	𥫗	bamboo
糸	糸	silk
雨	雨	rain
肉	月	flesh
艸	艹	grass
衣	衤	clothes
足	𧾷	foot
辵	辶	travel
邑	阝	city
阜	阝	mound

* Either 火 or 灬 may appear at the bottom of a character.

Most of these changes occur when the radical is to one side of the character. Wherever the radical appears it will widen or lengthen to fit the shape of the character.

There are two reasons why radicals are important. The first is that most dictionaries list their words according to radicals. After all, since there is no such thing as an "alphabetical order" in Chinese, there must be some way to be able to look up words. You must eventually be able to determine which is the radical of the word you want to look up. More on dictionaries and how to determine the radical will follow.

The second reason radicals are important is that knowing them makes it far easier to learn and remember new characters. In fact, it is almost impossible to remember how to write by memorizing all the strokes; it is much easier to say "man + mouth + bird" etc. Your becoming aware of radicals will be a short cut to your learning many more new words.

Notes on Character Meanings

When two or more characters are combined, they will sometimes emphasize the meaning of one or two of the words, or they may mean something else. For example:

Character	Definition
朋	companion
友	friend
朋友	friend
大	large
家	family
大家	all of them(people)

Combining characters often forms idioms:

Character	Definition
天	sky
下	under
一	one
家	family
天下	the world
天下一家	everyone in the world should treat each other as if all belonging to a big family

An adjective character duplicated emphasizes the meaning:

Character	Definition	Character	Definition
好	good	好好	very good
快	quick	快快	hurry

Antonyms put together form a noun:

Character	Definition	Character	Definition
大	big	大小	size
小	small		
快	fast	快慢	speed
慢	slow		

Nouns repeated means "all of" that noun. For example:

Character	Definition
人人	all people, everybody
次次	all the time, every time
個個	all, every one

Many words are formed by two or more characters. Examples of these compound words are:

Character	Definition
已經	already
所以	therefore
除非	unless
生意	business
出世	to be born
打理	look after

These words must be learned as pairs.

Calligraphy

Calligraphy, or beautiful writing, is very important in Chinese. As in any other language, there are simpler words and there are longer and more difficult ones. In Chinese, no matter how simple or complicated the characters may look, there is a pattern to follow to correctly write them. It is a basic pattern which can be applied to any character. Chiese stresses beauty and balance in each character. If the correct stroke order is not followed, the character will look lopsided.

Characters should be written from top to bottom and from left to right. For example:

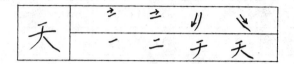

If any strokes are to be enclosed in a box they should be written before the box is closed. For example:

日	correct	❘	⼎	冃	日
	incorrect	❘	冂	口	日

One exception to the pattern is the radical 辵 , which is written as ⻌ . Although ⻌ comes first in the character, the inside part is written first before closing with ⻌ . For example:

近	correct	⼃	⼁	⼁	⼁	⼁	沂	近
	incorrect	⼂	⼁	⼁	⼁	⼁	沂	近

There are eight basic strokes. They are:

Stroke	⼂	⼀	❘	⼅	⼀	⼃	⼃	⼂
Example	永	大	中	永	永	永	永	永

When writing with a brush, the calligrapher will put emphasis on certain parts of the stroke:

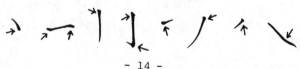

- 14 -

The arrows above show places where, for each type of stroke, the calligrapher should increase pressure in the brush to make the points heavier and darker. Similarly, the arrows below show the places in each stroke where thin, sharp points should be left:

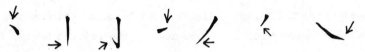

This alternating of heavy and light is the way a good calligrapher transmits his strength from the brush to the paper. It is one reason for the beauty of Chinese characters.

Good calligraphy comes with practice as does any other skill. To practice Chinese calligraphy, specially designed paper that has nine small boxes in each large square (called "nine square box" paper) is used to aid in the imitation of printed samples of good calligraphy.

Variations in Forms

In mainland China there is a trend today toward the simplification of characters. Many words already have a simplified form in use, with others being introduced daily. An example is the word for "side.

Long
Form   Simplified
Form

To give all the simplified characters is beyond the

scope of this book; there are whole dictionaries devoted to this subject. The simplified forms are not being used in Taiwan, and only some of them are being used in the United States.

There are actually six different forms of each Chinese character. The first is the printed "Square", also known as the Sung Dynasty form. The second is the printed Script form, which is the one used in the character charts in this book. The third is handwritten Script. The fourth, which is called Grass, is a more free-flowing and less recognizable hand-written script. The fifth style is used in large banners, and the sixth is Seal style, used in making seals for a person's signature. Examples of these styles for the character 張 illustrate the differences:

Square	張
Printed Script	張
Handwritten Script	张
Grass	怅
Banner	張
Seal	𤲃

Sometimes there will be a variation between printed forms of characters. For example, the word for "for" can be found either as 為 or 為. Both forms are correct.

Layout of Books

Chinese text is usually laid out vertically from top to bottom, with lines progressing from right to left.

Chinese books are therefore read, from the Western point
of view, from back to front. However, in Western countries,
to conform to what is familiar, often characters will be
printed horizontally from left to right.

The Dictionary

There are several types of Chinese dictionaries avail-
able. There are of course English to Chinese, Chinese to
English, and Chinese to Chinese dictionaries. There is a
Chinese phonetic alphabet and a dictionary for going from
pronounciation to character. There are also specialized
dictionaries, such as for simplified characters, or for al-
ternate forms. It is not recommended that the beginning
student use a Chinese dictionary because a good dictionary
will have many more characters than are needed, which makes
it difficult to find basic words. This book will be more
useful. In addition, this book tells how to pronounce the
word in Cantonese, which most dictionaries do not. In any
case, when you do want to use a dictionary, you will need to
know how to look up words. After all, there is no alphabet
in Chinese. There are two systems used by dictionaries for
listing words. The first is by radical and the second is
the "Bing" 5-stroke system.

The "Bing" system is a newer system, not yet popular,
and is only used in a few dictionaries. To look up a character under this system you must first determine which stroke
of the character is written first. You turn to this section
and determine which is the second stroke, turn to that sub-
section, then count the remaining number of strokes. The
words will be listed in ascending order of the number of
strokes. The reason it is called "Bing" is because there is
a character pronounced *bing* that has one of every type of
stroke:

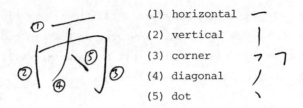

(1) horizontal —
(2) vertical |
(3) corner ㄱ ㄱ
(4) diagonal ノ
(5) dot ╲

This system has the advantage that it is easier to determine the stroke order of a character than its radical.

The radical system, used in most dictionaries and in this book, requires you to determine the radical of the word. To do this, break the character up into its parts:

(1) 想 ⇒ 噐   (3) 姐 ⇒ 口口
(2) 但 ⇒ 唱   (4) 台 ⇒ 吕

There are endless rules and endless exceptions for determining the radical. However, here a few rules that work almost always:

In case (1), the larger portion, the bottom half, will be the radical.

In case (2), the larger portion, the left half, will be the radical.

In case (3), if there are equal size parts, the one on the left is usually the radical.

In case (4), the part which is the more common will be the radical.

Now the exceptions to the rules. Certain very common elements, when present in a character, will almost always be the radical of the word. These are:

亻 口 忄 (忄) 辶 刀 (刂) 木 氵 門

Thus, the radical of 台 is 口 ; the radical of 想 is 心 ; the radical of 划 is 刂 . Here are some more examples:

- 18 -

Word	Radical
明	日
這	辶
男	田
所	戶
信	亻

    The fifty most common radicals are indicated by a star
(*) in the Table of Radicals.

    Because there are many words where it is not at all ob-
vious which is the radical, many dictionaries provide a glossary that tells what the radical is. If all else fails you
can still look up every element in the character. Once you
have the radical, count the number of strokes in it and con-
sult the radical chart at this number and find the radical
with a page number. All words having this radical will be
grouped in the same section at this page number. Then, count
the number of strokes remaining in the character and refer to
the page having that number to find the character.

HOW TO USE THIS BOOK

This book can be used both as a glossary and as an aid
to the learning of new characters. The characters are arranged
according to the number of strokes in the radical. Within each
radical section the characters are listed in order of the number of strokes of the character. So, to find a word, determine the radical as described in the previous section on dictionaries. Refer to the radical index for the page number of
that section. The top of each page tells the radical section
and the numbers in parenthesis give the range of number of
strokes of the words listed on that page.

For each character listed, the following information is
given:

Char.	Stroke Order	English Definitions *Cantonese* *Yale Mand.* *Pinyin Mand.*

The box to the right of the character shows the correct
stroke order for writing. The next box to the right gives
(a) one or two English definitions (b) Cantonese pronounciation in the Yale system, and (c) Mandarin pronounciation in
the Yale and Pinyin systems. An explanation of these systems
as well as a comparison chart between Yale, Pinyin, Wade-
Giles and the CNPA is given in the next section.

To find a word from the English meaning, refer to the
index at the back of the book. Sometimes more than one page
number is given; refer to all of these as different characters are often used to differentiate fine shades of meaning.

The best way to learn characters from this book is to
become aware of radicals and how they are combined to form

new words. Write each new word at least ten times - this
will help you to remember it. Say the word out loud, using
the pronounciation and tone charts - this will also aid your
memory. It is suggested to study no more than ten words a
day. Each day, review all the words studied in the previous
days. After a while try to pick up some Chinese materials
such as menus or newspapers. These will be difficult at
first and even after learning a good number of the characters
in this book may still be hard to understand. The reason for
this is that for total comprehension, a familiarity with the
grammar and idiomatic expressions of Mandarin is needed.
However, using this book will give you a very good idea of
the nature of the subject matter. The book in conjunction
with a first year course in Mandarin would be ideal.

GUIDE TO PRONOUNCIATION

The Dialects

The Chinese language has over fifty different dialects. This has resulted from the lack of communication between different parts of China which existed for many centuries. In fact, in the old days most Chinese lived their whole life without leaving their home county - as a result almost every county has a different speaking dialect. Today, there are two major dialects in Chinese: Mandarin and Cantonese. However, they are different enough that speakers of the two dialects cannot understand each other. To solve this problem, the government in Mainland China declared Mandarin the official language of China, requiring everyone to learn it. Mandarin is also spoken in Taiwan. Cantonese is still spoken in the Canton Province. In addition, it is the language of Hong Kong, Macau, Singapore, and is spoken by the vast majority of Chinese living in the United States, Canada, Great Britain, Viet Nam, Thailand and Malaysia. There are even sub-dialects of Cantonese such as Taishanese. Taishanese is part of the "*sei-yàp*"(four counties) whereas the Hong Kong dialect can also be called "*sàam-yàp*"(three counties). Other important dialects include Shanghainese, Fukkein, Mongolian, Junshai and others. However, although there are over fifty different dialects the written language is common to all of them. Therefore, a man in Peking can read the same newspaper as a man living in Hong Kong. Thus, if spoken language fails to communicate an idea, writing can always be used.

The written language is patterned after Mandarin. All words in Mandarin can be written out but not all words in Cantonese can be written. Therefore some characters have been created. Examples of these are:

Word	Cantonese	Definition
咗	jó	past tense
冇	móuh	none
係	haih	is
嘅	ge	possessive suffix
唔	m̀h	not
哋	deih	plural
啱	ngàam	correct
咁	gám	so
乜	màt	what
嘢	yéh	thing

They are mostly made up phonetically. Some phrases are
formed by combining existing words with these artificial
ones, such as:

Word	Cantonese	Definition
冇得頂	móuh dàk díng	incredible
唔抵得	m̀h dái dàk	cannot stand it
你開胃	néih hòi waih	you think it is so easy for you

Romanization Systems

This section explains the methods of romanization used
in this book. In an effort to give the Westerner an idea of

- 24 -

the correct pronounciation of Chinese, several romanization systems were developed, each with its own merits. For Cantonese, probably the best and most universally used is the Yale system. This system is used in this book with a few minor improvements. In Mandarin, the Yale system is also popular. However, with the recent adoption of Pinyin as the official romanization system of China, this system is becoming popular in the U.S. Both systems are used in this book. In addition, a comparative chart between Yale, Pinyin, Wade-Giles and the CNPA(Chinese National Phonetic Alphabet) is given. It will be well worth your while to study the tone and pronounciation charts. Practicing reading the words out loud is most beneficial.

The following charts are presented:

1. Cantonese: Yale to English

Initials	As in English
f,h,k,kw,l, m,n,p,s,t,w,y	same as English
b	b in bill
ch	between *ts* and *ch*
d	t in stale
g	k in skill
gw	qu in squat
j	between *j* and *ds* in odds
ng	ng in king

Finals

Short	Long	As in English	
a		a	in father
ai	aai	ai	in eye
ak	aak	ock	in lock
am	aam	om	in bomb
an	aan	on	in gone
ang	aang	ong	in gong
ap	aap	op	in operate
at	aat	ot	in cot
au	aau	ow	in how
e		ea	in measure
ei		ay	in bay
ek		eck	in neck
eng		eng	in Engels
eu		o	in work (ə)
eui		o	in work + e in seen
euk		ork	in work - r
eun		o	in work + n
eung		o	in work + ng in king
eut		o	in work + t

Finals

Short	Long	As in English
i	*e*	in seen
ik	*ick*	in lick
im	*eem*	in seem
in	*in*	in seen
ing	*ing*	in single
ip	*eep*	in weep
it	eat	
iu	you	
o	*aw*	in crawl
oi	*oy*	in boy
ok	*alk*	in talk
on	*awn*	in awning
ong	*ong*	in long
ot	ought	
ou	*o*	in tow
u	you	
ui	*ooey*	in phooey
uk	*uke*	in duke
un	*une*	in tune
ung	*oon*	in soon + *g*
ut	*oot*	in boot
yu	you	
yun	*y* + *une*	in tune
yut	you + *t*	

Note that for the three low tones, an *h* is added after the last vowel in the Final (see tone chart).

2. Cantonese: Tones

The system presented in this book is a "modified-Yale" system. It uses six tones, instead of Yale's seven, com-

- 27 -

bining the high level tone with the high falling, as these
are virtually indistinguishable. An *h* after the last vowel
in a Final denotes the lower tones. Although Yale does not
use the *h* for words beginning with *m, n,* or *ng,* for sim-
plicity this book will use the *h* with all initials.

Name of Tone	Symbol	*Pitch Diagram	Example
High Falling	\	5 4 3 2 1	分 *fàn*
High Rising	/	5 4 3 2 1	粉 *fán*
Middle Level	None	5 4 3 2 1	訓 *fan*
Low Falling	`\h`	5 4 3 2 1	焚 *fàhn*
Low Rising	`/h`	5 4 3 2 1	憤 *fáhn*
Low Level	(None) *h*	5 4 3 2 1	份 *fahn*

* 5 - highest pitch

3. Mandarin: Yale to English

Initials

Yale	As in English
b,ch,d,f,g,h, j,k,l,m,n,p, r,sh,t,w,y	same as English
dz	add d to z
sy	add s to y
sz	z in zoo
ts	add t to s

Finals

Yale	As in English	
(y)i	ea	in tea
(w)u	oo	in cool
(y)u	e	in she
a	a	in father
ai	i	in rise
an	on	in honest
ang	own	in gown
au	ow	in cow
e (ye)	ea	in pleasure
ei	ay	in pay
en	un	in fun
eng	ung	in lung
er	er	in mother
in	ean	in bean
ing	ing	in king
ou	o	in go
un	oon	in moon
ung	own + g	
wo	ar	in war (r silent)

4. Mandarin: Tones

There are four tones in Mandarin, plus a neutral tone used in ending words. Yale and Pinyin have the same tone markings.

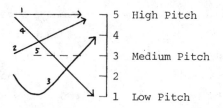

	5	High Pitch
	4	
	3	Medium Pitch
	2	
	1	Low Pitch

Name of Tone	Symbol	Number on Pitch Chart	Example
Upper Level	—	1	搭 *dā*
Upper Rising	／	2	答 *dá*
Lower Rising	⌄	3	打 *dǎ*
Upper Falling	＼	4	大 *dà*
Neutral	None	5	快快 *kwaikwai*

5. Mandarin: CNPA to Yale

The CNPA, or Chinese National Phonetic Alphabect, was developed as an aid in the pronounciation of characters. It is used primarily in Taiwan and is usually found in dictionaries. This table relates the symbols to the Yale romanization.

CNPA	Yale	CNPA	Yale
ㄅ	b	ㄚ	a
ㄆ	p	ㄛ	wo
ㄇ	m	ㄜ	e
ㄈ	f	ㄝ	e(ye)
ㄉ	d	ㄞ	ai
ㄊ	t	ㄟ	ei
ㄋ	n	ㄠ	au
ㄌ	l	ㄡ	ou
ㄍ	g	ㄢ	an
ㄎ	k	ㄣ	en
ㄏ	h	ㄤ	ang
ㄐ	j	ㄥ	eng
ㄑ	ch(y)	ㄦ	er
ㄒ	sy	ㄧㄥ	ing
ㄓ	j(r)	ㄧㄣ	un
ㄔ	ch		
ㄕ	sh	ㄧ	(y)i
ㄖ	r	ㄨ	(w)u
ㄗ	dz	ㄩ	(y)u
ㄘ	ts		
ㄙ	sz		

<u>Mandarin: Comparison of Yale, Pinyin, Wade-Giles and CNPA</u>

Yale	Pinyin	Wade-Giles	CNPA
a	*a*	*a*	ㄚ
ai	*ai*	*ai*	ㄞ
an	*an*	*an*	ㄢ
ang	*ang*	*ang*	ㄤ
au	*ao*	*ao*	ㄠ
ba	*ba*	*pa*	ㄅㄚ
bai	*bai*	*pai*	ㄅㄞ
ban	*ban*	*pan*	ㄅㄢ
bang	*bang*	*pang*	ㄅㄤ
bau	*bao*	*pao*	ㄅㄠ
bei	*bei*	*pei*	ㄅㄟ
ben	*ben*	*pen*	ㄅㄣ
beng	*beng*	*peng*	ㄅㄥ
bi	*bi*	*pi*	ㄅㄧ
bin	*bin*	*pin*	ㄅㄧㄣ
bing	*bing*	*ping*	ㄅㄧㄥ
bou	*bou*	*pou*	ㄅㄡ
bu	*bu*	*pu*	ㄅㄨ
bwo	*bo*	*po*	ㄅㄛ
byan	*bian*	*pien*	ㄅㄧㄢ
byau	*biao*	*piao*	ㄅㄧㄠ
bye	*bie*	*pieh*	ㄅㄧㄝ
cha	*cha*	*ch'a*	ㄔㄚ
chai	*chai*	*ch'ai*	ㄔㄞ
chan	*chan*	*ch'an*	ㄔㄢ
chang	*chang*	*ch'ang*	ㄔㄤ
chau	*chao*	*ch'ao*	ㄔㄠ
che	*che*	*ch'e*	ㄔㄜ
chen	*chen*	*ch'en*	ㄔㄣ

cheng	cheng	ch'eng	ㄔㄥ
chi	qi	ch'i	ㄑㄧ
chin	qin	ch'in	ㄑㄧㄣ
ching	qing	ch'ing	ㄑㄧㄥ
chou	chou	ch'ou	ㄔㄡ
chr	chi	ch'ih	ㄔ
chu	chu	ch'u	ㄔㄨ
chung	chong	ch'ung	ㄔㄨㄥ
chwa	chua	ch'ua	ㄔㄨㄚ
chwai	chuai	ch'uai	ㄔㄨㄞ
chwan	chuan	ch'uan	ㄔㄨㄢ
chwang	chuang	ch'uang	ㄔㄨㄤ
chwei	chui	ch'ui	ㄔㄨㄟ
chwo	chuo	ch'uo	ㄔㄨㄛ
chwun	chun	ch'un	ㄔㄨㄣ
chya	qia	ch'ia	ㄑㄧㄚ
chyan	qian	ch'ien	ㄑㄧㄢ
chyang	qiang	ch'iang	ㄑㄧㄤ
chyau	qiao	ch'iao	ㄑㄧㄠ
chye	qie	ch'ieh	ㄑㄧㄝ
chyou	qiu	ch'iu	ㄑㄧㄡ
chyu	qu	ch'ü	ㄑㄩ
chyun	qun	ch'ün	ㄑㄩㄣ
chyung	qiong	ch'iung	ㄑㄩㄥ
chwan	quan	ch'üan	ㄑㄩㄢ
chywe	que	ch'üeh	ㄑㄩㄝ
da	da	ta	ㄉㄚ
dai	dai	tai	ㄉㄞ
dan	dan	tan	ㄉㄢ
dang	dang	tang	ㄉㄤ
dau	dao	tao	ㄉㄠ
de	de	te	ㄉㄜ
dei	dei	tei	ㄉㄟ

deng	deng	teng	ㄉㄥ
di	di	ti	ㄉㄧ
ding	ding	ting	ㄉㄧㄥ
dou	dou	tou	ㄉㄡ
du	du	tu	ㄉㄨ
dung	dong	tung	ㄉㄨㄥ
dwan	duan	tuan	ㄉㄨㄢ
dwei	dui	tui	ㄉㄨㄟ
dwun	dun	tun	ㄉㄨㄣ
dwo	duo	to	ㄉㄨㄛ
dyan	dian	tien	ㄉㄧㄢ
dyau	diao	tiao	ㄉㄧㄠ
dye	die	tieh	ㄉㄧㄝ
dyou	diu	tiu	ㄉㄧㄡ
dz	zi	tzu	ㄗ
dza	za	tsa	ㄗㄚ
dzai	zai	tsai	ㄗㄞ
dzan	zan	tsan	ㄗㄢ
dzang	zang	tsang	ㄗㄤ
dzau	zao	tsao	ㄗㄠ
dze	ze	tse	ㄗㄜ
dzei	zei	tsei	ㄗㄟ
dzen	zen	tsen	ㄗㄣ
dzeng	zeng	tseng	ㄗㄥ
dzou	zou	tsou	ㄗㄡ
dzu	zu	tsu	ㄗㄨ
dzung	zong	tsung	ㄗㄨㄥ
dzwan	zwan	tsuen	ㄗㄨㄢ
dzwei	zui	tsui	ㄗㄨㄟ
dzwo	zuo	tso	ㄗㄨㄛ
dzwun	zun	tsun	ㄗㄨㄣ
e	e	o	ㄜ
en	en	en	ㄣ

eng	eng	eng	ㄥ
er	er	erh	ㄦ
fa	fa	fa	ㄈㄚ
fan	fan	fan	ㄈㄢ
fang	fang	fang	ㄈㄤ
fei	fei	fei	ㄈㄟ
fen	fen	fen	ㄈㄣ
feng	feng	feng	ㄈㄥ
fou	fou	fou	ㄈㄡ
fu	fu	fu	ㄈㄨ
fwo	fo	fo	ㄈㄛ
ga	ga	ka	ㄍㄚ
gai	gai	kai	ㄍㄞ
gan	gan	kan	ㄍㄢ
gang	gang	kang	ㄍㄤ
gau	gao	kao	ㄍㄠ
ge	ge	ko	ㄍㄜ
gei	gei	kei	ㄍㄟ
gen	gen	ken	ㄍㄣ
geng	geng	keng	ㄍㄥ
gou	gou	kou	ㄍㄡ
gu	gu	ku	ㄍㄨ
gung	gong	kung	ㄍㄨㄥ
gwa	gua	kua	ㄍㄨㄚ
gwai	guai	kuai	ㄍㄨㄞ
gwan	guan	kuan	ㄍㄨㄢ
gwang	guang	kuang	ㄍㄨㄤ
gwei	gui	kui	ㄍㄨㄟ
gwo	guo	kuo	ㄍㄨㄛ
gwun	gun	kun	ㄍㄨㄣ
ha	ha	ha	ㄏㄚ
hai	hai	hai	ㄏㄞ

han	han	han	ㄏㄢ
hang	hang	hang	ㄏㄤ
hau	hao	hao	ㄏㄠ
he	he	ho	ㄏㄜ
hei	hei	hei	ㄏㄟ
hen	hen	hen	ㄏㄣ
heng	heng	heng	ㄏㄥ
hou	hou	hou	ㄏㄡ
hu	hu	hu	ㄏㄨ
hung	hung	hung	ㄏㄨㄥ
hwa	hua	hua	ㄏㄨㄚ
hwai	huai	huai	ㄏㄨㄞ
hwan	huan	huan	ㄏㄨㄢ
hwang	huang	huang	ㄏㄨㄤ
hwei	hui	hui	ㄏㄨㄟ
hwo	huo	huo	ㄏㄨㄛ
hwun	hun	hun	ㄏㄨㄣ
ja	zha	cha	ㄓㄚ
jai	zhai	chai	ㄓㄞ
jan	zhan	chan	ㄓㄢ
jang	zhang	chang	ㄓㄤ
jau	zhao	chao	ㄓㄠ
je	zhe	che	ㄓㄜ
jei	zhei	chei	ㄓㄟ
jen	zhen	chen	ㄓㄣ
jeng	zheng	cheng	ㄓㄥ
ji	ji	chi	ㄐㄧ
jin	jin	chin	ㄐㄧㄣ
jing	jing	ching	ㄐㄧㄥ
jou	zhou	chou	ㄓㄡ
jr	zhi	chih	ㄓ
ju	zhu	chu	ㄓㄨ
jung	zhong	chung	ㄓㄨㄥ

jwa	zhua	chua	ㄓㄨㄚ
jwai	zhuai	chuai	ㄓㄨㄞ
jwan	zhuan	chuan	ㄓㄨㄢ
jwang	zhuang	chuang	ㄓㄨㄤ
jwei	zui	chui	ㄓㄨㄟ
jwo	zho	cho, chuo	ㄓㄨㄛ
jwun	zun	chun	ㄓㄨㄣ
jya	jia	chia	ㄐㄧㄚ
jyan	jian	chien	ㄐㄧㄢ
jyang	jiang	chiang	ㄐㄧㄤ
jyau	jiao	chiao	ㄐㄧㄠ
jye	jie	chieh	ㄐㄧㄝ
jyou	jiu	chiu	ㄐㄧㄡ
jyu	ju	chü	ㄐㄩ
jyun	jun	chün	ㄐㄩㄣ
jyung	jiong	chiung	ㄐㄩㄥ
jywan	juan	chüan	ㄐㄩㄢ
jywe	jue	chüeh	ㄐㄩㄝ
ka	ka	k'a	ㄎㄚ
kai	kai	k'ai	ㄎㄞ
kan	kan	k'an	ㄎㄢ
kang	kang	k'ang	ㄎㄤ
kau	kao	k'ao	ㄎㄠ
ke	ke	k'o	ㄎㄜ
ken	ken	k'en	ㄎㄣ
keng	keng	k'eng	ㄎㄥ
kou	kou	k'ou	ㄎㄡ
ku	ku	k'u	ㄎㄨ
kung	kong	k'ung	ㄎㄨㄥ
kwa	kua	k'ua	ㄎㄨㄚ
kwai	kuai	k'uai	ㄎㄨㄞ
kwan	kuan	k'uan	ㄎㄨㄢ
kwang	kuang	k'uang	ㄎㄨㄤ

kwei	*kui*	*k'uei*	ㄎㄨㄟ
kwo	*kuo*	*k'uo*	ㄎㄨㄛ
kwun	*kun*	*k'un*	ㄎㄨㄣ
la	*la*	*la*	ㄌㄚ
lai	*lai*	*lai*	ㄌㄞ
lan	*lan*	*lan*	ㄌㄢ
lang	*lang*	*lang*	ㄌㄤ
lau	*lao*	*lao*	ㄌㄠ
le	*le*	*le*	ㄌㄜ
lei	*lei*	*lei*	ㄌㄟ
leng	*leng*	*leng*	ㄌㄥ
li	*li*	*li*	ㄌㄧ
lin	*lin*	*lin*	ㄌㄧㄣ
ling	*ling*	*ling*	ㄌㄧㄥ
lou	*lou*	*lou*	ㄌㄡ
lu	*lu*	*lu*	ㄌㄨ
lung	*long*	*lung*	ㄌㄨㄥ
lwan	*luan*	*luan*	ㄌㄨㄢ
lwo	*luo*	*lo, luo*	ㄌㄨㄛ
lwun	*lun*	*lun*	ㄌㄨㄣ
lya	*lia*	*lia*	ㄌㄧㄚ
lyan	*lian*	*lien*	ㄌㄧㄢ
lyang	*liang*	*liang*	ㄌㄧㄤ
lyau	*liao*	*liao*	ㄌㄧㄠ
lye	*lie*	*lieh*	ㄌㄧㄝ
lyou	*liu*	*liu*	ㄌㄧㄡ
lyu	*lü*	*lü*	ㄌㄩ
lywan	*luan*	*lüan*	ㄌㄩㄢ
lywe	*lüe*	*lüeh*	ㄌㄩㄝ
ma	*ma*	*ma*	ㄇㄚ
mai	*mai*	*mai*	ㄇㄞ
man	*man*	*man*	ㄇㄢ

mang	mang	mang	ㄇㄤ
mau	mao	mao	ㄇㄠ
me	me	me	ㄇㄜ
mei	mei	mei	ㄇㄟ
men	men	men	ㄇㄣ
meng	meng	meng	ㄇㄥ
mi	mi	mi	ㄇㄧ
min	min	min	ㄇㄧㄣ
ming	ming	ming	ㄇㄧㄥ
mou	mou	mou	ㄇㄡ
mu	mu	mu	ㄇㄨ
mwo	mo	mo	ㄇㄛ
myan	mian	mien	ㄇㄧㄢ
myau	miao	miao	ㄇㄧㄠ
mye	mie	mieh	ㄇㄧㄝ
myou	miu	miu	ㄇㄧㄡ
na	na	na	ㄋㄚ
nai	nai	nai	ㄋㄞ
nan	nan	nan	ㄋㄢ
nang	nang	nang	ㄋㄤ
nau	nao	nao	ㄋㄠ
ne	ne	ne	ㄋㄜ
nei	nei	nei	ㄋㄟ
nen	nen	nen	ㄋㄣ
neng	neng	neng	ㄋㄥ
ni	ni	ni	ㄋㄧ
nin	nin	nin	ㄋㄧㄣ
ning	ning	ning	ㄋㄧㄥ
nou	nou	nou	ㄋㄡ
nu	nu	nu	ㄋㄨ
nung	nong	nung	ㄋㄨㄥ
nwan	nuan	nuan	ㄋㄨㄢ
nwo	nuo	no, nuo	ㄋㄨㄛ

nwun	nun	nun	ㄋㄨㄣ
nyan	nian	nien	ㄋㄧㄢ
nyang	niang	niang	ㄋㄧㄤ
nyau	niao	niao	ㄋㄧㄠ
nye	nie	nieh	ㄋㄧㄝ
nyou	niu	niu	ㄋㄧㄡ
nyu	nü	nü	ㄋㄩ
nywe	nüe	nüeh	ㄋㄩㄝ
ou	ou	ou	ㄡ
pa	pa	p'a	ㄆㄚ
pai	pai	p'ai	ㄆㄞ
pan	pan	p'an	ㄆㄢ
pang	pang	p'ang	ㄆㄤ
pau	pao	p'ao	ㄆㄠ
pei	pei	p'ei	ㄆㄟ
pen	pen	p'en	ㄆㄧㄢ
peng	peng	p'eng	ㄆㄥ
pi	pi	p'i	ㄆㄧ
pin	pin	p'in	ㄆㄧㄣ
ping	ping	p'ing	ㄆㄧㄥ
pou	pou	p'ou	ㄆㄡ
pu	pu	p'u	ㄆㄨ
pwo	po	p'o	ㄆㄛ
pyan	pian	p'ien	ㄆㄧㄢ
pyau	piao	p'iao	ㄆㄧㄠ
pye	pie	p'ieh	ㄆㄧㄝ
r	ri	jih	ㄖ
ran	ran	jan	ㄖㄢ
rang	rang	jang	ㄖㄤ
rau	rao	jao	ㄖㄠ
re	re	je	ㄖㄜ

ren	ren	jen	ㄖ ㄣ
reng	reng	jeng	ㄖ ㄥ
rou	rou	jou	ㄖ ㄡ
ru	ru	ju	ㄖ ㄨ
rung	rong	jung	ㄖ ㄨ ㄥ
rwan	ruan	juan	ㄖ ㄨ ㄢ
rwei	rui	jui	ㄖ ㄨ ㄟ
rwo	ruo	jo, juo	ㄖ ㄨ ㄛ
rwun	run	jun	ㄖ ㄨ ㄣ
sa	sa	sa	ㄙ ㄚ
sai	sai	sai	ㄙ ㄞ
san	san	san	ㄙ ㄢ
sang	sang	sang	ㄙ ㄤ
sau	sao	sao	ㄙ ㄠ
se	se	se	ㄙ ㄜ
sen	sen	sen	ㄙ ㄣ
seng	seng	seng	ㄙ ㄥ
sha	sha	sha	ㄕ ㄚ
shai	shai	shai	ㄕ ㄞ
shan	shan	shan	ㄕ ㄢ
shang	shang	shang	ㄕ ㄤ
shau	shao	shao	ㄕ ㄠ
she	she	she	ㄕ ㄜ
shei	shei	shei	ㄕ ㄟ
shen	shen	shen	ㄕ ㄣ
sheng	sheng	sheng	ㄕ ㄥ
shou	shou	shou	ㄕ ㄡ
shr	shi	shih	ㄕ
shu	shu	shu	ㄕ ㄨ
shwa	shua	shua	ㄕ ㄨ ㄚ
shwai	shuai	shuai	ㄕ ㄨ ㄞ
shwan	shuan	shuan	ㄕ ㄨ ㄢ
shwang	shuang	shuang	ㄕ ㄨ ㄤ

shwei	shui	shui	ㄕㄨㄟ
shwo	shuo	shuo	ㄕㄨㄛ
shwun	shun	shun	ㄕㄨㄣ
sou	sou	sou	ㄙㄡ
su	su	su	ㄙㄨ
sung	song	sung	ㄙㄨㄥ
swan	suan	suan	ㄙㄨㄢ
swei	sui	sui	ㄙㄨㄟ
swo	suo	so, suo	ㄙㄨㄛ
swun	sun	sun	ㄙㄨㄣ
sya	xa	hsia	ㄒㄧㄚ
syan	xian	hsian	ㄒㄧㄢ
syang	xiang	hsiang	ㄒㄧㄤ
syau	xiao	hsiao	ㄒㄧㄠ
sye	xie	hsieh	ㄒㄧㄝ
syi	xi	hsi	ㄒㄧ
syin	xin	hsin	ㄒㄧㄣ
sying	xing	hsing	ㄒㄧㄥ
syou	xiu	hsiu	ㄒㄧㄡ
syu	xu	hsü	ㄒㄩ
syun	xun	hsün	ㄒㄩㄣ
syung	xiong	hsiung	ㄒㄩㄥ
sywan	xuan	hsüan	ㄒㄩㄢ
sywe	xue	hsüeh	ㄒㄩㄝ
sz	si	ssu	ㄙ
ta	ta	t'a	ㄊㄚ
tai	tai	t'ai	ㄊㄞ
tan	tan	t'an	ㄊㄢ
tang	tang	t'ang	ㄊㄤ
tau	tao	t'ao	ㄊㄠ
te	te	t'e	ㄊㄜ
teng	teng	t'eng	ㄊㄥ
ti	ti	t'i	ㄊㄧ

ting	ting	t'ing	ㄊㄧㄥ
tou	tou	t'ou	ㄊㄡ
tsa	ca	ts'a	ㄘㄚ
tsai	cai	ts'ai	ㄘㄞ
tsan	can	ts'an	ㄘㄢ
tsang	cang	ts'ang	ㄘㄤ
tsau	cao	ts'ao	ㄘㄠ
tse	ce	ts'e	ㄘㄜ
tsen	cen	ts'en	ㄘㄣ
tseng	ceng	ts'eng	ㄘㄥ
tsou	cou	ts'ou	ㄘㄡ
tsu	cu	ts'u	ㄘㄨ
tsung	cong	ts'ung	ㄘㄨㄥ
tswan	cuan	ts'uan	ㄘㄨㄢ
tswei	cui	ts'ui	ㄘㄨㄟ
tswo	cuo	ts'o	ㄘㄨㄛ
tswun	cun	ts'un	ㄘㄨㄣ
tsz	ci	tz'u	ㄘ
tu	tu	t'u	ㄊㄨ
tung	tong	t'ung	ㄊㄨㄥ
twan	tuan	t'uan	ㄊㄨㄢ
twei	tui	t'ui	ㄊㄨㄟ
two	tuo	t'o, t'uo	ㄊㄨㄛ
twun	tun	t'un	ㄊㄨㄣ
tyan	tian	t'ian	ㄊㄧㄢ
tyau	tiao	t'iao	ㄊㄧㄠ
tye	tie	t'ieh	ㄊㄧㄝ
wa	wa	wa	ㄨㄚ
wai	wai	wai	ㄨㄞ
wan	wan	wan	ㄨㄢ
wang	wang	wang	ㄨㄤ
wei	wei	wei	ㄨㄟ
wen	wen	wen	ㄨㄣ

weng	weng	weng	ㄨㄥ
wo	wo	wo	ㄨㄛ
wu	wu	wu	ㄨ
ya	ya	ya	ㄧㄚ
yai	yai	yai	ㄧㄞ
yan	yan	yen	ㄧㄢ
yang	yang	yang	ㄧㄤ
yau	yao	yao	ㄧㄠ
ye	ye	yeh	ㄧㄝ
yi	yi	i	ㄧ
yin	yin	yin	ㄧㄣ
ying	ying	ying	ㄧㄥ
you	you	yu	ㄧㄡ
yu	yu	yü	ㄩ
yung	yong	yung	ㄩㄥ
ywan	yuan	yüan	ㄩㄢ
ywe	yue	yüeh	ㄩㄝ
ywun	yun	yün	ㄩㄣ

TABLE OF RADICALS

Number	Radical		Meaning	Page No.

One Stroke:

Number	Radical		Meaning	Page No.
1	一		horizontal	53
2	丨		vertical	54
3	丶		dot	54
4	丿		diagonal	55
5	乙		second	55
6	亅		hook	56

Two Strokes:

Number	Radical		Meaning	Page No.
7	二		two	56
8	亠		cap	57
9	* 人	亻	man	58
10	儿		long legs	69
11	入		enter	70
12	八	丷	eight	70
13	冂		borders	71
14	冖		crown	72
15	冫		ice	72
16	几		table	73
17	凵		can	74
18	* 刀	刂	knife	74
19	* 力		strength	77
20	勹		wrap	79
21	匕		spoon	80
22	匚		basket	80
23	匸		box	81
24	十		ten	81
25	卜		foretell	82
26	卩	㔾	seal	83

27	厂		cliff	83
28	厶		go	84
29	又		also	84

Three Strokes:

30	* 口		mouth	85
31	* 囗		fence	94
32	* 土	土	earth	95
33	士		soldier	100
34	夂		summer	101
35	夕		evening	101
36	* 大		big	102
37	* 女		woman	104
38	子		son	109
39	* 宀		roof	110
40	寸		inch	114
41	小		small	115
42	尤		lame	115
43	尸		foot	116
44	* 山		mountain	117
45	巛	川	stream	119
46	工		work	119
47	己		self	120
48	* 巾		napkin	121
49	干		interfere	123
50	幺		fine	123
51	* 广		shelter	124
52	廴		court	126
53	廾		play	126
54	弋		shoot	126
55	弓		bow	127
56	彐	彑	broom	128
57	彡		shape	128

58	*	彳		double man	129
59	*	心	忄	heart	131
60		戈		sword	141
61		戶	户	family	142
62	*	手	扌	hand	142
63		支		support	158
64		攴	攵	tap	158
65	*	文		literature	161
66		斗		measure	161
67		斤		catty	161
68		方		square	162
69		无	旡	since	163
70	*	日		sun	163
71		曰		say	168
72		月		moon	169
73	*	木		wood	169
74		欠		owe	182
75		止		stop	183
76		歹		bad	184
77		殳		kill	184
78		毋		do not	185
79		比		compare	185
80		毛		hair	186
81		氏		clan	186
82		气		air	186
83	*	水	氵	water	187
84	*	火	灬	fire	199
85		爪	爫	claw	203
86		父		father	204
87		爻		two x's	204
88		爿		bed	205
89		片		slice	205
90		牙		tooth	205

| 91 | * 牛 牛 | ox | 205 |
| 92 | * 犬 犭 | dog | 206 |

Five Strokes:

93	玄 玄	deep	208
94	* 玉 王	jade	208
95	瓜	melon	210
96	瓦	tile	210
97	甘	sweet	211
98	生	live	211
99	用	use	211
100	* 田	field	211
101	疋	cloth	213
102	* 疒	sickness	213
103	癶	climb	215
104	白	white	215
105	皮	skin	215
106	皿	vessel	216
107	* 目 四	eye	217
108	矛	lance	219
109	矢	arrow	219
110	* 石	stone	219
111	示 礻	show	221
112	内	track	222
113	* 禾	grain	222
114	穴	cave	224
115	立	stand	225

Six Strokes:

116	* 竹 𥫗	bamboo	226
117	* 米	rice	229
118	* 糸 糹	silk	230
119	缶	pottery	235

- 48 -

120		网	net	235
121		羊	sheep	236
122		羽	羽	feather	237
123		老	耂	old	238
124		而	yet	238
125		耒	plough	238
126		耳	ear	239
127		聿	learn	240
128	*	肉	月	meat	240
129		臣	officer	244
130		自	from	245
131		至	reach	245
132		臼	uncle	245
133		舌	tongue	246
134		舛	dance	246
135		舟	beat	246
136		艮	good	247
137		色	color	247
138	*	艸	艹	grass	248
139		虍	tiger	254
140	*	虫	insect	254
141		血	wood	257
142		行	walk	258
143	*	衣	衤	clothes	258
144		西	西	west	261

Seven Strokes:

145		見	see	261
146		角	horn	262
147	*	言	speech	262
148		谷	valley	270
149		豆	bean	270
150		豕	pig	270

151		豸		leopard	271
152	*	貝		shell	271
153		赤		red	274
154		走	走	run	275
155	*	足	足	leg	276
156		身		body	277
157	*	車		vehicle	278
158		辛		difficult	279
159		辰		time	280
160	*	辵	辶	travel	280
161	*	邑	阝	county	285
162		酉		chief	286
163		釆		free	287
164		里		mile	288

Eight Strokes:

165	*	金	金	gold	288
166		長	長	long	292
167	*	門		door	293
168	*	阜	阝	mound	294
169		隶		secondary	296
170		隹		single	297
171	*	雨	雨	rain	298
172		青		green	299
173		非		not	300

Nine Strokes:

174		面	face	300
175		革	revolution	300
176		韋	leather	301
177		音	sound	301
178	*	頁	page	301
179		風	wind	304

180	飛		fly	304
181	* 食	食	eat	304
182	首		head	306
183	香		fragrant	306

Ten Strokes:

184	* 馬	horse	306
185	骨	bone	308
186	高	tall	308
187	髟	whisker	308
188	鬥	fight	309
189	鬯	wine	309
190	鬲	caldron	309
191	鬼	ghost	309

Eleven Strokes:

192	* 魚	fish	310
193	* 鳥	bird	311
194	鹵	salt	312
195	鹿	deer	312
196	麥	wheat	313
197	麻	hemp	313

Twelve Strokes:

198	黃	yellow	313
199	黍	millet	313
200	黑	black	314

Thirteen Strokes:

201	鼎	tripod	314
202	鼓	drum	314
203	鼠	rat	315

Fourteen Strokes:

204	鼻	nose	315
205	齊	even	315

Fifteen Strokes:

206	齒	front tooth	315

Sixteen Strokes:

207	龍	dragon	316

Seventeen Strokes:

208	龜	turtle	316
209	龠	flute	316

*   The fifty most common radicals

		一 Section
一	一	One *yàt* *yī*　　　　　*yī*
丁	一 丁	A servant *dīng* *dīng*　　　　*dīng*
七	一 七	Seven *chàt* *chī*　　　　　*qī*
三	一 二 三	Three *sàam* *sān*　　　　　*sān*
丈	一 ナ 丈	Measurement of 10 Chin. feet *jeuhng* *jàng*　　　　*zhàng*
上	丨 卜 上	To ascend; up *seuhng* *shàng*　　　　*shàng*
下	一 丁 下	To descend; down *hah* *syà*　　　　　*xà*
不	一 フ 才 不	No, not *bàt* *bù*　　　　　*bù*
丐	一 丁 亍 丐	Beggar *kọi* *gài*　　　　　*gài*
冇	一 ナ 才 冇	None, don't have *móuh* *mǒu*　　　　*mǒu*
丑	フ 刀 丑 丑	Clown *cháu* *chǒu*　　　　*chǒu*

且	｜ 冂 月 月 且	Besides, moreover *ché* *chyě*　　　　*qiě*
世	一 十 廿 廿 世	Generation *sai* *shŕ*　　　　*shì*
丘	ノ イ 斤 斤 丘	Hillock *yau* *chyōu*　　　　*qiū*
丙	一 丆 闩 丙 丙	The third of the ten stems *bǐng* *bǐng*　　　　*bǐng*
丢	ノ 亠 千 壬 丢 丢	To throw, lose *diu* *dyāu*　　　　*diāo*
並	丶 丷 丷 并 并 並 並	Side by side, also *bihng* *bìng*　　　　*bìng*
	｜	Section
中	丶 口 口 中	Middle, center *jùng* *jùng*　　　　*zhōng*
串	丶 口 口 吕 串	String *chyun* *chwān*　　　　*chuān*
	丶	Section
丸	ノ 九 丸	Pill *yún* *wǎn*　　　　*wǎn*
丹	ノ 刀 丹 丹	Red, pill *dàan* *dān*　　　　*dān*

主	丶 一 十 主 主	God, master, owner jyú jǔ zhǔ
	丿	Section
乃	𠃌 乃	Then náaih nǎi nǎi
久	丿 𠂉 久	A long time gáu jyóu jiǔ
之	丶 ㇇ 之	Of jì jr̄ zhī
乍	丿 𠂉 𠂉 乍 乍	Suddenly ja jà zhà
乏	丿 𠂉 ラ 乏	To lack faht fá fá
乖	丿 一 千 千 千 千 乖 乖	Obedient gwāai gwāi guāi
乘	乖 乖 乘	To multiply; ride on a vehicle sìhng chéng chéng
	乙	Section
乙	乙	The second of the ten stems yuht yí yī
九	丿 九	Nine gáu jyóu jiǔ

乙 (2-12) 亅 (1-5) 二 (2)

乞	ノ 气 乞	To beg *haht* *chi* *qi*
也	⊃ 也 也	Also, still *yaah* *yě* *yě*
乳	ノ ベ ベ ☆ 匆 严 乎 乳	Milk, the breast *yúh* *rǔ* *rǔ*
乾	一 十 十 古 古 吉 直 車 車 軟 乾	Dry *gòn* *gān* *gān*
亂	ノ ノ ベ ベ 乡 乡 乡 孚 畟 爵 爵 簡 亂	Disorder *lyuhn* *lwàn* *luàn*
	亅	Section
了	⊐ 了	To finish *liuh* *lyǎu, le* *liǎo, le*
予	⊐ マ 予 予	To give *yúh* *yú* *yú*
事	一 一 亓 亓 写 写 写 事	Affairs, matters *sih* *shr* *shì*
	二	Section
二	一 二	Two *yih* *èr* *èr*
云	一 二 云 云	To say *wàhn* *yún* *yún*

互	一 工 亏 互	Each other *wuh* hù hù
五	一 丁 五 五	Five *ńg* wǔ wǔ
井	一 二 于 井	A well *jéng* jǐng jǐng
些	丨 丨 丨 丨 此 此 此 些	Few *sè* syē xiē
亞	一 丅 丆 亐 亞 亞 亞 亞	Second a yǎ yǎ

亠   Section

亡	、 亠 亡	To die *mòhng* wáng wáng
交	、 亠 亣 六 亣 交	To hand over *gaàu* jyāu jiāo
亦	、 亠 亣 亣 亣 亦	Also *yihk* yī yī
享	、 亠 亠 古 古 亨 亨 享	To enjoy *héung* syǎng xiǎng
京	、 亠 亠 古 亨 亨 京 京	Capital, metropolis *gìng* jīng jīng
亭	、 亠 亠 古 古 古 高 高 亭	Pavilion *tìhng* tīng tīng

亮	` 亠 六 古 古 亭 亮 亮 亮	Bright *leuhng* *lyàng* *liàng*
	人	Section
人	丿 人	Man, people *yàhn* *rén* *rén*
什	丿 亻 仁 什	Assorted *sahm* *shè* *shè*
仁	亻 仁 仁	Benevolent *yàhn* *rén* *rén*
仇	亻 仏 仇	To hate; enemy *sàuh* *chóu* *chóu*
仆	亻 亻 仆	To fall forward *pùk* *pū* *pū*
今	丿 人 今 今	At present *gàm* *jīn* *jīn*
介	人 个 介	To introduce, lie between *gaai* *jyè* *jiè*
仍	亻 仔 仍	Still *yìhng* *réng* *réng*
仔	亻 仁 仔 仔	Child, son *jái* *dz* *zǐ*
仕	亻 仁 仕 仕	Gentleman, scholar *sih* *shr* *shì*

他	亻仁仲他	He, others tā̀ tā̄　　　tā̄
仗	亻仁付仗	To rely on; battle jeung jaǹg　　　zhàng
付	亻仁什付	To pay, give to fu fù　　　fù
仙	亻仆仙仙	Immortal; an angel sìn syān　　　xiān
代	亻仁代代	To represent, substitute; doih　　　dynasty dài　　　dài
令	人亼今令	To command, cause; A law; your lihng lìng　　　lìng
以	㇀㇀以以	By, with yíh yǐ　　　yǐ
仰	亻亻仃仰仰	To regard with respect yéuhng yǎng　　　yǎng
仲	亻亻仃仲仲	The middle one juhng jung　　　zhōng
件	亻亻伫仁件	Item, piece gihn jyàn　　　jiàn
任	亻亻仁仟任	To appoint, let; duty yahm rèn　　　rèn
企	人个个企企	To stand kéih chi　　　qì

伉	亻亻广伫伉	Married couple kong kàng kàng
伊	亻亻ヿ仔仔伊	She, you yī yi yī
伍	亻亻亻仃伍伍	Five; a company of soldiers ńgh wǔ wǔ
伏	亻亻仁仕伏伏	To hide fuhk fú fú
伐	亻亻代伐伐	To attack faht fá fá
休	亻亻仁什休休	To rest, stop yàu syōu xiū
伙	亻亻仏伩伙	Assistant, fellow fó hwo huǒ
全	人人仐全全	Complete chyùhn chywán quán
份	亻亻仏伀份	Part, portion fahn fèn fèn
伯	亻亻仢伯伯伯	Father's elder brother, uncle, senior baak bwó bó
估	亻亻仕仕估估	To estimate, guess gú gu gǔ
伴	亻亻伩伩伜伴	To accompany; companion buhn bàn bàn

伶	亻亻亻伶伶伶	Actor/actress; lonely lihng líng líng
伸	亻亻亻伂伅伸	To stretch, extend sàn shēn shēn
何	亻亻亻侗侗何	Which, what hòh hé hé
似	亻亻亻似似	Similar chíh sz̀ sì
但	亻亻亻伃但但	But, however daahn dàn dàn
佈	亻亻亻佈佑佈	To spread, inform bou bù bù
位	亻亻亻位位位	Seat, person, position wái, waih wèi wèi
低	亻亻亻低低低	Low dài dī dī
住	亻亻亻住住住	To live in, stop jyuh jù zhù
佐	亻亻亻佐佐佐	To assist; junior official jo dzwǒ zuǒ
佔	亻亻亻佔佔佔	To seize by force jim jàn zhàn
你	亻亻亻你你你	You néih nǐ nǐ

人 (5-6)

佛	亻亻亻亻佛佛	Buddha *faht* *fwǒ* *fó*
作	亻亻亻竹作作	To make, write *jok* *dzwò* *zùo*
佩	亻亻们佩佩佩 佩	To respect; a pendant *pui* *pèi* *pèi*
佳	亻亻亻佳佳佳佳	Good *gaai* *jyā* *jiā*
佻	亻亻竹杪杪佻	Frivolous *tiu* *tyáu* *tiáo*
使	亻亻亻佢伖使使	To cause, command; a messenger *sí* *shr* *shǐ*
來	一丆夾夾本來來	To come *lòih* *laí* *laí*
侈	亻亻伀佟侈	Extravagant *chí* *shr* *shǐ*
例	亻亻亻佰佟佟 佟	Regulation, example *laih* *lì* *lì*
侍	亻亻亻佳佳侍侍	To wait upon, serve *sih* *shr* *shì*
侏	亻亻亻佟件侏侏	Dwarf *jyù* *jū* *zhū*
供	亻亻亻佚供供供	To supply, provide *gung* *gung* *gòng*

- 62 -

依	亻亻亻亻亻依 依	To rely on yì *yi* *yī*
侮	亻亻亻侮侮侮 侮侮	To insult móuh *wǔ* *wǔ*
侯	亻亻亻侯侯侯 侯侯	Marquis hàuh *hóu* *hóu*
侵	亻亻亻亻侵侵 侵侵	To invade cham *chīn* *qīn*
侶	亻亻亻亻伊侶	Companion léuih *lyǔ* *lǚ*
侷	亻亻伊侷侷侷 侷	Cramped guhk *jyú* *jú*
便	亻亻亻亻便便 便便	Convenient bihn *byan* *bian*
係	亻亻亻係係係 係係	To be, relation haih *sỳi* *xì*
促	亻亻亻亻亻促 促	To urge; hurried chuk *tsu* *cù*
俊	亻亻亻俊俊俊 俊俊	Handsome jeun *jìn* *jìn*
俏	亻亻亻亻俏俏 俏	Pretty chiu *chyàu* *qiào*
俗	亻亻亻俗俗俗 俗俗	Custom, common juhk *sú* *sú*

俘	亻亻'亻'亻'亻'亻'亻'亻乎 俘	Captive, war prisoner fù fú fú
保	亻亻'亻'亻'亻'二亻呆 保	To protect, guarantee bóu baǔ baǒ
俟	亻亻'亻厶亻矢亻矣俟 俟	To wait; till aài sz`      si`
俠	亻亻'亻'亻夾亻夾俠 俠	Hero hahp syá xá
信	亻亻'亻广亻言亻言信 信	To believe, trust; A letter seun syìn xìn
修	亻亻'亻'亻攵修攸修 修 修	To fix, study sāu syōu xīu
俯	亻亻'亻广亻广亻府俯 俯 俯	To bend down fǔ fǔ fu
俱	亻亻'亻们们俱俱俱 俱 俱	All, entirely keùi jyū jū
倆	亻亻'亻广亻两亻兩倆 倆 倆	Both leúhng lyǎng liǎng
倂	亻亻'亻亻亻倂	To combine ping pīng pīng
倉	丿人仌今仝全 仐貪倉倉	Warehouse chòng tsāng cāng
倍	亻亻'亻广亻立亻倍倍 倍 倍	To double, increase púih bei bèi

們	亻亻亻亻們們們們們 們	Word denoting plural *mùhn* *mén*　　　　　*mén*
倒	亻亻亻仁伍伍倒倒 倒	To fall over, pour; inverted *dóu* *dǎu*　　　　*daǒ*
候	亻亻亻仁仔仔候候 候	To wait *hauh* *hòu*　　　　*hòu*
倚	亻亻亻亻伟倍倚 倍倚	To rely on, lean towards *yí* *yī*　　　　*yī*
借	亻亻亻仕借借借 借借	To borrow, lend *je* *jye*　　　*yìe*
倡	亻亻亻们们倡	To originate *chēung* *chāng*　　*chāng*
倣	亻亻仁仿仿 仿仿倣	To imitate *fóng* *fǎng*　　*fǎng*
值	亻亻亻仿值值 值值	Price, worth; on duty *jihk* *jr*　　　*zhi*
倘	亻亻们们们们 倘倘倘	If, suppose *tóng* *tǎng*　　*tǎng*
個	亻亻们佣佣個個 個個	Measure word for objects *go* *gè*　　*gè*
俾	亻亻们伯伯俾 俾俾俾	To enable, allow *béi* *bi*　　*bì*
假	亻亻亻仮仮假假 假假假	To pretend; false; holiday *ga, ga* *jyǎ*　*jiǎ*

偉	亻 亻 亻 什 亻 佇 偉 佇 佇 佇 偉 偉	Great wáih wěi wěi
偕	亻 亻 亻 佧 佨 佳 偕 偕 偕	To accompany gàai jye̅ jie̅
做	亻 亻 什 什 佑 估 佔 做 做 做	To do, make jouh dzwò zuò
偽	亻 亻 亻 伊 伊 伊 偽 偽 偽	Hypocritical, fake ngaih wěi wěi
健	亻 亻 亻 伊 伊 信 信 偉 健 健	Strong, healthy gihn jyan jiàn
側	亻 亻 们 侗 但 但 侗 偵 偵 側	To lean against; a side jàk tse̅ ce̅
停	亻 亻 亻 仁 佇 佇 信 信 停 停	To stop tìhng tíng tíng
偵	亻 亻 什 忱 佑 佑 佾 偵 偵 偵	To inspect; detective jing je̅n zhe̅n
偶	亻 亻 们 侗 侗 侶 偶 偶 偶 偶	Idol, mate; accidental ngáuh ǒu ǒu
偷	亻 亻 亻 伶 伶 佮 偷 偷 偷 偷	To steal tàu to̅u to̅u
傢	亻 亻 亻 佇 佇 傢 傢 傢 傢 傢	Funiture gà jya jia
傅	亻 亻 亻 什 付 佛 佛 佛 傅 傅 傅	Teacher, expert fú fù fù

傑	亻 亻' 亻' 仪 仍 仳 伀 伀 傑 傑 傑	Hero, eminent figure *giht* *jyé*　　　　*jié*
傘	ノ 人 介 夵 夵 夵 夵 夵 傘	An umbrella *saan* *sǎn*　　　　*sǎn*
備	亻 亻' 亻' 仴 仴 伊 伊 伖 俻 俻 備	To prepare, get ready *beih* *bei*　　　　*bei*
傲	亻 亻' 仕 仕 佳 佳 俜 俜 俽 傲 傲	To be proud, haughty *ngouh* *au*　　　　*ao*
催	亻 亻' 仙 仙 伊 伊 伐 伄 俳 催 催	To urge, hasten *chēui* *tswēi*　　　　*cūi*
傭	亻 亻' 广 广 庐 庐 俏 俯 傭 傭 傭	Servant *yuhng* *yung*　　　　*yong*
傳	亻 亻' 亻' 伃 俑 伬 傴 傳 傳 傳	To preach, spread; biography *chyùhn, jyúhn, jyuhn* *chwàn, jwàn　chuán, zhùan*
債	亻 亻' 仕 佳 佳 佳 俵 債 債 債 債	A debt *jaai* *jài*　　　　*zhài*
傷	亻 亻' 亻' 作 俏 佲 佲 傷 傷 傷	To injure, wound *sēung* *shāng*　　　　*shāng*
傾	亻 亻' 亻' 仴 仴 伺 俰 倾 傾 傾 傾	To pour, lean towards *kìng* *ching*　　　　*qing*
僅	亻 亻' 亻' 仕 佚 佳 借 僅 僅 僅 僅	Simply, barely *gán* *jǐn*　　　　*jǐn*
僕	亻 亻' 亻' 仴 仴 仴 僕 僕 僕 僕 僕	A servant *buhk* *bú*　　　　*bú*

僚	亻 亻ˊ 亻ˊ 伏 伏 侊 侊 倅 倅 倅 僚 僚 僚	A colleague liuh lyáu — liáo
僥	亻 亻ˊ 亻ˊ 仹 仹 佬 倖 倖 僥	Lucky hiu jyǎu — jiāo
僧	亻 亻ˊ 亻ˊ 亻ˊ 伶 俌 倘 倘 倘 僧 僧 僧	Buddhist monk jang sēng — sēng
僑	亻 亻ˊ 亻ˊ 伇 伒 佟 佟 倃 倃 倃 僑 僑 僑	Emigrants, overseas Chinese kiùh chyáu — qiáo
像	亻 亻ˊ 亻ˊ 伒 佀 佀 伊 倏 傍 傍 像 像 像	To resemble; an image jeuhng syáng — xiàng
傻	亻 亻ˋ 亻ˊ 仙 佃 佃 伨 伨 傎 傻 傻 傻	Stupid, silly sòh sha — shǎ
價	亻 亻ˊ 亻ˊ 佀 伬 價 價 價 價 價 價 價 價	Price, value ga jya — jià
億	亻 亻ˋ 亻ˊ 亻ˊ 佇 佇 佇 倍 倍 倍 億 億 億	A hundred million yik yi — yì
儉	亻 亻ˋ 亻ˊ 佇 伶 伶 伶 倫 儉 儉 儉	Thrifty gihm jyǎn — jiǎn
儀	亻 亻ˋ 亻ˊ 亻ˊ 佯 佯 伴 倖 倖 倖 儀 儀 儀	Manners, instruments, ceremony yìh yi — yí
僻	亻 亻ˊ 亻ˊ 佇 佲 倨 倨 倨 倨 僻 僻 僻 僻	Depraved, secluded pik pi — pì
儒	亻 亻ˋ 亻ˊ 伀 伓 倔 儒 儒 儒 儒 儒 儒 儒	Scholar yùh rú — rú

優	亻 亻 亻 亻 佢 佢 佢 佢 佢 佢 優 優 優 優 優 優 優	Excellent *yàu* *you* *yōu*
儲	亻 亻 亻 亻 信 信 信 信 信 佶 佶 佶 佶 儲 儲 儲	To store, save *chýuh* *chu* *chú*
儷	亻 亻 亻 佪 佪 佪 儷 儷 儷 儷 儷 儷 儷 儷 儷 儷 儷	A couple *laih* *lí* *lì*
儿		Section
允	ㄥ ㄠ ㄠ 允	To promise, allow *wáhn* *yǔn* *yǔn*
元	一 二 亍 元	The chief; a dollar *yùhn* *yẃan* *yuán*
兄	丿 口 口 ㄗ 兄	An elder brother *hìng* *syūng* *xiōng*
充	丶 亠 云 云 充 充	To fill *chùng* *chūng* *chōng*
兆	丿 丿 兆 兆 兆 兆	An omen; a million *siuh* *jàu* *zhào*
兇	ㄴ 凵 凶 凶 凶 兇	Fierce, cruel *hùng* *syūng* *xiōng*
先	丿 一 牛 生 牛 先	First, before *sìn* *syān* *xiān*
光	丨 丬 丬 业 ㇀ 光	Light *gwòng* *gwāng* *guāng*

ㄦ (5-9) 入 (2-6) 八

克	一 十 ナ ナ 古 古 克 克	To overcome; a gram haak kè　　　　kè
兌	ノ 八 ャ 分 台 宁 兌	To exchange deui dwèi　　　duì
免	ノ ク ク 舟 舟 臽 免 免	Free from, avoid míhn myǎn　　　mian
兒	ノ 亻 亻 亻 臼 臼 臼 兒	A son, child yìh er　　　　er
兔	ノ ハ 勹 白 甶 免 兔 兔	A rabbit tou tù　　　　tù
兜	ノ 亻 亻 伯 伯 伯 伯 伯 伯 兜 ノ 兜	A helmet daù dōu　　　dōu
入		Section
入	ノ 入	To enter yahp rù　　　　rù
內	丨 冂 冂 內	Inside, within noih nèi　　　nèi
兩	一 冂 冂 雨 雨 雨 兩	An ounce, tael; two leuhng lyǎng　　liǎng
八		Section
八	ノ 八	Eight baat bā　　　　bā

- 70 -

公	ノ 八 公 公	Public; old man gung gūng gōng
六	丶 亠 宀 六	Six luhk lyòu liù
共	一 十 卄 芷 共 共	All, together guhng gǔng gòng
兵	ノ イ ト 斤 丘 兵 兵	A soldier bing bǐng bīng
其	一 十 卄 芇 甘 其 其	A possessive pronoun kèih chí qí
具	丨 冂 月 月 目 且 具	A tool geuih jyù jù
典	丶 冂 巾 曲 曲 曲 典	Dictionary din dyǎn diǎn
兼	ノ 八 公 亼 仐 全 争 争 弇 兼	In addition gim jyān jiān
冀	丨 コ ナ 北 北 北 背 背 皆 皆 皆 曹 冀 萱 冀	To hope kei jì jì
	冂	Section
册	丿 刀 册 册	A volume of a book chaak tsè cè
再	一 丆 冂 丙 再 再	Again joi dzài zài

- 71 -

冒	丶冂冃日冃冃 冃冒冒	To feign, risk *mouh* màu　　　mào
冕	丶冂冃日冃冃冃 冃冃冕冕冕	A crown *mihn* myǎn　　　miǎn
	冖	Section
冗	丶冖冖冗	Wordy *yúng* rǔng　　　rǒng
冠	丶冖冖冖冠冠 冠冠冠	A crown; premiere *gun, gun* gwàn　　　guān
	冫	Section
冬	丿夂夂冬冬	Winter *dung* dǔng　　　dōng
冱	丶冫冫冱冱冱	Icy *wuh* hù　　　hù
冶	冫冫冶冶冶冶	To melt *yéh* yě　　　yě
冷	冫冫冫冷冷 冷	Cold *laahng* lěng　　　lěng
冰	冫冫冰冰冰	Ice *bing* bing　　　bīng
准	冫冫冫冫冫冫 准准准	To allow, approve *jéun* jwǔn　　　zǔn

凋	冫 冫 汩 汩 汩 / 汩 汩 汩 凋	To wither, fade chàuh dyāu — diāo
凍	冫 冫 沪 沪 涑 涑 / 涑 涑 凍	To freeze; cold dung dung — dong
淨	冫 冫 冫 冫 沴 沴 / 沴 沴 淨	Clean jihng jing — jing
淒	冫 冫 汀 沯 沽 沽 淒 / 淒 淒 淒	Sad; windy and rainy chài chī — qi
凜	冫 冫 汙 汙 沱 沱 滴 / 滴 滴 滴 凜 凜 凜	Shivering lahm lin — lin
凝	冫 冫 冰 冰 冰 涘 涘 涘 / 涘 涘 凝 凝 凝 凝	To coagulate, freeze yih ning — ning

| | 几 | Section |

几	丿 几	A small table gei jī — jī
凡	丿 几 凡	Common; every faàhn fán — fán
凰	丿 几 几 凡 凡 凨 / 凨 凨 凰 凰 凰	Phoenix wòhng hwang — huáng
凱	丨 山 山 屵 屵 岂 岂 岂 / 岂 岂 剀 凱	Victory ngoi kai — kai
凳	フ ㇅ 癶 癶 癶 癶 癶 癶 / 癶 癶 癶 癶 登 凳	A stool, bench dang deng — deng

		凵	Section
凶	凵 凵 凵 凶		Evil *hùng* *syung* *xiong*
凸	丨 丄 丄 凸 凸 凸		To protrude *daht* *tú* *tú*
凹	丨 冂 凵 凹 凹 凹		Indentation *nàp* *aō* *aō*
出	凵 凵 屮 出 出		To go out *chèut* *chū* *chū*
函	乛 了 了 函 函 函 函		A letter, note *haahm* *hán* *hán*
		刀	Section
刀	乛 刀		A knife, sword, chopper *dōu* *dāu* *dao*
刁	乛 刁		Sneaky *diù* *dyāu* *diāo*
刃	乛 刀 刃		The edge of a sword *yahn* *ren* *rèn*
分	丿 八 分 分		To divide, distribute; a minute *fàn* *fēn* *fēn*
切	一 十 切 切		To cut, slice *chit* *chyē* *qiē*

刊	一 二 干 刊 刊	To publish; a publication hóhn kān　　　　　　kān
划	一 弋 弋 戈 划 划	To row a boat wà hwa　　　　　　hua
列	一 丆 歹 歹 列 列	To list liht lyè　　　　　　liè
刑	一 二 干 开 刑 刑	Punishment ying sying　　　　　xing
删	） 刀 刑 册 册 删 删	To pare saan shān　　　　　shān
初	` ラ ネ ネ ネ 初 衤刀	Beginning, at first cho chū　　　　　chū
判	` 丷 ⺌ 兰 半 判	To judge; decision pun pàn　　　　　pàn
别	` 口 口 므 另 别	To part, distinguish; do not biht bye　　　　　bie
利	ノ 二 千 禾 禾 利	To benefit; interest leih lì　　　　　lì
刮	ノ 二 千 千 舌 舌 刮	To scrape gwaat gwā　　　　　guā
到	一 工 云 至 至 至 到	To reach, attain dou dau　　　　　dào
制	ノ ト 上 午 告 朱 制	To regulate, ration jai jì　　　　　jì

刀 (6-8)

刷	ㄱ ㄱ ㄕ ㄕ 尸 屄 屌 刷	To brush *chaat* *shwā*　　　　　shūa
券	、 ㄚ ㄥ 羊 美 美 券 券	A bond, ticket, coupon *gwun* *chwàn*　　　　chùan
刻	、 亠 亠 亥 亥 亥 刻	To carve, engrave *hàk* *kè*　　　　　kè
刺	一 ㄏ ㄍ 市 束 束 刺	To stab, sting; a thorn *chih* *tsz*　　　　　cì
剎	ノ ㄨ ㄌ 羊 矛 杀 剎	A buddhist monastery; instant *saat* *shà*　　　　　shà
剃	、 ㄚ 亠 ㄢ 肖 弟 弟 剃	To shave *tai* *tì*　　　　　tì
則	ㄧ ㄇ ㄇ 目 目 貝 貝 則	A rule, law; then *jak* *dze*　　　　　zē
削	ㄧ ㄑ 竹 小 ㄓ 肖 肖 削	To deprive of *seuk* *sywe*　　　　　xùe
前	、 ㄚ 亠 亠 广 肖 肖 前 前	Before, in front of; former *chihn* *chyan*　　　　qian
剗	一 ㄊ 戈 戈 戔 剗	To trim, spade *chàn* *chǎn*　　　　　chǎn
剖	、 亠 亠 立 立 音 音 音 剖	To dissect *faú* *poù*　　　　　poǔ
剛	ㄧ ㄇ 冂 冈 冈 用 罔 岡 剛	Firm; recently *gong* *gang*　　　　　gāng

- 76 -

剝	丨 夕 夕 夅 틀 틀 틀 彔 彔 剝	To strip, peel mòk bwō buō
副	一 丆 丆 百 百 高 高 畐 畐 副	To aid; an assistant fu fù fù
剪	丶 丷 丷 丷 芇 芇 肖 前 剪 剪	To cut with scissors; scissors jin jyǎn jiǎn
割	丶 宀 宀 宆 宆 宝 宝 宑 害 害 割	To cut goht gē gē
剩	丿 一 千 禾 禾 禾 乘 乘 乘 乘 剩	To retain; remaining sihng sheng shèng
創	丿 人 亼 今 今 今 會 會 倉 倉 創	To start, create; a wound chong chwàng chuàng
劃	一 コ ᄏ 급 급 書 書 書 書 畫 畫 劃	To mark; a plan waahk hwà huà
劉	丿 乊 乊 俰 刪 岎 丣 罗 娶 娶 翠 劉	To slaughter; a last name làuh lyóu liú
劇	丨 ⺊ 上 广 广 庐 虍 虎 虏 虏 虏 豦 劇	An opera; extremely kehk jyù jù
劈	コ コ 尸 尺 启 启 启 启 䂂 䂃 辟 辟 劈	To chop, split open pek pi pī
劍	丿 人 亼 亼 合 合 合 僉 僉 劍	A sword gim jyàn jiàn
	力	Section

- 77 -

力 (3-9)

力	フ 力	Strength, energy *lihk* lì · lì
功	一 丁 工 巧 功	Merit, achievement *guhng* gung · gōng
加	力 加 加 加	To add, increase *gà* jyā · jiā
劣	丶 丿 小 少 劣	Bad, inferior *lyut* lyè · lìe
助	丨 冂 日 日 且 助	To help; assistance *joh* jù · zhù
努	ㄑ ㄨ 女 如 奴 努	To strive *louh* nǔ · nǔ
劫	一 十 土 去 去 劫	To rob *gip* jyé · jié
勁	一 ㄍ 巠 巠 巠 巠 勁	Strength *ging* jing · jìng
勃	一 十 ㄓ 古 声 亨 亨 勃	Flourishing; suddenly *buht* bwó · bó
勇	フ マ ア 丹 丹 丹 甬 勇	Brave; a soldier *yuhng* yung · yǒng
勉	丿 ㄅ ⺈ 굼 由 岛 免 免 勉	To encourage *mihn* myan · miǎn
動	丿 一 ㄏ 台 台 旨 重 重 重 動	To act; motion *duhng* dung · dòng

- 78 -

Character	Stroke order	Meaning / Readings
勒	丶 十 艹 甘 艻 苩 苩 莒 革 勒	A harness lahk le`, léi     le`, léi
務	ㄱ マ マ 予 矛 矛 豺 矛攵 務 務	A duty mouh wù wù
勝	丿 刀 月 月 月 月' 肝 胖 朕 勝	To win, conquer sing shĕng shĕng
勞	丶 ⸜ ⺌ 火 炏 炏 炏 炏 勞	To work hard; labor louh laú láo
募	丶 十 卄 卝 艾 苩 莒 草 莫 募	To enlist, raise mouh mù mù
勢	一 十 土 走 圥 夫 去 坴 刲 刲 埶 執 勢	Authority sai shr shì
勤	丶 十 艹 甘 甘 艻 苩 莒 革 革 堇 勤	Diligent kàhn chín qín
勳	丿 ⼍ 仁 台 台 台 台 旬 車 重 重 熏 勳	Merits fan syun xūn
勵	一 厂 厂 厃 厈 厍 厉 厉 厉 厎 厲 厲 厲 勵	To encourage laih lì lì
勸	丶 ⼍ 卄 卝 艾 甘 莒 茆 苭 莖 莖 莖 莖 萑 勸	To advise, persuade, admonish hyun chywàn quàn
	勹	Section
勻	丿 勹 勽 勻	Equally, evenly gwàn ywún yún

勹 (2-3) 匕 (2-9) 匚 (4)

勾	′ 勹 勺 勾	To hook, entice *ngàu* *gōu* *gōu*
勿	′ 勹 勺 勿	Do not *maht* *wù* *wù*
包	′ 勹 勺 勺 包	To wrap, include; a bundle *baàu* *baū* *baō*
匆	′ 勹 勺 勿 匆	Hurried *chùng* *tsung* *cōng*
匈	′ 勹 勺 匇 匈 匈	Tumultuous *hung* *syūng* *xiōng*
	匕	Section
匕	′ 匕	A ladle, dagger *bei* *bǐ* *bǐ*
化	′ 亻 化	To transform *fa* *hwa* *huà*
北	l ⺆ ⺊ ⺊匕 北	North *bàk* *běi* *běi*
匙	l ⼌ 日 日 旦 早 是 昻 是 匙	A spoon, key *sìh* *shr* *shí*
	匚	Section
匠	一 厂 匚 匠 匠 匠 匠	A workman, craftsman *jeuhng* *jyang* *jiàng*

匪	一 丁 厂 厅 厈 匪 匪 匪 匪	A robber, thief féi fěi fēi
	匚	Section
匹	一 匚 匸 匹	A unit for cloth and horse pàt pǐ pǐ
匿	匚 匚 匚 匚 匠 匿 匿 匿 匿	To hide; secret, anonymous lìk nì nì
區	匚 匚 匚 匚 匚 區	A district keui chyū qū
	十	Section
十	一 十	Ten sahp shŕ shí
千	丿 千	A thousand, many chīn chyān qiān
廿	一 十 卄 廿	Twenty yah nyàn niàn
升	丿 匚 千 升	To ascend, rise sīng shēng shēng
卅	一 十 卄 卅	Thirty sà sa sà
午	丿 丿 上 午	Noon nģh wǔ wǔ

- 81 -

半	丶 丶 丷 丷 半	Half *bun* *bàn* *bàn*
卒	丶 一 宀 亠 亢 卒	A soldier *jyut* *dzú* *zú*
卓	丨 ㆑ 卜 占 占 卣 卓 卓	Distinguished *cheuk* *jwó* *zhó*
協	十 十 协 协 協 協	To aid; an agreement *hihp* *syé* *xié*
卑	丿 亻 白 白 卑 卑 卑 卑 卑	Inferior, humble *bēi* *bēi* *bēi*
南	十 十 内 两 两 南 南 南	South *naahm* *nàn* *nán*
博	十 十 廿 卄 博 博 博 博 博 博 博	To gamble; an expanse *bok* *bwó* *bó*
	卜	Section
卜	丨 卜	To foretell *bùk* *bǔ* *bǔ*
卡	丨 卜 上 卡	Caught between *kaat* *chyǎ* *qiǎ*
占	卜 卜 占 占	To foretell *jìm* *jān* *zhān*
卦	一 十 土 丰 圭 圭 卦	A stick for fortune telling *gwa* *gwà* *guà*

卪		Section
印	´ ⺁ ⺒ 臼 印	To stamp, print; seal *yan* *yìn* *yìn*
危	´ ⺈ ⺈ ⼴ 产 危	Danger *ngaih* *wei* *wéi*
却	一 十 土 去 去 去ㄱ 却	To refuse; nevetheless *keuk* *chywe* *què*
卵	´ ⺒ 自 自 卵 卵	Eggs *leun* *lwǎn* *luǎn*
卷	丶 ⺍ ⺍ 兰 半 关 卷 卷	A roll, volume of a book *gwún* *jywàn* *juàn*
即	´ ⺈ 白 白 自 良 白 即	Immediately *jik* *ji* *jí*
卸	´ ⺊ ⺊ 午 午 牟 缶 卸	To unload, get rid of *yik* *sye* *xiè*
厂		Section
厚	一 厂 厂 厂 厈 厔 厚 厚 厚	Thick, generous *hauh* *hou* *hòu*
原	厂 厂 ⺁ 所 盾 盾 原 原 原	The origin *yuhn* *ywan* *yuán*
厕	厂 厂 厉 厕 厚 厚 厚 厠 厠 厠	Toilet *chi* *tse* *cè*

厨	厂 厂 厈 厈 厈 厈 厈 居 居 厝 厨 厨 厨 厨 厨	Kitchen *cheuih* *chú* 　　　　*chú*
厭	厂 厂 厈 戶 戶 戶 戶 屑 屑 屑 屑 厭 厭 厭 厭	Bored, bothered by *yim* *yàn* 　　　　*yàn*
厲	厂 厂 厈 厈 厈 厈 厈 厈 厝 厝 厲 厲 厲 厲	Strict *laih* *lì* 　　　　*lì*

厶　　Section

去	一 十 土 去 去	To go; previous *heui* *chyù* 　　　　*qù*
叄	厶 厶 厽 夕 矣 叄 叄 叄	Three *saàm* *sān* 　　　　*sān*
參	厶 厽 厽 幺 矣 矣 參 參	To consult, participate *chàam* *tsān* 　　　　*cān*

又　　Section

又	乃 又	Again, also *yauh* *yòu* 　　　　*yòu*
叉	又 叉	To cross; a fork *chā* *chā* 　　　　*chā*
及	乃 乃 及	And, about *kahp* *jí* 　　　　*jí*
反	ノ 厂 厃 反	To turn over, oppose; opposite *faán* *fǎn* 　　　　*fǎn*

友	一 ナ 友	A friend, companion *yáuh* *yǒu* *yǒu*
取	一 丁 丌 丌 丌 耳 取	To take, get *chéui* *chyǔ* *qǔ*
叔	丨 卜 上 才 未 未 叔	Father's younger brother, *suk* uncle *shū* *shú*
受	丿 爫 爫 爫 爫 爫 受	To accept, receive *sauh* *shòu* *shòu*
叛	丶 丷 丷 半 半 半 尗 叛	To rebel, revolt *buhn* *pān* *pān*
叢	丨 丨丨 丨丨 丨丨 业 业 世 世 丵 丵 丵 丵 丵 丵 叢	Crowded, thick; dense *chuhng* *tsúng* *cóng*

	口	Section
口	丨 冂 口	A mouth, hole, opening *háu* *kǒu* *kǒu*
古	一 十 古	Ancient, old, primitive *gú* *gu* *gǔ*
句	丿 勹 句	A sentence, phrase *geui* *jyù* *jù*
另	口 号 另	Other *lihng* *lìng* *lìng*
只	口 尸 只	Only, simply *jí* *jr* *zhǐ*

可	一 口 可	To be willing, be able *hó* *ke* (ˇ) *ke* (ˇ)
叫	口 叫 叫	To shout, call, name *giu* *jyaù* *jiao* (ˋ)
史	口 史 史	History *si* *shr* (ˇ) *shǐ*
叮	口 口 叮	To sting, reiterate *ding* *dīng* *dīng*
召	フ 刀 召	To call *jiuh* *jaù* *zhào*
司	ㄱ ㄋ 司	To control, manage; superint- *si* endant *sz* *sī*
叭	口 叭 叭	A trumpet *bà* *bā* *bā*
台	ㄥ ㄥ 台	A stage *tòih* *tái* *tái*
右	一 ナ 右	The right side *yauh* *yoù* *yòu*
吃	口 吖 吖 吃	To eat *hek* *chr* *chī*
各	ノ ク 夂 各	Every, each *gok* *gé* *gé*
名	ノ ク 夕 名	To name; name *mihng* *míng* *míng*

吉	一 十 士 吉	Good luck *gàt* *jī* *jī*
合	丿 人 人 合	To combine, close *hahp* *hé* *hé*
同	丨 冂 同 同	Identical, together *tùhng* *túng* *tóng*
后	丿 厂 斤 后	A queen *hauh* *hòu* *hòu*
向	丿 亻 冋 向	Towards; direction *heung* *syàng* *xiàng*
吏	一 口 吏 吏	A government official *leih* *lì* *lì*
吐	口 口 吐 吐	To vomit, spit *tou* *tǔ* *tǔ*
含	丿 人 人 今 含	To hold, endure *hahm* *hán* *hán*
吵	口 叫 叫 吵 吵	To annoy, quarrel *cháau* *chǎu* *chǎo*
告	丿 广 屮 牛 告	To announce; impeach *gou* *gau* *gao*
吝	丶 亠 文 文 吝	Miserly *leuhn* *lìn* *lìn*
吠	口 口 吠 吠 吠	To bark (dog) *faih* *fèi* *fèi*

吹	口 口' 吵 吹 吹	To blow, puff cheui _chwēi_ _chūi_
吼	口 口' 吇 吇 吼	To roar; the cry of a beast haau _hǒu_ _hǒu_
呀	口 口' 吒 吇 呀	An exclamation, a creak a _ya_ _ya_
君	丁 ユ ヨ 尹 君	A ruler, prince gwan _jyūn_ _jūn_
否	一 丆 オ 不 否	To refuse; no fau _fǒu_ _fǒu_
吞	ノ ー チ 天 吞	To swallow tan _twūn_ _tūn_
吧	口 口' 吧 吧 吧	A final article bah _ba_ _ba_
吾	一 丁 五 五 吾	I, we, my ngh _wú_ _wú_
吸	口 吋 吸 吸	To inhale kap _syi_ _xī_
呈	口 口 兕 早 呈	To offer, present to superior chihng _chéng_ _chēng_
吻	口 口' 吻 吻 吻	The corners of the mouth, mahn speech _wěn_ _wěn_
呆	口 口 呆 呆 呆	Silly, foolish ngoih _aī_ _aī_

周	) 刀 月 用 用 周	To surround; provide for *jau* *jōu*　　　　*zhōu*
呢	口 口ˋ 口ˋ 叩 叩, 呢	A final article *le* *ne*　　　　*ne*
味	口 口ˉ 口ニ 吁 咔 味	To taste; flavor, smell *meih* *wèi*　　　　*wèi*
命	) 人 合 合 命	To command; luck, fate *mihng* *mìng*　　　　*mìng*
和	) ニ 千 禾 禾 和	Peace, harmony *woh* *hé*　　　　*hé*
呻	口 口) 叩 叩 叩 呻	To groan *san* *shēn*　　　　*shēn*
咀	口 口) 叩 叩 叩 咀	Mouth; to chew *jeui* *jyǔ*　　　　*ju*
呼	口 口ˊ 叩ˊ 叩ˊ 呼 呼	To call, exhale *fu* *hu*　　　　*hu*
哈	口 口ˊ 叭 叭 哈	An exclamation of joy; to sip *ha* *ha*　　　　*ha*
品	口 品 品	An article, rank *ban* *pin*　　　　*pin*
咳	口 口ˋ 吽 咹 咳 咳 咳	To cough *kat* *ké*　　　　*ke*
咬	口 口ˋ 口ˊ 吘 咹 吃, 咬	To bite *ngáau* *yau*　　　　*yao*

哀	、 一 亠 亩 亩 亩 哀 哀	Sorrow oi ai ai
咽	口 叮 叨 叨 咽 咽 咽	A throat yin yan yan
哨	口 口' 叮' 口' 叮' 哨 哨 哨	To guard; an outpost saau shàu shào
哺	口 叮一 叶 叶 哺 哺 哺 哺	To feed a child bouh bǔ bǔ
員	口 早 吊 吊 吊 員 員 員	A member of a profession yuhn ywán yúan
唐	、 一 广 庁 庁 庁 庠 唐	The Tang Dynasty; boastful tòhng táng táng
哥	一 т 可 哥 哥	An elder brother gò ge ge
哭	口 叩 哭 哭 哭 哭	To cry, weep hùk ku ku
哮	口 口 叶 吐 哮 哮 哮 哮	To roar, howl haau syāu xiāo
唉	口 叱 叱 吟 吟 哈 哞 唉	Oh! eh! aài ai ai
唇	一 厂 厂 厇 辰 辰 辰 唇	Lips seuhn chwun chún
哲	一 扌 扌 扌 扩 折 折 哲	Wise jit jé zhé

- 90 -

問	丨 冂 冂 冂 冂 門 門 門 門 問	To ask *mahn* wèn wèn
售	丿 亻 亻 忄 亻 隹 隹 隹 售	To sell *sauh* shòu shòu
唯	口 口 口 口 叮 唯 啡 唯 唯	To answer; only *wạih* wei wéi
唱	口 口 口 叮 唱 唱 唱	To sing *cheung* chàng chàng
商	丶 一 六 亠 宀 商 产 商 商 商	To trade; a merchant *seụng* shāng shāng
啓	丶 丶 亠 户 户 户 户 改 啓	To open, explain *kái* chǐ qǐ
喚	口 口 口 口 叭 叭 叻 吶 啮 喚 喚	To call *wuhn* hwàn huàn
啦	口 口 吖 吖 吖 吖 呀 啦 啦	A final article *lạ* le le
啊	口 口 吋 阝 哌 啊 啊	An exclamation of surprise *oh* a a
善	丶 丶 丷 亠 羊 羊 羊 美 美 善	good, skillful *sihn* shàn shàn
單	口 口 吅 吅 吅 吅 吅 單 單	Single; a bill *dàan* dān dān
喜	一 十 士 吉 吉 吉 吉 喜	Joy, happiness *héi* sỷi xǐ

字	筆順	意味
喊	口 ロ ロ 叮 叮 咸 喊 喊 喊	To cry, call *haam* *hǎn* *han*
喪	一 十 寸 声 戸 声 喪 喪	To die, mourn *song* *sāng* *sāng*
啼	口 ロ ロ ロ 叱 唪 唪 啼 啼 啼	To crow, cry *taih* *tí* *tí*
喂	口 ロ ロ 맥 唎 唎 喂 喂 喂 喂	Hello *waih* *wèi* *wèi*
喧	口 ロ ロ 吽 吽 吟 唁 喧 喧 喧	Noisy; an argument *hyun* *sywan* *xuan*
喝	口 ロ ロ 呵 唱 唱 喝 喝 喝 喝 喝	To drink; shout *hot* *hè* *hē*
啞	口 ロ 一 吓 吓 咕 唘 唘 啞	Mute, silent *á* *yǎ* *yǎ*
嗜	口 ロ 叶 吐 味 味 咾 嗜 嗜 嗜 嗜	To be fond of; a hobby *siuh* *shr* *shi*
嗓	口 ロ 叺 叺 哐 喿 喿 嗓 嗓	The throat, voice *song* *sǎng* *sǎng*
嗟	口 ロ ロ ロ 吀 咩 咩 嗟 嗟 嗟	To sign, mourn *je* *jye* *jie*
嗅	口 ロ 叩 叭 吶 咱 咱 嗅 嗅 嗅	To smell *chau* *syou* *xiu*
嗚	口 ロ 叮 吖 吖 咱 嗚 嗚 嗚	An expression for a sigh *wù* *wū* *wū*

嗎	口 口一 口丁 口下 口F 口开 嗎 嗎 嗎	A question mark *mà* *ma* *ma*
嘔	口 口一 口匚 口叵 嘔 嘔	To vomit *ngáu* *ǒu, òu* *ǒu, òu*
嘉	一 十 士 吉 吉 喜 喜 嘉 嘉 嘉	To praise; good *gā* *jya* *jiā*
嗽	口 口一 口戸 口申 口束 口束 嗽 嗽 嗽 嗽	To cough, clear throat *sau* *sòu* *sòu*
嘗	丨 丬 ⺌ ⺌ 尚 尚 尝 尝 尝 嘗 嘗 嘗	To taste, try *seùhng* *cháng* *cháng*
嘆	口 口丨 口廿 口廿 口廿 嘆 嘆 嘆 嘆 嘆	To sigh, moan *taan* *tàn* *tàn*
噴	口 口一 口十 口土 口卉 口卉 噴 噴 噴 噴 噴 噴	To eject, blow out *pan* *pēn* *pēn*
噤	口 口一 口十 口木 口林 口林 噤 噤 噤 噤 噤	To refrain from speaking *kàm* *jìn* *jìn*
嘴	口 口丨 口卜 口止 口此 口此 口此 嘴 嘴 嘴 嘴 嘴 嘴 嘴	The mouth *jéui* *dzwěi* *zuǐ*
器	口 吅 吅 哭 哭 哭 器 器	Tool, employ *hei* *chī* *qī*
噸	口 口一 口匚 口屯 口屯 口屯 口屯 噸 噸 噸 噸 噸 噸 噸	A ton *deùn* *dwún* *dún*
噬	口 口丿 口𠂉 口竹 口竹 口竹 口竹 噬 噬 噬 噬	To bite *saih* *shr̀* *shì*

嚇	ㅁ ㅁ` ㅁ⁺ ㅁ⁺ 吽 啈 啈 嚇 嚇	To frighten, threaten *haak* *syá*　　　　*xà*
嚴	ㅁ ㅁㅁ ㅁㅁ 严 严 严 严 严 严 严 严 严 严 厰 嚴	Strict, severe *yìhm* *yán*　　　　*yán*
嚷	ㅁ ㅁ` ㅁ` 亠 吣 嘹 嘹 嘘 嚯 嘖 嚷 嚷 嚷	To shout, scold *yeuhng* *rang*　　　　*rang*
嚼	ㅁ ㅁ` ㅁ` ㅁ` 呬 呬 嘬 嚕 嚕 嚕 嚕 嘬 嚕 嚼 嚼	To chew *jeuk* *jyáu*　　　　*jiao*
囂	ㅁ ㅁㅁ ㅁㅁ ㅃ 罒 罤 罤 罤 囂 囂 囂 囂 囂	Clamor *hyùn* *syāu*　　　　*xiāo*
囊	一 一 由 由 毒 事 嘉 嘉 毒 壹 壼 夒 嚢 囊	A bag, purse *nòhng* *nang*　　　　*nang*
囑	ㅁ ㅁ` ㅁ` ㅁ` 叩 叺 呀 喉 喉 喔 喉 喔 喔 囑 囑 囑 囑	To instruct, order *jùk* *jǔ*　　　　*zhǔ*
	囗	Section
四	ㅣ 冂 四 四	Four *sei* *sz*　　　　*sì*
囚	ㅣ 冂 冈 冈 囚	To imprison *chàuh* *chyóu*　　　　*qiù*
回	ㅣ 冂 冋 同 回	To return *wùih* *hwéi*　　　　*huí*
因	ㅣ 冂 冋 冈 冈 因	Because, a reason *yàn* *yín*　　　　*yīn*

- 94 -

困	丨 冂 冂 用 困 困 困	Fatigued, exhausted *kwan* *kwùn*　　*kùn*
固	丨 冂 冂 用 固 固 固 固	Strong, stubborn *gu* *gú*　　*gù*
圈	丨 冂 冂 冂 冂 冃 圀 圀 圂 圈 圈	To surround; a circle *hyùn* *chywàn*　　*quàn*
國	丨 冂 冂 冂 同 同 同 國 國 國 國	A country, empire *gwok* *gwó*　　*gúo*
圍	丨 冂 冂 冃 冃 圍 圍 圍 圍 圍 圍 圍	To surround, an enclosure *waih* *wéi*　　*wéi*
圓	冂 冂 冂 冂 冃 冃 冃 冃 冃 圓 圓 圓	Round, circular *yùhn* *yán*　　*yán*
園	冂 冂 冂 冃 冃 園 園 園 園 園 園	A park, yard, garden *yùhn* *yán*　　*yán*
圖	冂 冂 冂 冃 冃 圉 圉 圉 圕 圖 圖 圖	A library *toùh shyu gwún* *túshūgwǎn*　　*túshūguǎn*
圖	冂 冂 冂 冂 冂 圉 圉 圖 圖 圖	A picture, drawing, plan *toùh* *tú*　　*tú*
團	冂 冂 冂 同 同 圓 圓 團 團 團 團 團 團	A lump, mass, group *tyùhn* *twán*　　*tún*
	土	Section
土	一 十 土	Earth, ground *tóu* *tǔ*　　*tǔ*

在	一 ナ 才 右 右 在	To exist; in, at, on joih dzài　　　　zài
地	一 十 土 圫 地 地	The ground, earth deih dì　　　　dì
址	土 圤 圤 圤 圵 址	A place, address ji jr̆　　　　zhǐ
均	土 圵 圴 均 均	To equalize gwàn jyun　　　　jun
坐	丿 人 从 坐 坐 坐	To sit, stay joh dzwò　　　　zùo
坑	土 圵 圹 圹 坑	A ditch, pit haàng kēng　　　　kēng
坊	土 圵 圹 圩 坊	A lane, street fóng fāng　　　　fāng
坦	土 圵 圯 坦 坦 坦	Level, smooth táan tān　　　　tān
垂	丿 一 二 立 垂 垂 垂 垂	To hang, drop seùih chwēi　　　　chúi
垃	土 圵 圹 坃 坊 垃	Waste, dirt laahp le　　　　lè
坡	土 圵 圹 圹 坡 坡	A slope bò pwō　　　　pō
坪	土 圵 圹 圲 坪 坪	Level ground pìhng píng　　　　píng

坤	土 圠 坰 坰 坦 坤	The earth; feminine *kwàn* *kwūn* *kūn*
垣	土 圹 圹 坧 垣 垣 垣	A wall, defense *wùhn* *ywán* *yuán*
城	土 圹 圹 坊 城 城 城	A city, town *sìhng* *shéng* *shéng*
型	一 二 于 开 开 刑 刑 型 型	A mold, pattern *yìhng* *syíng* *xíng*
埋	土 圠 坰 坰 坦 坤 埋 埋	To bury, hide *màaih* *mǎi* *mǎi*
堆	土 圵 圵 圻 圻 圻 堆 堆 堆	To pile, heap up *dèui* *dwēi* *duī*
堂	丨 丬 ⺌ ⺌ 尚 尚 尚 尚 堂 堂 堂	A hall, court *tòhng* *táng* *táng*
培	土 圵 圵 圹 坟 垃 培 培 培	To cultivate, nourish *pùih* *péi* *péi*
執	土 圭 圭 幸 幸 幸 幸 執 執	To grasp, hold *jàp* *jŕ* *zhí*
域	土 圹 圹 坷 坷 垣 域 域 域	A region, frontier *wihk* *yù* *yù*
堅	一 丅 五 臣 臣 臤 臤 堅 堅 堅	Strong, firm, durable *gìn* *jyān* *zhuān*
基	丨 十 卄 廿 甘 其 其 其 基 基 基	A foundation, beginning *gèi* *jī* *jī*

土 (8-10)

字	筆順	意味
埠	土 圵 圵 坥 坥 埠 埠	A wharf, port *fauh* bù　　　　bù
堵	土 圵 圵 圵 坺 堵 堵 堵 堵	To obstruct *dou* dǔ　　　　dǔ
報	土 圭 幸 幸 幸 幸 報 報 報 報	To inform, report; a newspaper *bou* bàu　　　　bào
堪	土 圵 圵 坩 坩 坩 堪 堪 堪 堪	To endure; capable *ham* kān　　　　kān
場	土 圵 圯 坍 坍 坦 坦 場 場 場	A yard, field *cheuhng* chǎng　　　　chǎng
堡	ノ イ 仁 仃 仍 仔 仔 保 保 保 保 堡	A fort *bou* bǎu　　　　bǎo
堤	土 圵 坍 坍 坦 坦 埕 埕 堤 堤	An embankment, barrier *taih* tí　　　　tí
塗	丶 冫 氵 氵 汁 汵 汵 涂 涂 涂 塗 塗	To smear; mud *touh* tú　　　　tú
塘	土 圵 圹 圹 坷 坷 塘 塘 塘 塘 塘	A pool, embankment *tohng* tǎng　　　　tǎng
塞	丶 宀 宀 宀 宀 宷 宷 寒 寒 塞	To close up; a frontier *choi* sāi　　　　sāi
填	土 圵 圵 坊 坑 坑 填 填 填 填 填	To fill up *tihn* tyán　　　　tián
塌	土 圵 圹 坍 坍 埕 埕 塌 塌	To crumble *taap* tā　　　　tā

- 98 -

塢	土 圠 圤 圹 圸 圸 塢 塢 塢	A low wall *wuh* *wū*　　　　　*wū*
塊	土 圠 圤 圳 坥 坤 坤 塊 塊 塊 塊	A piece, lump *faai* *kwài*　　　　　*kuài*
塔	圠 圡 圳 圤 圤 坅 坆 塔 塔 塔	A pagoda, tower *taap* *tǎ*　　　　　*tǎ*
境	圠 圡 圡 圹 圸 圸 垃 培 培 培 培 境 境	A region, boundary *gíng* *jìng*　　　　　*jìng*
墊	土 圭 圭 坴 幸 幸 執 執 執 墊	To place under, pay up *jin* *dyān*　　　　　*diān*
墓	丶 丷 艹 艹 苩 苩 苩 莫 莫 莫 墓	A grave *mouh* *mù*　　　　　*mù*
塾	丶 亠 亠 六 古 亨 亨 亨 亯 孰 孰 孰 塾	A school *suhk* *shú*　　　　　*shú*
墅	丶 口 日 日 甲 里 里 里 野 野 野 墅	A house in the country *seuih* *shù*　　　　　*shù*
塵	丶 一 广 广 户 庐 庐 鹿 鹿 塵	Dust, dirt *chàhn* *chén*　　　　　*chén*
隆	⁊ ㇇ 阝 阝 阝 阽 阹 防 防 陽 陽 隊 隆	To fall *seuih* *jwèi*　　　　　*zuì*
墮	⁊ 了 阝 阝 阝 阣 阼 阼 陀 陏 陏 隋 隋 墮	To fall down, sink *doh* *dè*　　　　　*dè*
增	土 圡 圤 圳 圸 圸 坳 坳 堆 墻 墙 增	To increase, add to *jeng* *dzēng*　　　　　*zēng*

墟	土 圤 圵 圩 圩 圹 圹 圹 圹 塘 墟 墟 墟	A market, wasteland *heui* *syu* *xu*
墳	土 圵 圵 圵 圵 圹 圹 墳 墳 墳 墳 墳	A grave *fáhn* *fén* *fén*
墨	丶 ⼍ ⼞ 四 四 甲 甲 黒 黒 黒 墨	Blank ink, dark *mahk* *me* *me*
壁	⼀ ⼍ 尸 尺 启 启 启 启 启 启 壁 辟 辟 壁	A wall, defense *bik* *bì* *bì*
墾	丿 丿 ⼃ 夕 多 多 豸 豸 豹 豹 貇 貇 墾	To plow land, cultivate *hán* *kén* *kén*
壇	土 圵 圹 圹 圹 圹 坫 坫 壇 壇 壇 壇 壇 壇	An altar *taàhn* *tán* *tán*
壓	⼀ ⼚ 厂 厅 戶 戶 戶 屑 屑 厭 厭 厭 壓 壓	To crush, repress *ngaat* *yā* *yā*
壘	丶 ⼍ ⼞ 田 田 畾 畾 畾 壘	A rampart *leúih* *lěi* *lěi*
壞	土 圵 圹 圹 坮 坮 坮 塄 塄 塄 壞 壞 壞 壞	Ruined, broken *waaih* *hwài* *huài*
壤	土 圵 圹 圹 坮 坮 坮 埨 埨 壇 壤 壤 壤 壤	Soil, rich earth *yeuhng* *rǎng* *rǎng*
<div align="center">士</div>		Section
士	⼀ ⼗ 士	A soldier, officer *sih* *shr* *shì*

壯	ㄥ ㄐ ㄐ 壮 壮 壯	To encourage; strong *jong* *jwang* *zhuàng*
壹	士 士 吉 志 壳 壳 壹 壹 壹 壹	One; uniform *yat* *yī* *yī*
壺	士 士 吉 志 壺 壺 壺 壺 壺 壺	A jug, pot *wuh* *hú* *hú*
壻	士 圹 圻 圻 圻 壻 坧 壻 壻 壻	A son-in-law, husband *saih* *syù* *xù*
壽	士 生 吉 吉 壴 壴 壽 壽 壽 壽 壽 壽	Age, longevity *sauh* *shòu* *shòu*
夊		Section
夏	一 丆 丆 丆 万 百 百 百 頁 頁 夏	Summer *hah* *syà* *xià*
夕		Section
夕	丿 夕 夕	Evening, sunset *jihk* *syì* *xì*
外	夕 外	Outside, foreign; without *ngoih* *waì* *wài*
多	夕 多	Many, much *dò* *dwō* *duō*
夜	丶 亠 广 疒 夵 夜	Night, dark *yeh* *yè* *yè*

夠	夕 多 多 豹 豹 豹 豹	Enough *gau* *goù*　　　　　*goù*
夢	丶 丶 艹 艹 芇 苩 苗 茁 苗 蕚 夢	To dream *muhng* *meng*　　　　*meng*
夥	丶 口 日 日 旦 果 果 果 夥 夥	Companion; many *ló* *hwo*　　　　*huǒ*

大　Section

大	一 ナ 大	Big, very *daaih* *dà*　　　　*dà*
天	一 天	The sky, day; God *tin* *tyān*　　　*tiān*
太	大 太	Extreme, very *taai* *tai*　　　　*tai*
夫	一 夫	A husband, servant *fu* *fū*　　　　*fū*
夭	ノ 夭	To die young, fresh *diu* *yau*　　　*yāo*
失	ノ 广 失	To miss, lose *sat* *shr*　　　　*shī*
央	丶 冂 央	To beg; center *yeung* *yang*　　　*yāng*
夷	一 ⼻ 三 弓 夷 夷	Even; barbarians *yih* *yí*　　　　*yí*

夾	一 厂 丙 夾 夾 夾	To squeeze, press *gaap* *jyā* *jiā*
奇	大 查 杳 杳 奇 奇	Remarkable, rare *keih* *chí* *qí*
奈	大 太 杏 夲 奈 奈	However, a means *noih* *nài* *nài*
奉	一 二 三 丰 夹 表 奏 奉	To wait on, receive *fuhng* *fèng* *fèng*
奔	大 太 本 本 奔 奔	To run, hurry *ban* *bēn* *bēn*
奏	一 二 三 丰 夹 表 奏 奏 奏	To play music *jau* *dzòu* *zòu*
契	一 二 三 丰 封 韧 契	To adopt; a contract *kai* *chì* *qì*
套	大 太 本 本 杢 套 套 套	A case, envelope; series *tou* *tàu* *tào*
奢	大 太 本 夲 夲 夲 奓 奢 奢	Wasteful, extravagant *che* *shē* *shē*
奥	' 亻 冂 向 向 向 向 向 雨 奥 奥	Mysterious *ou* *aù* *aò*
奪	大 太 本 本 本 奔 奔 奋 奞 奞 奪 奪	To take by force, seize *dyuht* *dwó* *dúo*
獎	ㄥ ㄐ ㄐ ㅒ ㅒ 爿 将 将 㳚 將 將 獎	To praise; a prize *jéung* *jyǎng* *jiǎng*

奮	大 太 大 木 本 本 杏 奞 奞 奞 奞 奞 奞 奮 奮 奮	To stir up; vigorous fahn fèn fèn
	女	Section
女	く 女 女	A girl, woman, female néuih nyǔ nǔ
奴	女 女 奴	To enslave; a slave nouh nú nú
奶	女 奶 奶	The breast; milk náaih nǎi nǎi
妃	女 女 妃	An imperial concubine fēi fēi fēi
妄	、 一 亡 亡 亡 妄	Foolishly mong wàng wàng
奸	女 女 奸 奸	Wicked, corrupt gaan jyān jiān
她	女 奶 奶 她	She tā tā tā
好	女 女 好 好	Good, very hóu hǎu hǎo
如	女 女 如 如	If; like, as yùh rú rú
妙	女 女 妙 妙 妙 妙	Wonderful, perfect miuh myàu miào

妖	女 女' 妖 妖 妖	Magical *yiu* *yāu*　　　　*yāo*
妨	女 女' 妨 妨 妨	To hinder *fong* *fang*　　　　*fang*
妥	ノ ⺈ ⺈ ⺈ ⺈ ⺈ 妥	Secure, stable *tóh* *twǒ*　　　　*tuǒ*
妗	女 女' 妗 妗 妗	A sister-in-law *kahm* *jín*　　　　*jín*
妒	女 女' 妒 妒 妒	To be jealous, envious *douh* *dù*　　　　*dù*
妓	女 女' 妓 妓 妓	A prostitute *geih* *jì*　　　　*jì*
妻	一 ラ ⺕ ⺕ 妻 妻	A wife *chāi* *chī*　　　　*qī*
妾	⺊ ⺀ ⺀ ⺀ 立 妾	A concubine *chip* *chye*　　　　*qiè*
妹	女 女' 妹 妹 妹 妹	A younger sister *mui* *mei*　　　　*mei*
姊	女 女' 姊 姊 姊	An elder sister *jí* *dz*　　　　*zǐ*
姐	女 女' 姐 姐 姐 姐	An elder sister *je* *jyě*　　　　*jiě*
姑	女 女' 姑 姑 姑 姑	Father's sister, aunt *gu* *gū*　　　　*gū*

始	女 女ˊ 女ˊ 始 始 始	To begin; an origin *chi* shǐ shǐ
姓	女 女ˊ 女ˊ 姓 姓 姓	A family name, surname *sing* syìng xìng
委	ノ 一 千 禾 禾 委	To commit, delegate *wai* wěi wěi
姆	女 女ˊ 如 姆 姆 姆	An old woman, baby sitter *mouh* mǔ mǔ
姨	女 女ˊ 妒 妒 姨 姨 姨	Wife or mother's sister, aunt *yi* yí yí
姻	女 女 如 姻 姻 姻 姻	Marriage *yan* yīn yīn
姿	丶 冫 冫ˊ 次 次 次 姿	Manner, style *ji* dz zī
威	一 厂 厂 屈 威 威 威	Dignity; solemn *wai* wēi wēi
姦	女 姦 姦	Adultery, to rape *gaan* jyān jiān
娃	女 女ˊ 好 娃 娃 娃 娃	Baby, little girl *wa* wá wá
姪	女 女ˊ 妒 姪 姪 姪 姪	A nephew or niece *jaht* jŕ zhí
娘	女 女 妒 娘 娘 娘 娘 娘	A wife, mother, young lady *neuhng* nyáng niáng

娟	女 女 如 如 妈 娟 娟 娟	Graceful, attractive gwùn jywan　　　　juān
娱	女 女 如 如 娯 娯 娯 娯	To amuse; joy yuh yú　　　　yú
娩	女 女 女 妒 娩 娩 娩 娩 娩	To give birth to; obliging míhn myǎn　　　　miǎn
婚	女 女 女 妒 娇 娇 娇 婚 婚	To marry; a wedding fàn hwūn　　　　hūn
婦	女 女 女 女 妇 妇 婦 婦 婦 婦	A woman, wife fúh fù　　　　fù
婆	丶 宀 氵 沪 沪 沙 波 波 婆	An old woman, mother-in-law, pòh　　　　grandmother pwo　　　　po
婢	女 女 女 妒 娴 娴 娴 娴 娴 婢	A slave girl, maid peíh bì　　　　bì
婊	女 女 女 妓 妓 妓 妓 婊 婊 婊	A prostitute biu byǎu　　　　biǎo
婪	木 木 木 木 林 婪	Greedy laahm lán　　　　lán
婉	女 女 女 妒 妒 妒 婉 婉 婉	Obliging yún wǎn　　　　wǎn
娶	一 丁 丌 丌 耳 耳 取 取 娶	Marriage; to marry chéui chyǔ　　　　qù
娼	女 女 如 妈 妈 妈	A prostitute cheùng chāng　　　　chāng

媒	女 奵 奵 娕 娕 娕 娕 媒 媒 媒	A match-maker *muih* *mei*　　　　`mei`
婿	女 奵 奵 奵 奵 妮 婿 婿 婿 婿	A son-in-law, husband *sai* *syu*　　　　`syu`
嫂	女 奵 奵 奵 奵' 奵¹ 妲 婌 嫂 嫂	The wife of an elder brother *sóu* *saŭ*　　　　*saŏ*
嫁	女 女' 奵 奵' 奵' 奵' 婇 婇 婇 嫁 嫁	To marry a husband *ga* *jya*　　　　`jia`
媳	女 女' 奵' 奵ᵀ 娟 娟 媦 媦 媦 媳 媳	A daughter-in-law *sik* *sýi*　　　　*xí*
嫉	女 女' 奵` 奵' 奵' 奵' 妎 婎 婎 嫉 嫉	Envy, jealousy *jaht* *jí*　　　　*jí*
嫌	女 女' 奵` 奵` 奵⁶ 妈 妈° 婍 婍 嫌 嫌	To dislike *yihm* *syán*　　　　*xián*
媽	女 奵` 奵` 奵ᶠ 妸 妸 妈 妈 媽	A mother *ma* *mā*　　　　*mā*
嫡	女 女` 奵` 奵` 妒 妒 婍 婍 婍 嫡 嫡	Legally related wife *dik* *dí*　　　　*dí*
嫩	女 女` 奵` 妐 妐 妯 妯 嫀 嫀 嫩 嫩 嫩	Tender, delicate *nyuhn* *nen*　　　　`nen`
嬌	女 女' 奵` 奵 妖 妖 婄 婄 婄 嬌 嬌	Charming, beautiful *giu* *jyāu*　　　　*jiāo*
嫻	女 奵 奵 奵 奵 奵' 婀 婀 婀 婀 嫻 嫻	Graceful, refined *haahn* *syán*　　　　*xián*

嬉	女 女 女゙ 女゙ 女゙ 姞 姞 姞 婅 婅 嬉 嬉 嬉	To play; amusement *hei* *syī*　　　　*xī*
嬰	丨 冂 冃 月 目 貝 貝 賏 嬰	A baby, infant *yīng* *yīng*　　　*yīng*
嬸	女 女゙ 女゙ 女゙ 妒 妒 妒 妒 妒 嬸 嬸 嬸 嬸	Wife of father's younger *sam*　　　　brother, aunt *shěn*　　　*shěn*
孀	女 女゙ 女゙ 女゙ 妒 妒 婷 婷 嫘 嫘 嬬 嬬 孀	A widow *seung* *shwāng*　　*shuāng*

子　　Section

子	⁊ 了 子	A son, boy, seed *ji* *dz*　　　　*zi*
孑	⁊ 了 孑	Only, single *diu* *jye*　　　　*jie*
孔	孑 孔	A hole; very *hung* *kǔng*　　　*kǒng*
孕	乃 乃 孕 孕 孕	To conceive; pregnant *yahn* *ywùn*　　　*yùn*
字	丶 丶 宀 宁 字 字	Character, letter, word *jih* *dz*　　　　*zì*
存	一 ナ 才 存	To keep, preserve *cheuhn* *twún*　　　*tún*
孝	一 十 土 耂 孝	Dutiful, filial *haau* *syàu*　　　*xiao*

孤	子 子 孑 孤 孤 孤	An orphan, lonely gu gū gū
季	ノ 一 千 禾 禾 季	A season; young gwai jì jì
孟	子 子 舌 舌 孟 孟	Senior, eldest maahng meng meng
孩	子 孑 孓 孖 孩 孩 孩	A child, baby haaih hái hái
孫	子 孑 孑 孫 孫 孫 孫 孫	A grandchild syun swūn sūn
孰	丶 一 亠 古 亨 享 孰 孰	Who, which suhk shú shú
孵	ノ イ ｲ 夘 卯 卵 卵 卵 卵 卵 卵 孵	To hatch, originate fu fū fū
學	ノ ｲ ｲ ｲ ｲ ｲ 段 阋 阋 阋 阋 學 學	To study, learn hohk sywe xúe
孺	子 孑 孑 孖 孖 孖 孖 孖 孖 孺 孺 孺	Small child, woman yuh rù, rú rù, rú
孿	丶 一 亠 亠 言 言 言 信 綜 綜 戀 孿	Twins lyuhn lywán luán
	宀	Section
它	丶 丷 宀 宀 它	It tà tā tā

宅	宀 宀 宅 宅	A residence *jaahk* *jè*　　　　　*zhè*
守	宀 宀 守 守	To guard, keep *sáu* *shǒu*　　　*shòu*
安	宀 宀 安 安	Peaceful, secure *on* *ān*　　　　　*ān*
宇	宀 宀 宇 宇	A house, universe *yúh* *yǔ*　　　　　*yǔ*
宋	宀 宀 宇 字 宋	The Sung Dynasty *sung* *sung*　　　　*sòng*
完	宀 宀 宀 宇 完	To finish, complete *yùhn* *wán*　　　　*wán*
宏	宀 宀 宀 宏 宏	Wide, vast *wàhng* *hung*　　　　*hóng*
定	宀 宀 宀 宇 宇 定	To decide; certain *dihng* *dìng*　　　　*dìng*
宙	宀 宀 宀 宙 宙 宙	Universe *jauh* *jou*　　　　　*zhòu*
官	宀 宀 宀 宁 官	An officer; sense organ *gun* *gwān*　　　　*guān*
宗	宀 宀 宀 宇 宗 宗	An ancestor, clan *jùng* *jūng*　　　　*zhōng*
宜	宀 宀 宫 宫 宜 宜	Should; suitable *yìh* *yí*　　　　　*yí*

室	宀 宀 空 宏 空 室 室	A room, office, apartment sat shr shì
宣	宀 宀 宀 宣 宣 宣 宣	To announce syun syan xian
客	宀 宀 宀 安 客 客 客	A guest, visitor, customer haak ke ke
容	宀 宀 宀 宀 宊 容 容 容	To contain, endure; manner yuhng rung rong
家	宀 宀 宀 宊 家 家 家 家	A home, family, household ga jya jia
宮	宀 宀 宀 宮 宮 宮	A palace, temple gung gung gong
宴	宀 宀 宀 宴 宴 宴	To feast, entertain yin yan yan
害	宀 宀 宀 害 害 害 害	To hurt, injure hoih hai hai
寄	宀 宀 宊 宊 寄 寄 寄	To send, stay at gei ji ji
宿	宀 宀 宀 宀 宿 宿 宿 宿	To pass the night suk su su
密	宀 宀 宓 宓 宓 密 密 密	Secret, close maht mi mi
寃	宀 宀 宀 宀 宊 寃 寃 寃 寃	Injustice yun ywan yuan

字	筆順	意味
寂	宀 宀 宀 宀 宀 宀 宀 宋 寂 寂	Silent, lonely jihk jí jì
寇	宀 宀 宀 宁 完 完 完 寇 寇	Robbers kau kòu kòu
富	宀 宀 宀 官 官 官 宮 宮 富 富	Rich, wealthy fu fù fù
寒	宀 宁 宁 宇 宙 宙 宙 寒 寒 寒	Cold, chilly, poor hohn hán hán
實	宀 宀 宁 宁 宁 宁 宇 宇 實 實	True, solid saht shŕ shí
寧	宀 宀 宀 宀 宀 宀 宮 宮 宮 窜 寧	Peaceful; rather nihng níng níng
寥	宀 宁 宁 宁 宙 宙 宙 寀 寥 寥	Empty; very few liuh lyau liáo
察	宀 宀 宀 宀 宀 宀 宛 宛 寂 察 察	To examine, consider chaat chā chā
寢	宀 宁 宁 宇 宇 宇 宇 宇 寢 寢 寢	To rest, go to bed cham chĭn qĭn
寡	宀 宀 宁 宁 官 官 官 官 寊 寡 寡	Few, alone; widowhood gwa gwă guă
寞	宀 宁 宁 宀 宛 宛 宙 宙 寞 寞	Lonely, quiet mohk mwo mò
寬	宀 宀 宁 宀 宛 宛 宵 宵 寊 寊 寬 寬	Wide, broad, large fun kwān kuān

審	宀宀宀宀宀宀 宋宋宋宋宋審審	To judge, investigate *sam* *shen* *shen*
寫	宀宀宀宀宀宀宀 宀寫寫寫	To write, copy *se* *sye* *xie*
寵	宀宀宀宀宀宀宵 宵宵宵宵宵寵寵	To love; spoil *chung* *chung* *chong*
寶	宀宀宀宀宀宀宀 宇宇宗宇寶寶寶	Precious, a jewel *bou* *bau* *bao*
	寸	Section
寸	一寸寸	A Chinese inch *chyun* *twun* *tun*
寺	一十土寺	A temple, buddhist monastery *ji* *sz* *si*
封	一十土圭圭圭圭 圭封封	To seal, close *fung* *feng* *feng*
射	丿亻竹身身身身 射	To shoot, squirt *seh* *she* *she*
將	㇄丬丬爿爿爿爿 爿將將將	To take; soon; a commander *jeung, jeung* *jyang* *jiang*
專	一厂厅百百申車 車專	Special, to attend to *jyun* *jwan* *zhuan*
尉	一コフ尸尸尸尿尿 尿尉	A military officer *wai* *wei* *wei*

尊	丶丷兴兴兴酋酋 酋酋尊	To honor, esteem *jyun* *dzwūn* *zūn*
尋	⼓⼐⺕⼱⺕⺕⺕ 帚帚尋	To search, find *chàhm* *syún* *xún*
對	⼀⼍⼍⼚业业业丵 业丵丵丵對	To compare; a pair; correct *deui* *dwei* *duì*
導	丶丷丷丷产产首首 首首首道道道導 寻	To lead, direct *douh* *dàu* *dǎo*

| | 小 | Section |

小	亅小小	Small, little *siú* *syǎu* *xiǎo*
少	小 少	A few; young *siu* *shǎu* *shǎo*
尖	小 业 半 尖	Pointed, sharp *jim* *jyān* *jiān*
尚	丨丨丬丬尚尚 尚尚	To esteem; yet, still *souhng* *shàng* *shàng*

| | 尢 | Section |

| 尤 | 一 十 尢 尤 | An error; furthermore, yet
yàuh
yóu   *yóu* |
| 就 | 丶亠亠方亨亨亨
京京尌就就 | To approach; then
jauh
jyòu   *jiù* |

尷	一十九尤尤尢尢尢尢尢尢尢尢尢尢尷尷尷尷尷	Embarrassment *gaam* *gān*　　　　*gān*
	尸	Section
尺	𠃌 コ 尸 尺	A Chinese foot, ruler *chek* *chř, chě*　　*chǐ, chě*
尼	𠃌 コ 尸 尸' 尼	A nun *nei* *ní*　　　　*ní*
尾	尸 尸' 尼 尾 尾	To follow; a tail, end *mej* *wei*　　　*wei*
局	尸 尸' 局 局 局	An office; chess *guhk* *jyu*　　　*jú*
尿	尸 尸 尿 尿 尿	Urine *niuh* *nyàu*　　　*niào*
居	尸 尸' 尸 尸 居 居	To live; a residence *geui* *jyu*　　　*jū*
屆	尸 尸' 尸 屏 屆 屆	To reach; a set time, a term *gàaih* *jyè*　　　*jiè*
屈	尸 尼 尼 屏 屈 屈	To stoop, give in *wàt* *chyu*　　　*qu*
屋	尸 尸' 居 居 居 屋 屋	A house, room *uk* *wū*　　　*wū*
屎	尸 尸' 尸' 屈 屏 屏 屎	Excrement *sí* *shr*　　　*shi*

屍	尸 尸 尸 房 房 房 屍	A corpse, carcass si shr　　　shī
展	尸 尸 尸 尿 屈 展 展 展	To expand, spread, exhibit jín jan　　　zhǎn
屑	尸 尸 尸 屑 屑 屑 屑 屑	A fragment, powder sit syè　　　xiè
屐	尸 尸 尸 屍 屍 屐 屐 屐	Wooden shoes kehk jì　　　jì
屏	尸 尸 尽 尿 居 屏 屏 屏 屏 屏	A screen, shelter pihng ping　　　píng
屜	尸 尸 尽 尿 屌 屉 屉 屉 屜	A drawer sit tì　　　tì
屠	尸 尸 尸 屋 屋 屋 屠 屠 屠	To slaughter; a butcher touh tú　　　tú
屢	尸 尸 尿 局 屑 屑 屑 屑 屢 屢 屢 屢	Frequently, often leuih lǔ　　　lǚ
履	尸 尸 尿 尿 尿 屏 屏 屈 屈 屈 屨 屨 履	To walk, act; shoes leuih lyuh　　　lǚ
層	尸 尸 尸 尿 屋 屋 屋 屑 屑 屑 層 層	Floors of a building chàhng tséng　　　céng
屬	尸 尸 尿 屍 屈 屏 屏 屏 屏 屚 屚 屬 屬 屬 屬 屬	To belong to, subject to suhk shū　　　shū
山		Section

- 117 -

山	丨 山 山	A hill, mountain, range _saan_ _shān_ _shān_
岔	丿 八 今 分 岔	Point where roads meet _cha_ _chā_ _chà_
岳	丿 亻 斤 丘 丘 岳	A wife's parents; lofty _ngohk_ mountain _ywe_ _yue_
岸	山 屵 屵 岸 岸 岸	The beach, shore _ngohn_ _an_ _an_
島	丿 亻 竹 白 臼 鳥 島	An island _dou_ _dǎu_ _dǎo_
峭	丨 山 山 山' 屵 屵 屵 峭 峭 峭	Steep, severe _chiu_ _chyàu_ _qiào_
峰	山 山' 屵 屵 峰 峰 峰 屵	The peak _fung_ _fēng_ _fēng_
峽	山 山' 屵 屾 屾 屾 峽	A mountain pass, gorge _hahp_ _syá_ _xá_
峻	山 山' 屵 屵 峻 峻 峻 峻	Steep, stern, severe _jeun_ _jìn_ _jìn_
崩	山 屵 岢 肯 肯 崩	To fall, collapse _bang_ _beng_ _bēng_
崗	山 屵 岢 岢 岢 岗 崗 崗 崗	The ridge of a hill, a mound _gong_ _gāng_ _gāng_
崖	山 屵 屵 岸 岸 崖 崖 崖 崖	A slope, cliff _ngaaih_ _yái_ _yái_

崇	山 屮 屮 屵 峀 峇 崈 崇 崇	To respect; high *suhng* *chúng*　　　*chóng*
崎	山 屵 山† 山木 岐 崎 崎 崎 崎	Uneven, rugged *kèih, kei* *chí*　　　*qí*
嶇	山 山 屺 屺 屺 屺 屺 嶇	Rugged and steep, uneven *kèui* *chyū*　　　*qū*
嶺	山 屵 屵 屵 岺 岺 岺 岺 岺 岺 嵿 嶺 嶺 嶺	Mountain range, ridge *líhng* *líng*　　　*líng*
嶼	山 山† 屿 屿 屿 屿 嶼 嶼 嶼 嶼 嶼 嶼 嶼 嶼	An island *jeuih* *yǔ*　　　*yǔ*
巔	山 屵 屶 屵 肯 肯 置 寘 寘 寘 寘 巔 巔 巔 巔	The top of a hill, peak *dìn* *dyān*　　　*diān*
巛		Section
川	ノ 丿丨 川	A stream, flow *chyun* *chwān*　　　*chuān*
州	` 丿 屮 州 州 州	A state, region *jàu* *jōu*　　　*zhōu*
巡	〈 巜 巛 彡巛 巡	To patrol *chèuhn* *syún*　　　*xún*
巢	巛 竹 竹 甾 甾 甾 甾 巢 巢	A nest *chàauh* *cháu*　　　*cháo*
工		Section

工	一 丁 工	To work, labor *gung* *gung*　　　　*gōng*
左	一 ナ 左	The left hand side *jó* *dzwo*　　　　*zuǒ*
巧	エ エ一 巧	Skillful, artful, ingenious *haáu* *chyǎu*　　　*qiǎo*
巨	一 丆 冋 巨	Great, huge *geuih* *jyù*　　　　*jù*
巫	一 丁 丌 丒 巫 巫	A wizard, witch *mouh* *wu*　　　　*wu*
差	丶 丷 丷 ꭅ 羊 羊 羊 差	To send; a mistake, a mes- *chāi, chaai*　　senger *chā, chāi, chà chā, chāi, chà*
己		Section
己	ㄱ コ 己	Oneself *géi* *ji*　　　　*ji*
已	ㄱ コ 已	To stop; already *yih* *yi*　　　　*yi*
巳	ㄱ コ 巳	The 6th of the branches *jih* *se*　　　　*se*
巴	ㄱ ㄱ ㄢ 巴	To adhere, attach to *ba* *bā*　　　　*bā*
巷	丨 十 艹 艹 芏 共 莽 巷	An alley, lane *hohng* *syang*　　　*xiàng*

巾		Section
巾	丨 冂 巾	A napkin, kerchief, towel *gān* *jīn*　　　　　*jīn*
布	一 ナ 布	Cloth, fabric *bou* *bu*　　　　　*bu*
市	、 亠 市	A city, town, market *sih* *shr*　　　　　*shi*
帆	巾 帄 帆 帆	A sail, canvas *faahn* *fan*　　　　　*fan*
希	ノ メ 产 羊 希	To hope; rare *hei* *syi*　　　　　*xi*
帕	巾 巾' 帕 帕 帕 帕	Kerchief *paak* *pa*　　　　　*pa*
帚	コ ヨ ヨ ヨ 帚 帚	A broom *gon* *jou*　　　　　*zhou*
帛	ノ 亻 冂 白 白 帛	Silk, fabric *baahk* *bwo*　　　　　*bo*
帖	巾 帄 帖 帖 帖 帖	A document, invitation *tip* *tye*　　　　　*tie*
帝	、 亠 亠 产 产 产 帝	A king; God *dai* *di*　　　　　*di*
帥	ノ 亻 阝 阝 自 帥	A general, leader *seui* *shwe, shwai*　　*shwe shuai*

師	´ ⺅ ⼍ ⼍ 𠂤 師	To follow as an example; *si* teacher *shr* *shi*
席	` 亠 广 广 庐 庐 庶 席	A mat, table *jihk* *syi* *xi*
帷	巾 巾´ 帐 帷 帷 帷 帷 帷 帷	A curtain, screen *waih* *wéi* *wéi*
帶	一 十 廿 卅 世 世 世 带 带	To bring; a belt *daai* *dai* *dai*
帳	巾 帜 帜 帐 帐 帐 帳 帳 帳	A curtain, screen *jeung* *jang* *zhang*
常	⼀ ⼁ ⺌ ⺌ 当 常 常 常 常	Always; a rule *seuhng* *chang* *chang*
幀	巾 巾´ 巾´ 帄 帄 帧 帧 帧 幀 幀	Measure word for picture *jing* *jeng* *zheng*
幅	巾 巾´ 帄´ 帄 帄 帄 帽 帽 幅 幅	A roll of map or pictures *fuk* *fu* *fu*
帽	巾 巾´ 帄 帄 帽 帽 帽 帽 帽 帽	A cap, hat *mou* *mau* *mao*
幕	⼀ 十 艹 艹 莫 莫 莫 莫 莫 幕	A screen, curtain *mohk* *mu* *mu*
幣	´ ⼋ 𠂉 𠂉 尚 尚 尚 敝 敝 敝 敝 幣	Money, wealth *baih* *bi* *bi*
幫	⼀ 十 土 圭 圭 封 封 封 封 封 幇 幇 幫	To help; a gang *bong* *bang* *bang*

幪	巾 巾' 巾' 巾艹 巾艹 巾艹 巾芦 巾芦 巾芦 幪 幪 幪	To cover up, protect *muhng* *meng*　　　*meng*
	干	Section
干	一 二 干	To interfere, oppose *gon* *gān*　　　*gān*
平	一 ㄱ ㄤ 立 平	Level, peaceful *pihng* *píng*　　　*píng*
年	ノ ㄣ ㄥ 二 午 年	A year, yearly *nihn* *nyán*　　　*nián*
幸	一 十 土 土 古 古 幸 幸 幸	Luck; happily *hehng* *syìng*　　　*xìng*
幹	一 十 十 古 古 古 直 卓 卓 斡 幹	To manage; business *gon* *gàn*　　　*gàn*
	幺	Section
幻	ㄥ ㄠ 幺 幻	Imaginary, unreal *waahn* *hwàn*　　　*huàn*
幼	幺 幻 幼	An early age *yau* *yòu*　　　*yòu*
幽	ㅣ 幻 幽 幽 幽	Dark, mysterious *yau* *yōu*　　　*yōu*
幾	幺 丝 丝 絲 丝 幾 幾 幾	Several; almost, some *géi, gèi* *jǐ, jī*　　　*jǐ, jī*

	广	Section
序	、 亠 广 庁 庁 庁 序	Preface, order, series jeuih syu xu
床	广 庁 庁 床 床	Bed, sofa chohng chwang chuang
底	广 庁 庁 底 底 底	The bottom, low dai di di
店	广 庁 庁 庁 店 店	A shop, store dim dyan dian
府	广 庁 庁 庁 府 府	A residence, storehouse fu fu fu
度	广 庁 庁 庁 庁 庋 度	To pass, a measure douh, dohk du,dwo du, duo
庭	广 庁 庁 庁 庭 庭 庭	A courtyard; straight tihng ting ting
座	广 庁 庁 庶 座 座 座	A seat, stand joh dzwo zuo
庫	广 庁 庁 庁 庁 庫 庫	A store house, treasury fu fu fu
庶	广 庁 庁 庁 庶 庶 庶	The people; various syu shu shu
庸	广 庁 庁 庁 庸 庸 庸 庸 庸	A service; common yuhng yung yong

康	广 庐 庐 庐 庐 庐 康 康 康	Healthy, peaceful hong kang kang
厢	广 广 厈 厈 床 床 厢 厢 厢 厢	A side room seung syang xiang
廁	广 广 庐 庐 庐 庐 庐 庐 庐 廁	A toilet chi tsz ci
廈	广 广 广 庐 庐 庐 庐 庐 庐 庐 廈	A large house, building hah sya xa
廉	广 广 广 广 庐 庐 庐 庐 庐 庐 廉	Honest, frugal lihm lyan lian
廊	广 广 庐 庐 庐 庐 庐 庐 廊 廊 廊	A porch long lang lang
廟	广 广 庐 庐 庐 庐 庐 庿 庿 庿 廟 廟	A temple miu myau miao
廢	广 庐 庐 庐 庐 庐 庐 庐 庐 庐 廢 廢	Ruined; to abandon fai fei fei
廠	广 广 广 广 庐 庐 庐 庐 庐 庐 庐 廠 廠	A factory, work-shop chong chang chang
廣	广 广 广 庐 庐 庐 庐 庐 庐 庐 廣 廣	To enlarge; broad gwong gwang guang
廚	广 广 庐 庐 庐 庐 庐 庐 庐 庐 廚 廚	A kitchen chyuh chu chu
龐	广 广 广 庐 庐 庐 庐 庐 庐 庐 庐 龐 龐	Great, huge pohng pang pang

廳	广 庁 庁 庌 庌 庌 庌 庌 庌 庌 廍 廍 廍 廍 廍 廳 廳	A hall, living room *teng* *tǐng* *tīng*
	廴	Section
廷	ノ ニ 千 壬 廷 廷	The imperial court *tihng* *tíng* *tíng*
延	ノ ノ イ 千 壬 延 延	To delay, postpone *yihn* *yán* *yán*
建	コ ユ ヨ 聿 聿 聿 肂 建	To build, set up *gin* *jyàn* *jiàn*
	廾	Section
弄	一 丁 干 王 王 弄 弄	To play, make *nuhng* *nùng* *nòng*
弊	ノ ソ イ 介 伇 伇 伇 伇 伇 伇 敝 敝 弊 弊	Defects *baih* *bì* *bì*
	弋	Section
式	一 二 三 弍 式	Two *yih* *er* *er*
式	一 二 干 王 式 式	Form, rule *sik* *shr* *shì*
弑	ノ メ 二 羊 羊 羊 羊 羊 彩 弒 弑	To murder a superior *si* *shr* *shì*

	弓	Section
弓	ㄱ ㄱ 弓	A bow guńg guńg gōng
引	弓 引	To lead, guide, introduce yáhn yǐn yǐn
弔	弓 弔	Compassionate; to hang diu dyau diào
弛	弓 弚 弛 弛	To relax, loosen chih shř shǐ
弟	` ˊ 兰 弟 弟	A younger brother daih dì dì
弧	弓 弓 弘 弧 弧 弧	A wooden bow wùh hú hú
弦	弓 弓 弦 弦 弦 弦	A string of an instrument yìhn syān xián
弱	弓 弓 弓 弱	Weak, young yeuhk rwò ruò
張	弓 弓 引 引 引 引 張 張 張	A sheet; to stretch; large jeung jāng zhāng
強	弓 弘 弘 弘 弘 強 強 強 強	To force; strong keuhng chýang qiǎng
彈	弓 弓 弓 弓 弓 弓 彈 彈 彈 彈 彈	To flick, play music, a bullet daahn, taàhn, dáan dàn, tán dàn, tán

彌	弓 弓 弓 弣 弥 弥 弥 弥 弥 彌 彌 彌	Still; to reach nèih mí mí
彎	丶 亠 亠 言 言 言 言 信 綰 綰 綰 綗 彎	A curve wàan wān wān
彐		Section
彗	一 二 三 丰 赳 彗 彗 彗	A broom, to sweep seuih hwèi huì
彙	乚 夕 牟 盤 牟 牟 牟 牟 盦 彔 彙 彙	To classify; a series wuih hwèi huì
彡		Section
形	一 二 于 开 开 形 形 形	Shape, appearance yìhng sýing xíng
彦	丶 亠 亠 文 立 产 彦	A refined cholar yihn yàn yàn
彩	丶 丷 爫 꿀 乎 푸 采 彩	Beautiful colors chòi tsài cǎi
彫	丿 刀 月 月 用 用 周 周 彫	To engrave, carve diu dyāu diāo
彪	丨 卜 ﾋ 广 卢 虎 虎 虎 彪	Tiger stripes; ornamental biu byāu biāo
彬	一 十 才 木 林 彬	Elegant and refined ban bīn bīn

彰	丶 亠 亠 产 立 产 音 音 音 音 章 章 彰	Splendid; to show *jeung* *jāng* *zhāng*
影	丶 冂 冃 日 旦 早 早 昙 昌 昙 景 景 影	To take picture or movie; a *ying* shadow *yíng* *yǐng*
	彳	Section
役	丶 彳 彳 彳 彳 役 役	To serve; a servant *yihk* *yi* *yì*
彷	彳 彳 彳 彷 彷	Resembling, alike *fong* *fǎng* *fǎng*
往	彳 彳 彳 行 往 往	Formerly; to pass *wohng* *wǎng* *wǎng*
征	彳 彳 行 行 征 征	To attack, tax *jing* *jēng* *zhèng*
彼	彳 彳 彳 衫 彼 彼	He, she, that *béi* *bǐ* *bǐ*
後	彳 彳 彳 往 往 後 後	Back, after, behind *hauh* *hòu* *hòu*
很	彳 彳 彳 伊 伊 很 很	Very *hán* *hěn* *hěn*
待	彳 彳 彳 往 往 待 待	To wait, act to *doih* *dài* *dài*
律	彳 彳 彳 伊 伊 律 律	A law, rule *leuht* *lyù* *lü*

徊	彳 彳 徊 徊 徊 徊 徊	To go back and forth *wuih* *hwéi* *huí*
徐	彳 彳 徐 徐 徐 徐 徐 徐	Slow, at ease *cheuih* *syú* *xú*
徒	彳 彳 彳 彳 彳 彳 徒 徒	A follower, disciple *touh* *tú* *tú*
徑	彳 彳 彳 彳 徑 徑 徑 徑	A path; straightforward *ging* *jing* *jing*
徘	彳 彳 彳 彳 彳 徘 徘 徘 徘	To walk aimlessly *puih* *pái* *pái*
從	彳 彳 彳 從 從 從 從 從	To follow, obey; from *chuhng* *tsúng* *cóng*
御	彳 彳 彳 彳 御 御 御 御	To drive, manage *yik* *yu* *yù*
徙	彳 彳 彳 彳 徙 徙 徙 徙	To move, shift *saai* *syi* *xi*
得	彳 彳 彳 得 得 得 得 得	To get, gain; can, may *dak* *de, dei* *de, dei*
徧	彳 彳 彳 彳 徧 徧 徧 徧 徧	Everywhere *piŋ* *byan* *bian*
復	彳 彳 彳 彳 復 復 復 復 復	To recover, obtain again *fuhk* *fú* *fú*
徨	彳 彳 彳 彳 徨 徨 徨 徨	Hesitating, confused *wohng* *hwáng* *huáng*

循	彳彳彳彳彳彳彳 彳彳彳	To follow, go around chèuhn syún xún
傍	彳彳彳彳彳彳 彳彳彳傍傍	To attach to, walk by the pòhng side of páng páng
微	彳彳彳彳彳彳 微微微微微	Small, slight; to dwindle mèih wéi wéi
徵	彳彳彳彳彳彳 彳彳徵徵徵徵	To seek, call jìng jēng zhēng
德	彳彳彳彳彳彳彳 德德德德 德德	Virtue, morality dàk dé dé
徹	彳彳彳彳彳彳彳 徹徹徹徹徹徹	To displace, go through chit shè shè
徽	彳彳彳彳彳彳彳 彳彳徽徽徽徽徽	A flag fāi hwēi huī
	心 Section	
心	丶心心心	The heart, mind; a motive sàm syīn xīn
必	心 必	Must, surely, certainly bit bì bì
忍	フ刀刃忍	To endure; patience, severe yan rěn rěn
忌	フマ己忌	To avoid, fear; jealous geih ji jì

忘	、 亠 亡 忘	To forget, neglect *mòhng* *wáng*　　　　*wǎng*
志	一 十 士 志	A will, target, determination *ji* *jì*　　　　*zhì*
忙	、 丿 忄 忄 忙 忙	Busy, occupied, hurried *mòhng* *máng*　　　　*máng*
忠	、 口 中 忠	Loyal, sincere *jùng* *jūng*　　　　*zhōng*
念	丿 人 仐 今 念	To think about; a thought *nihm* *nyàn*　　　　*niàn*
忽	丿 勹 勺 勿 忽	To neglect; suddenly *fāt* *hū*　　　　*hū*
快	忄 忄 忙 快 快	Fast, cheerful *faai* *kwài*　　　　*kuài*
性	忄 忄 忄 忤 性 性	Temper; sex *sing* *sying*　　　　*xìng*
急	丿 ⺈ 刍 刍 刍 急	Urgent, anxious, hasty *gāp* *ji*　　　　*jí*
怒	⺄ 女 女 如 奴 怒	Angry; resentment *nouh* *nù*　　　　*nù*
思	、 口 曰 田 田 思	To consider; a thought *si* *sē*　　　　*sē*
怠	⺈ 厶 台 台 台 怠	Lazy, careless *toih* *daì*　　　　*daì*

怪	忄 忄 忆 怪 怪 怪	To blame; strange *gwaai* *gwài*　　　*guài*
怎	丿 亇 个 乍 乍 怎	Why, how *jám* *dzěn*　　　*zěn*
怕	忄 忄 忄 怕 怕 怕	To fear, dread *pa* *pà*　　　*pà*
怯	忄 忄 忄 忄 怯 怯	Timid, cowardly *hip* *chyè*　　　*qiè*
怨	丿 勹 夕 夗 夗 怨	To complain, dislike *yun* *ywàn*　　　*yuàn*
怖	忄 忄 忄 怖 怖 怖	Afraid; to scare *bou* *bù*　　　*bu*
恒	忄 忄 忄 恒 恒 恒 恒	Permanent, constant *hàhng* *héng*　　　*héng*
恩	丨 冂 日 用 因 因 恩	Kindness, benevolence *yàn* *ēn*　　　*ēn*
恨	忄 忄 忄 忄 恨 恨 恨	To hate; resentment *hahn* *hen*　　　*hèn*
息	丿 亻 白 白 自 自 息	To rest; a breath *sik* *syí*　　　*xí*
恕	く 女 女 如 如 如 恕	To pardon, excuse *syu* *shu*　　　*shù*
恙	丶 丷 ⺍ 羊 羊 羊 恙	Sickness *yeuhng* *yàng*　　　*yàng*

恢	忄 忆 忆 恢 恢 恢 恢	Great; to enlarge *fui* *hwei* *huī*
恐	一 丁 工 丑 巩 巩 恐	Fearful *húng* *kung* *kǒng*
恭	丶 一 艹 艹 艹 共 苿 恭 恭 恭	To respect *gung* *gung* *gōng*
恰	忄 忄 忄 忄 恰 恰 恰	Exactly, fortunately *hap* *chya* *qià*
恤	忄 忄 忄 恤 恤 恤 恤	To sympathize, pity *syut* *syù* *xù*
悔	忄 忄 忄 忙 悔 悔 悔 悔	To regret, repent *fui* *hwei* *huǐ*
悟	忄 忄 忏 悟 悟 悟 悟 悟	To awake, become aware *ngh* *wu* *wù*
悠	丿 亻 仁 似 攸 攸 悠 悠	Sad, distant *yàuh* *yōu* *yōu*
您	丿 亻 仁 你 你 你 你 您	A respectful form of "you" *neih* *nín* *nín*
患	丶 冂 口 吕 串 患	To suffer; misery *waahn* *hwàn* *huàn*
悦	忄 忄 忄 忄 悦 悦 悦 悦	To please; delighted *yuht* *ywè* *yuè*
悉	丿 亻 亻 丄 乎 釆 釆 悉	To comprehend; completely *sik* *syī* *xī*

惟	忄 忄 忄 忄 忄 忄 惟 惟 惟	To think about; only waih wéi wéi
惋	忄 忄 忄 忄 忄 惋 惋 惋 惋	Surprised, annoyed yún wàn wàn
悽	忄 忄 忄 忄 忄 悽 悽 悽 悽	Grieved, sorrowful chāi chī qī
情	忄 忄 忄 忄 忄 情 情 情 情	Feelings, desires chìhng chíng qíng
惡	一 丁 工 亞 亞 亞 亞 亞 惡 惡	Mean, bad ok, wu è, wù è, wù
悼	忄 忄 忄 忄 忄 悼 悼 悼 悼	To grieve; sad douh dàu dào
悴	忄 忄 忄 忄 忄 悴 悴	Distressed, sad seuih tswèi cuì
悲	丿 亅 丬 非 非 非 悲	To be sad, grieve bēi bei bēi
惕	忄 忄 忄 惕 惕 惕 惕 惕	Respect, awe tik tì tì
悶	丨 冂 冂 門 門 門 門 門 悶	Depressed, bored muhn men mèn
惦	忄 忄 忄 忄 忄 惦 惦 惦	To think of dim dyàn diàn
惆	忄 忄 忄 惆 惆 惆 惆 惆	Vexed, grieved chàuh chou chóu

惠	一厂厅厉百亩 重重惠	To be kind to; benevolent waih hwei hui
惜	忄忄忄忄忄忄 惜惜惜	To regret; pity sik syi xi
惑	一厂厅百或或 或或惑	To doubt; suspicion waahk hwò huo
感	一厂厂厃厉戌 厉感感感	To influence; emotion gam gǎn gǎn
愛	ノ爫爫爫爫 恶爱爱爱	To love, be fond of; love oi ai ai
想	一十才木札机 相相相想	To think, want seúng syǎng xiǎng
惰	忄忄忄忄忄忄 惰惰惰惰	Lazy, sluggish doh dwò duò
愚	丶冂日日禺 禺禺禺禺愚	Foolish, dull yuh yú yu
惶	忄忄忄忄忄忄 悍悍悍惶	Nervous, frightened wòhng hwang huáng
愉	忄忄忄忄忄 愉愉愉愉愉	Happy, pleased yuh yú yú
愎	忄忄忄忄忄忄 怕悕愎愎	Stubborn bìk bì bì
意	丶二六立立音 音音音意	A thought, opinion yi yì yì

惻	忄 忆 怀 怌 怚 怚 怚 惧 惧 惻	To grieve for; pity *chăk* *tsè*　　　*cè*
愈	丿 亼 亼 亼 亼 亼 亼 亼 亼 愈 愈 愈	To exceed, recover *yuht* *yù*　　　*yù*
惱	忄 忄 忆 忆 惱 惱 惱 惱 惱	Displeased, irritated *nóuh* *naŭ*　　　*năo*
愕	忄 忄 忄 忄 忄 忄 惄 愕	Startled, frightened *ngouh* *è*　　　*è*
愁	丿 二 千 禾 禾 禾 利 秒 秋 愁	Sad, mournful *sàuh* *chóu*　　　*chóu*
惹	丶 艹 艹 艹 艹 艹 若 若 若 惹	To cause, tease *yeh* *rě*　　　*rě*
愧	忄 忄 忄 忄 忄 忄 怦 怦 愧 愧 愧	Ashamed, bashful *kwáih* *kwèi*　　　*kuì*
慇	丿 厂 户 户 启 启 殷 殷 殷 慇	Sorrowful, careful *yan* *yīn*　　　*yīn*
態	丶 厶 厶 台 台 台 能 能 能 態	Behavior, attitude *taai* *tai*　　　*tài*
慌	忄 忄 忄 忄 忄 忙 忙 恍 慌 慌	Nervous, excited *fong* *hwāng*　　　*huāng*
愴	忄 忄 忄 忄 忄 恰 恰 愴 愴 愴	Sad; to pity *chŏng* *chwàng*　　　*chuàng*
慈	丶 丷 艹 艹 艹 玄 兹 慈	Kind, motherly *chíh* *tsź*　　　*cí*

慶	丶亠广庐庐庐庐 庱慶慶慶	To congratulate, greet *hing* *syìng*　　　*xìng*
慨	忄忄忉忓忓忾 忾忾忾慨慨	Generous, noble *koi* *kai*　　　*kài*
慰	㇇㇐尸尸尼尽尉 尿尿尉尉慰	To soothe, console *wai* *wei*　　　*wèi*
慾	丶丷グ父谷谷 谷谷欲欲慾	Desire, appetite *yuhk* *yu*　　　*yù*
慷	忄忄忙忙忭忭 忭忭忭忭慷慷	Generous, warm-hearted *hong* *hāng*　　　*hāng*
慢	忄忄忉忉忉恨 恨愠愠慢慢	Slow, negligent *maahn* *man*　　　*màn*
憂	一丆了丂百百百 直恵恵憂憂	To worry; sorrow *yau* *yōu*　　　*yōu*
慮	丶卜丄广庐虍虎 虏虏虑虑慮	Anxious, concerned *leuih* *lyù*　　　*lù*
慟	忄忄忙忙怡怡 怡悀悀悀慟慟	Grief; excited *tung* *túng*　　　*tòng*
慣	忄忄忦忦忛忛 忛慣慣慣慣慣	Custom; habitual *gwaan* *gwan*　　　*guàn*
慘	忄忄忪忪忪忪 惂惂慘慘	Sad, cruel *chăam* *tsăn*　　　*căn*
慫	丿丷彳彳彳从从 从從從慫	To alarm, arouse *sung* *súng*　　　*sŏng*

慚	忄忄忄忄恒恒恒 愅愅慚慚	Ashamed *chaahm* *tsán* *cán*
慧	一二三丰转转彗 彗慧	Intelligent; wisdom *waih* *hwèi* *hùi*
憔	忄忄忄忄忄忄忄 忄忄惟惟憔	Distressed and pining *chyuh* *chyáu* *qiáo*
憎	忄忄忄忄忄忄 忄忄忄憎憎憎	To dislike, hate *jàng* *dzēng* *zēng*
憐	忄忄忄忄忄忄忄 忄憐憐憐憐憐	To pity, sympathize *lìhn* *lyán* *lián*
憫	忄忄忄忄忄忄忄 忄忄忄憫憫憫	To pity, sympathize *máhn* *mǐn* *mǐn*
憮	忄忄忄忄忄忄忄 憮憮憮憮	Charming; to cherish *mou* *wǔ* *wǔ*
憑	丶冫冫冯冯馮馮 馮憑	To rely on; evidence *pàhng* *píng* *píng*
憲	丶宀宀宇宇宇 宇宇害害憲	A law, constitution *hin* *syan* *xiān*
應	丶亠广广广府府 府府府雁雁應	To answer; should *ying* *yìng* *yīng*
憶	忄忄忄忄忄忄忄 憶憶憶憶	To remember, reflect *yik* *yì* *yì*
懂	忄忄忄忄忄忄 懂懂懂懂懂懂	To understand, know *dúng* *dǔng* *dǒng*

懊	忄 忄′ 忄″ 忄向 忄向 忄向 忄向 懊 懊 懊 懊 懊 懊	To regret; irritated ou aù aò
懇	ノ イ ⺈ 夕 夕 夗 夗 夗 豸′ 豹 貇 貇 貇 懇	To beg; sincerely han kén kèn
憾	忄 忄′ 忄厂 忄厂 忄厂 忄咸 忄咸 忄咸 忄咸 憾 憾	Hatred, regret hahm haǹ haǹ
憤	忄 忄′ 忄″ 忄十 忄土 忄圭 忄貴 忄貴 忄貴 憤 忄貴 憤	Anger, zeal fáhn feǹ feǹ
懈	忄 忄′ 忄″ 忄厂 忄角 忄角 忄角 忄角″ 懈′ 懈 懈 懈 懈	Slow, idle haaih syè xiè
懦	忄 忄′ 忄″ 忄厂 忄雨 忄需 忄需 忄需 忄需 懦 懦 懦	Cowardly, weak noh nwō nuō
懸	l 冂 月 且 県 県 県 県′ 県′ 県′ 県縣 縣 縣 懸	To hang; different yùhn syán xián
懶	忄 忄′ 忄″ 忄厄 忄申 忄束 忄束 忄束′ 懶 懶 懶 懶 懶	Lazy, sluggish láahn lán lán
懷	忄 忄′ 忄十 忄十 忄十 忄亩 忄亩 忄亩 忄亩 忄亩 懷 懷 懷 懷	To cherish; the bosom waàih hwai huái
懺	忄 忄′ 忄″ 忄″ 忄″ 忄″ 忄″ 忄″ 懺 懺 懺 懺 懺 懺	To regret, repent chaam chàn chàn
懼	忄 忄′ 忄目 忄目 忄目 忄目 忄貝 忄貝 忄貝 懼 懼 懼 懼 懼	To fear, dread geuih jyu jù
戀	㇐ 亠 六 言 言 言 言 信 䜌 䜌 䜌 䜌 戀 戀	To long for, lust after lyun lyàn liàn

	戈	Section
戊	一 厂 戊 戊 戊	The 5th of the 10 stems *mou* *wù*　　　　*wù*
戌	一 厂 F 戌 戌 戌	The 11th of the 12 branches *seut* *syu*　　　　*xū*
戎	一 二 于 戎 戎 戎	Weapons, soldiers *yung* *rúng*　　　　*róng*
戍	一 厂 斥 戍 戍 戍	To guard the frontier *syu* *shù*　　　　*shù*
成	一 厂 斤 成 成 成	To finish, succeed *sihng* *chéng*　　　　*chéng*
我	ノ 一 十 才 我 我 我	I, me *ngoh* *wǒ*　　　　*wǒ*
戒	一 二 于 开 戒 戒 戒	To caution; limit *gaai* *jye*　　　　*jiè*
或	一 、 戸 口 豆 或 或	Or; perhaps, probably *waahk* *hwo*　　　　*huò*
戚	一 厂 厂 斥 斥 斥 斥 床 戚 戚 戚	To be related to; pity *chik* *chī*　　　　*qī*
截	一 十 土 圭 圭 奉 奉 青 青 截 截 截	To cut off, intercept *jiht* *jye*　　　　*jíe*
戰	丶 ᵛ ᵛ ᵛᵛ ᵖ ᵖᵖ 뽀 뽀 𤯔 單 單 戰 戰 戰	To fight; war *jin* *jan*　　　　*zhàn*

戲	丨卜乜卢卢卢虎虎虚虚 虚虚虚戲	A play; to joke *hei* *syi* *xi*
戴	一十壸壸壸壸青青青 青青壸壹壸戴	To wear, carry *daai* *dai* *dai*
	戸	Section
戸	丶丶コ戸	A door, gate, family *wuh* *hu* *hu*
房	戸戸戸房房	A room, house, apartment *fohng* *fang* *fang*
所	丶厂戸戸'所 所 所	A building; that which *so* *swo* *suo*
扇	戸房房肩扇	A fan *sin* *shan* *shan*
扉	戸戸戸戸扇扉	A one-leaf door *fei* *fei* *fei*
	手	Section
手	丿二三手	A hand, arm *sau* *shou* *shou*
才	一十才	Talent; ability *choih* *tsai* *cai*
扎	一十才扎	To fasten; a letter *jaat* *fa* *zha*

打	扌 扌 打	To hit; a dozen *dá* *dǎ*　　　　*da*
扒	扌 扌 扒	A pickpocket; to scratch *pàh* *pā*　　　　*pa*
扔	扌 扔 扔	To throw, fling *ying* *rēng*　　　　*rēng*
托	扌 扌 扌 托	To support with the hand *tohk* *twō*　　　　*tūo*
扛	扌 扌 扛 扛	To carry on shoulders by 2 men *gòng* *gāng*　　　　*gāng*
扣	扌 扌 扣 扣	To deduct, knock *kau* *kou*　　　　*kòu*
抓	扌 扌 扌 扪 抓	To scratch, seize *jaáu* *jwā*　　　　*zhūa*
投	扌 扌 扣 投 投	To throw, join *tàuh* *toù*　　　　*tòu*
把	扌 扌 扣 把	To hold; a handle *bá* *bǎ*　　　　*bǎ*
折	扌 扌 扌 折 折	To break, discount *jit* *jé*　　　　*zhé*
技	扌 扌 扌 技 技	Skill, talent *geih* *ji*　　　　*jì*
批	扌 扌 扒 批 批 批	To sell wholesale, criticize *pài* *pī*　　　　*pī*

- 143 -

手 (4-5)

找	才 才 扌 找 找 找	To seek, find *jaáu* *jáu* *zhǎo*
承	一 了 了 了 手 斉 承 承	To receive, consent *sìhng* *chéng* *chéng*
扭	才 打 扪 扭 扭	To twist, grasp *náu* *nyóu* *niǔ*
扮	才 扌 扒 扮 扮	To dress up, disguise *baahn* *bàn* *bàn*
抄	才 扌 扚 抄 抄	To copy, confiscate *chāau* *chāu* *chāo*
抗	才 扌 扩 扩 抗	To resist, object *kong* *kàng* *kàng*
扶	才 扌 扶 扶 扶	To assist, support *fùh* *fú* *fú*
抒	才 扌 扩 抒 抒	To pour out, state freely *yìk* *shū* *shū*
扯	才 扌 扗 扯 扯	To pull, drag *ché* *chě* *chě*
抑	才 扌 扣 抑 抑	To restrain; or else *yìk* *yì* *yì*
抖	才 扌 扩 抖	To shake, tremble *dáu* *dǒu* *dǒu*
拜	丿 二 三 手 手 钅 拜	To respect, worship *baai* *bài* *bài*

- 144 -

拒	扌 才 扗 拒 拒	To refuse, resist *keuih* *jyu* *ju*
抛	扌 扌 扚 扚 抛	To throw, cast *paau* *pau* *pao*
拖	扌 扌 扩 扗 拃 拖	To drag out, tow *to* *two* *tuo*
拘	扌 扌 扚 扚 拘 拘	To seize, arrest *keui* *jyu* *ju*
押	扌 扌 扩 护 担 押	To arrest; seal; mortgage *at* *ya, ya* *ya, ya*
拔	扌 扌 扙 拔 拔 拔	To pull up *baht* *ba* *ba*
抬	扌 扌 扑 抬 抬 抬	To carry between 2 people, raise *toih* *tai* *tai*
抵	扌 扌 扺 扺 抵 抵	To mortgage; resist *dai* *di* *di*
招	扌 扌 护 扨 招 招	To invite *jiu* *jau* *zhao*
抽	扌 扌 扣 扣 抽 抽	To draw out *chau* *chou* *chou*
拌	扌 扌 扌 扞 拦 拌	To mix; throw away *buhn* *ban* *ban*
披	扌 扌 扩 护 披 披	To put on, spread out *pei* *pi* *pi*

拐	扌 扌 扩 扩 拐 拐	To kidnap; swindle gwáai gwāi　　　　　guǎi
抱	扌 扌 扌 抝 抱 抱	To carry; feel pou bàu　　　　　bào
拍	扌 扌 扌 折 拍 拍	To hit, pat paak bwo　　　　　bō
拙	扌 扌 扌 扣 拙 拙	Unskillful, clumsy chyut jwó　　　　　zhó
拉	扌 扌 扩 扩 拉 拉	To pull, bend laài lā　　　　　lā
拇	扌 扎 扨 抠 拇 拇	The thumb móuh mǔ　　　　　mǔ
拂	扌 扌 扩 拐 拂 拂	To wipe off, shake off fat fú　　　　　fú
拆	扌 扌 扩 折 折 拆	To pull down, destroy chaak chè　　　　　chè
抹	扌 扌 扩 村 材 抹	To wipe, rub mut mwó　　　　　mó
拼	扌 扌 扌 扩 拦 拤 拼	To pronounce, combine ping pīn　　　　　pīn
挑	扌 扌 扌 扒 扒 挑 挑	To carry on shoulder, select tiù tyau　　　　　tiāo
按	扌 扌 扌 扩 扲 按 按	To press, stop; according to on an　　　　　àn

挖	扌 扌 扩 护 护 护 挖	To dig, excavate *waat* wā　　　　wā
拷	扌 扌 扩 拷 挎 拷 拷	To torture *haau* kaǔ　　　　kaǒ
拾	扌 扌 扑 扒 抡 拾 拾	To pick up; ten *sahp* shŕ　　　　shí
括	扌 扌 扩 扦 括 括 括	To include, enclose *kut* gwā　　　　guā
持	扌 扌 扌 扩 拦 持 持	To hold, support *chih* chŕ　　　　chí
拭	扌 扌 扌 拮 拮 拭 拭 拭	To wipe, rub *sik* shŕ　　　　shì
指	扌 扒 扒 扗 指 指 指	To point out, instruct; a finger *ji* jř　　　　zhǐ
拴	扌 扌 扑 抡 抡 拴 拴	To fasten, strap up *saan* shwān　　　　shuān
拿	丿 人 스 스 合 合 合 亽 合 盒 拿	To take hold, bring *nàh* ná　　　　ná
拳	丶 丷 丷 兰 乡 乡 芣 卷 叁 拳	The fist; boxing *kyùhn* chýwan　　　　qúan
挈	一 二 三 丰 丰刀 初 初 初 挈 挈	To carry, assit *kit* chyé　　　　qìe
挪	扌 扎 扐 扭 挪 挪 挪	To shift, rub *nàh* nwó　　　　nuó

挫	才 扌 扌 扩 挫 挫 挫	To oppress *cho* *tswò* *cuò*
振	才 扌 扩 护 护 振 振 振	To agitate, excite *jan* *jeǹ* *zhèn*
捉	才 扌 扩 护 护 护 捉 捉	To catch, arrest *juk* *jwō* *zhō*
捕	才 扌 扌 扗 拆 捕 捕 捕	To catch, arrest *bouh* *bǔ* *bǔ*
捆	才 扌 扪 捆 捆 捆 捆 捆	To tie together, bind *kwán* *kwǔn* *kǔn*
挾	才 扌 扩 护 挷 挾 挾	To hold under the arm *hihp* *syé* *xié*
捍	才 扌 扩 护 捍 捏 捏 捍	To defend, guard *hóhn* *haǹ* *haǹ*
捎	才 扌 扪 扪 扪 捎 捎 捎	To send, select *saāu* *shāu* *shāo*
挨	才 扩 扩 扩 挨 挨 挨 挨	To suffer; near *aaī* *aī* *aī*
捐	才 扩 护 护 护 捐 捐 捐	To contribute, subscribe *gyun* *jywān* *juān*
挺	才 扌 扚 扌 挺 挺 挺	To straighten; upright *tihng* *tiǹg* *tǐng*
挽	才 扌 扩 护 挽 挽 挽 挽 挽	To lead, pull *waan* *waǹ* *wǎn*

採	扌 扌 扩 抨 抨 採 抨 採 採	To pick, gather *choi* *tsai* *cai*
推	扌 扌 扗 扩 扩 推 推 推	To push *teui* *twei* *tui*
掛	扌 扌 扗 扗 拝 拝 挂 掛 掛	To hang up, register *gwa* *gwa* *gua*
捨	扌 扌 扙 扲 扲 扲 捨 捨	To bestow, give up *se* *she* *she*
掃	扌 扌 扨 扪 扫 扫 掃 掃 椊	To sweep; a broom *sou* *sau* *sao*
措	扌 扌 扩 扸 拱 拱 措 措 措	To manage, arrange *chou* *tswo* *cuo*
掌	丨 丬 屮 屵 当 当 尚 尚 堂 堂 堂 掌	The palm; to manage *jeung* *jang* *zhang*
掀	扌 扌 扩 扩 折 折 掀 掀 掀	To lift up, pull aside *yan* *syan* *xian*
掂	扌 扌 扩 扩 扤 扤 掂 掂	To weigh in the hand *dim* *dyan* *dian*
掘	扌 扌 扝 护 扝 扝 掘 掘 掘	To dig, excavate *gwaht* *jywe* *jue*
授	扌 扌 扜 扜 扜 扜 捼 捼 授	To impart, grant *sauh* *shou* *shou*
捧	扌 扌 扞 扞 扶 扶 捧 捧 捧	To hold up, offer *bung* *peng* *peng*

掖	扌 扌 扩 挤 扩 扩 掖 掖 掖	The arm-pit; to lead yihk yi yi
掮	扌 扌 扩 护 护 护 护 掮 掮	To carry up on the shoulder gin chyán qian
捲	扌 扌 扩 扩 扩 扮 扶 捲 捲	To roll up gyún jywán juan
掠	扌 扌 扩 扩 拧 拧 护 护 掠	To rob, strike leuhk lywe lüe
捶	扌 扌 扩 扩 扩 护 护 捶 捶	To beat, strike seuih shwei shui
掉	扌 扌 扩 扩 护 护 护 捍 掉	To fall, move diuh dyàu diao
排	扌 扌 扩 排 排 排	To arrange, line up paaih pái pai
掙	扌 扌 扩 扩 扩 护 挣 挣 掙	To get free from jang jeng zheng
掏	扌 扌 扚 扚 扚 掏 掏 掏 掏	To draw out touh táu tao
探	扌 扌 扩 护 护 护 择 探 探	To visit, search taam tan tan
控	扌 扌 扌 扩 护 护 护 挖 控	To impeach, control hung kung kong
捫	扌 扌 扩 押 押 押 捫 捫 捫	To feel, cover muhn men men

接	扌 扌 扩 扩 扩 护 接 接 接	To receive, connect *jip* *jyē* *jiē*
捷	扌 扌 扩 扲 捛 捷 捗 捷 捷	Prompt; to win *jiht* *jye* *jié*
掩	扌 扌 扩 扷 扲 捧 捧 掩	To cover, close *yim* *yǎn* *yǎn*
掣	丿 亠 上 卡 卢 朱 串 制 制 制 掣 掣	To obstruct, hinder, pull *jai* *chè* *chè*
換	扌 扌 扩 扲 拚 换 换 换 换 換	To change, substitute *wuhn* *hwàn* *huàn*
揚	扌 扌 扪 扪 担 担 捛 揚 揚 楊	To wave, raise *yeuhng* *yáng* *yáng*
提	扌 扌 扪 扪 抇 担 捏 捏 捏 捏 提	To carry, mention *taih* *tí* *tí*
描	扌 扌 扩 扩 扲 扲 拱 措 描 描	To sketch, describe *miuh* *myáu* *miáo*
揸	扌 扌 扌 扲 扶 扶 拝 拹 揸 揸	To squeeze, hold *jà* *jā* *zhā*
揶	扌 扌 扩 扣 扣 抇 挿 挪 挪	To ridicule *ye* *yé* *yé*
揮	扌 扌 扩 扩 扣 扣 挏 挏 揖 揮	To wave; shake *fai* *hwēi* *hūi*
插	扌 扌 扩 扦 扦 扻 扻 挿 挿 插	To insert, interrupt *chaap* *chā* *chā*

援	扌 扩 扩 扩 捿 抒 护 挘 援 援	To rescue, help wuhn ywán yuán
揉	扌 扩 扩 捁 抒 抒 捹 挓 揉 揉	To twist, make flexible yauh róu róu
揍	扌 扩 扩 拧 揍 扶 挟 捧 捧 揍	To beat up jau dzòu zòu
揩	扌 扐 扐 批 批 批 扲 揩 揩 揩	To rub, clean gaai kāi kāi
揖	扌 扩 护 护 护 拧 挏 揖 揖	To bow, salute yap yī yī
揭	扌 扩 扩 押 扫 护 挕 揭 揭 揭	To uncover, take off kit jyē jiē
揪	扌 扌 扩 扌 材 拃 捸 挊 揪 揪	To pick up, grasp chau jyōu jiū
搥	扌 扌 扩 扣 扫 拍 拍 搥 搥	To strike, beat cheuih chwéi chúi
搖	扌 扩 扩 扩 扲 扲 拴 捁 搖 搖	To shake, annoy yiuh yáu yáo
搗	扌 扌 扩 护 护 扣 拘 搗 搗 搗	To beat, attack dóu dǎu dǎo
搜	扌 扌 扌 扩 扌 护 挡 挿 搜 搜	To search for, examine sáu sōu sōu
搓	扌 扌 扩 扩 扶 揯 拌 搓 搓 搓	To roll between the hands chò tswō cuō

搧	扌 扌 扩 护 护 护 搧 搧 搧	To agitate, fan *sin* *shan*　　　*shān*
搾	扌 扌 扩 扩 拃 搾 搾 搾 搾 搾	To squeeze *ja* *jà*　　　*zhà*
搬	扌 扌 扩 扩 扚 拚 搬 搬 搬 搬 搬	To move, remove *bun* *bān*　　　*bān*
搭	扌 扌 扌 扩 扩 扚 扚 扻 搭 搭 搭	To build, ride *daap* *dā*　　　*dā*
損	扌 扌 扩 护 护 捐 捐 捐 捐 損 損	To destroy, injure *syún* *swún*　　　*sǔn*
搶	扌 扌 扐 扐 捈 捈 捈 捈 搶 搶	To rob, snatch *cheung* *chyǎng*　　　*qiǎng*
搏	扌 扌 扞 村 捕 捕 捕 捕 搏 搏 搏	To strike, seize *bok* *bwo*　　　*bó*
搽	扌 扌 扩 扩 扚 扚 扚 搽 搽 搽 搽	To rub on *chàh* *chá*　　　*chá*
搔	扌 扚 杈 扨 扨 扨 搔 搔 搔 搔 搔	To scratch *sou* *sāu*　　　*sāo*
摸	扌 扌 扩 扩 扩 扚 扚 捁 搢 摸 摸	To feel, grope *mo* *mwo*　　　*mō*
摧	扌 扌 扚 扚 扚 扩 扩 扚 拚 搒 摧 摧	To destroy *cheui* *tswēi*　　　*cuī*
摔	扌 扌 扩 扩 拉 拉 扺 拉 拉 搂 摔	To throw down *syut* *shwāi*　　　*shuāi*

手 (11-12)

摟	扌 扌 扩 扩 扞 扻 摂 扴 搟 搟 摟 摟	To embrace, drag làu lou　　　lòu
摒	扌 扌 扩 护 护 护 扜 扜 扜 摒	To expel, remove pihng ping　　　pìng
摻	扌 扩 扩 扗 拯 挴 换 捈 摻 摻	To mix, help chaahm chān　　　chān
摩	丶 亠 广 广 庁 庌 床 麻 麻 歴 磨 麼 摩	To rub, handle mò mwó　　　mó
摑	扌 扌 扪 扪 扪 捫 捫 捫 摑 摑	To slap gok chwó　　　chuó
摘	扌 扌 扩 扩 扩 挤 捐 摘 摘 摘 摘	To pick, pluck jaahk jāi, jé　　zhāi, zhe
摺	扌 扌 扌 扫 扫 挕 挕 摺 摺 摺	To fold up jip jé　　　zhé
摹	丶 丷 艹 艻 苩 苩 苩 莒 草 莫 莫 蓦 摹	To imitate, follow a pattern mouh mwó　　　mó
撥	扌 扌 扩 扩 拶 拶 拶 捗 撥 撥 撥 撥	To distribute, allot buht bwó　　　bō
撕	扌 扌 扩 拱 拱 拱 揸 揸 揸 撕 撕 撕	To tear, break into pieces si sz　　　si
撚	扌 扌 扚 扚 抄 抄 撚 撚 撚 撚	To tease; twist jim nyán　　　nian
撤	扌 扌 扩 扩 拉 护 挦 捔 捔 揹 捔 撤 撤	To withdraw, dismiss chit chè　　　chè

- 154 -

撮	扌 扌 扩 押 捏 捏 捏 捏 撮 撮 撮	To bring together, pinch *chyut* *tswo* *cuo*
撲	扌 扌 扩 扩 扑 扑 拌 拌 撲 撲 撲	To strike *pok* *pū* *pū*
撓	扌 扌 扩 扩 桂 拮 捁 撓 撓	To disturb *naauh* *nàu* *nào*
撞	扌 扌 扩 扩 扩 拉 拧 挡 撞 撞 撞 撞	To knock, collide *johng* *chwang* *chuáng*
撈	扌 扌 扌 扩 扰 扱 撇 撇 撈 撈	To dredge *louh* *làu* *lāo*
撩	扌 扩 扩 扶 扶 扶 拺 捁 捁 捁 捁 撩	To stir up, tickle *liuh* *lyáu* *liáo*
撬	扌 扌 扩 扩 扩 托 撬 撬	To force open *giuh* *chyàu* *qiào*
播	扌 扌 扩 拧 拌 採 採 撐 撟 播 播	To spread, disseminate *bo* *bwō* *bō*
撐	扌 扌 扩 扑 挡 挡 捁 擋 擋 擋 擋	To prop up, support *chaang* *chēng* *chēng*
撇	扌 扌 扩 扰 捭 捕 捕 捕 撇 撇 撇	To abandon, cast away *pit* *pye* *piē*
撒	扌 扌 扩 扩 捭 拌 措 措 措 措 撒 撒	To cast, distribute *saat* *sā* *sā*
撫	扌 扌 扩 拧 撫 撫 撫	To soothe, console *fu* *fu* *fu*

撙	扌 扌 扩 扩 挡 措 搢 搢 撙 撙 撙	To economise, regulate *jeun* *jwǔn*　　　　*zǔn*
操	扌 扌 扩 扩 拐 揑 摇 撡 撡 操	To control, drill, manage *chou* *tsau*　　　　*cāo*
擋	扌 扌 扌 扩 扩 挡 挡 挡 挡 捎 擋 擋	To oppose, obstruct *dong* *dang*　　　　*dǎng*
擅	扌 扌 扩 扩 拍 揗 揗 揗 揗 擅 擅 擅	To act without authority *sihn* *shàn*　　　　*shàn*
撻	扌 扌 扌 扩 括 括 撻 撻 撻 撻 撻	To whip *taat* *tà*　　　　*tà*
擎	丶 丶 艹 𡗗 芍 苟 苟 苟 敬 敬 敬 擎	To elevate; engine *kihng* *jìng*　　　　*jìng*
擔	扌 扌 扌 扩 扩 扩 掀 掐 擔 擔 擔 擔	To carry, support *daàm, daam* *dàn, dàn*　　*dān, dàn*
擁	扌 扌 扩 扩 挌 挤 挤 挤 挤 挤 擁 擁	To crowd, embrace *yǔng* *yǔng*　　　　*yōng*
擂	扌 扌 扩 扩 抨 揨 揨 撂 擂 擂 擂	To pound, grind *leuih* *léi*　　　　*lei*
擇	扌 扌 扩 扩 押 押 押 捏 捏 擇 摆 擇	To choose, prefer *jaahk* *jé*　　　　*zhé*
據	扌 扌 扌 扩 扩 扩 捈 掳 掳 擄 擄 據	To base on, occupy *geui* *jyù*　　　　*jù*
撼	扌 扌 扩 扩 扦 振 振 掁 掁 揻 撼 撼	To shake *hahm* *hàn*　　　　*hàn*

擄	扌扩扩扩扩护护 扩护挊擄擄擄擄	To capture, rob fú lǔ lǔ
擊	一厂石石白車重車 軎軎軗軗擊	To strike, attack gik jí jí
擠	扌扌扩扩扩扩挤 挤挤挤挤挤擠	To squeeze; crowded jài jǐ jǐ
擱	扌扫扫担捫捫捫 捫捫擱擱擱擱	To put aside gok gē gē
擦	扌扌扩扩扩护护 护挼挼擦擦	To rub; a brush chat tsā cā
擡	扌扌扌扩扩扗拮拮 搢搢擡擡擡擡擡	To carry on shoulder tòih taí taí
擰	扌扌扌扩扩挧挧 挓挓擖撨擰擰	To twist, spin nihng níng níng
擬	扌扑扑扩挡挭挭挭 擃擃擃擬擬擬	To intend, plan yíh nǐ nǐ
擴	扌扌扩扩扩护护 护搪擔擔擴擴	To stretch, enlarge kong kwó kuò
擾	扌扌扩扩扪挦挦 挦挦擾擾擾擾	To annoy, trouble yiú raú raó
擲	扌扌扩扩挧挧挦 揹揹揹摸摸擲擲	To throw, fling jaahk jí zhí
擺	扌扌扩押押押押 捫捫擺擺擺	To display, swing baai baí baí

攏	扌 扩 护 护 护 捔 捔 捔 捔 揺 揺 揺 攏 攏	To assemble, grasp *luhng* *lung* long
攔	扌 扎 扣 扣 扣 扣 押 押 押 押 押 攔 攔 攔 攔 攔	To stop, obstruct *laahn* *lan* lan
攝	扌 扌 扌 扩 扪 扪 拥 拥 揖 攝	To gather, photograph *sip* *she* she
攜	扌 扩 扩 护 护 扶 拂 攜 攜 攜 攜 攜 攜	To carry, lead by hand *kwaih* *shi* xi
攤	扌 扩 扩 扩 扩 拋 措 措 摸 摸 摸 摸 攤 攤 攤	To spread; a stall *taan* *tan* tan
攢	扌 扌 扩 扩 扩 扩 挋 挋 摂 摂 摂 摂 攢 攢 攢	To collect *jyun* *jan* zhan
攣	丶 亠 三 亖 言 言 言 绉 绉 绉 绉 攣	Bent, crooked *lyuhn* *lywan* luan
攪	扌 扩 扚 挌 挌 挌 挌 挌 挌 挌 挌 挌 挌 攪	To stir, mix *gaau* *jyau* jiao
攬	扌 扌 扌 扌 扩 扣 扣 扣 扣 扣 挋 挋 挋 挋 攬	To grasp, monopolize *laam* *lan* lan
支		Section
支	一 十 圡 支	To support; a branch *ji* *jr* zhi
攴		Section

收	レ 屮 屮 屮 屮 收	To receive, gather *sau* *shōu* *shōu*
改	ㄱ ㄱ 己 己 改 改	To change, correct *goi* *gái* *gǎi*
攻	一 丁 工 攻	To attack, work at *gung* *gūng* *gōng*
放	、 一 方 方 放	To allow, release *fong* *fáng* *fàng*
政	一 丁 下 正 正 政	Government, laws *jing* *jeng* *zhèng*
故	一 十 古 古 古 故	Reason; old *gu* *gu* *gù*
效	、 一 ナ 六 亥 交 效	To imitate; effect *haauh* *syau* *xiào*
救	一 寸 寸 求 求 求 求 救	To save, rescue *gau* *jyou* *jiù*
教	ノ メ 土 并 考 考 考 教	To teach; a religion *gaau* *jyau* *jiào*
敗	丨 冂 冃 目 目 貝 貝 敗	To defeat, ruin *baaih* *bai* *bài*
敏	ノ ㇇ 乞 勾 每 每 每 敏	Quick, clever *mahn* *min* *mǐn*
敍	ノ 人 仐 仐 佘 余 斜 斜 敍	To converse, put in order *jeuih* *syu* *xù*

散	丶十卄艹芏莆莆 菁菁散	To scatter, break up *saan* *sàn*　　　　*sàn*
敢	一丁工干开乔 乔乔敢	To dare, venture *gám* *gǎn*　　　　*gǎn*
敦	丶亠六古古亯 亨亨敦	To urge; honest *deun* *dwun*　　　　*dun*
敝	丶丷丷忄伜術術 啇敝	Bad, poor *baih* *bì*　　　　*bì*
敞	丨丬丬丬肖肖尚 尚敞	Spacious; to disclose *tóng* *cháng*　　　*chǎng*
敬	丶丨艹艹艹艻 苟苟苟敬	To respect; honorable *ging* *jìng*　　　　*jìng*
敲	丶亠六古古高 高高高'高'歊敲	To beat; a club *haau* *chyau*　　　*qiāo*
敵	丶亠六古古㐭 啇啇商商敵	To fight against; enemy *dihk* *dí*　　　　*dí*
敷	一十扌甫甫甫甫 重專尃敷	To announce; sufficient *fu* *fu*　　　　*fu*
數	丶口日日罒吕吕 串婁婁婁數	To count; a number; several *sóu, sou* *shǔ, shù*　　*shǔ, shù*
整	广厂厈束束束敕 敕敕整整整	To arrange; even *jíng* *jěng*　　　*zhěng*
斃	八个个術術術敝 敝敝斃斃斃斃	To die *baih* *bì*　　　　*bì*

		文 Section	
文	丶 二 亍 文	Literature, language *mahn* *wén*	*wén*
斑	一 T F 王 王 珏 珏 玟 斑	Striped *baan* *bān*	*bān*
斐	丨 丨 非 非 非 斐	Elegant, graceful *fei* *fěi*	*fěi*
斌	文 文 坟 妌 妌 妌 斑 斌 斌	Graceful, genteel *ban* *bīn*	*bīn*

		斗 Section	
斗	丶 冫 二 斗	10 pints measure *dau* *dǒu*	*dǒu*
料	丶 丷 二 半 半 米 料	Estimate; material *liuh* *lyàu*	*liào*
斜	丿 亼 厶 合 余 余 余 斜	Slanting, distorted *che, chèh* *sýe*	*xíe*
斟	丨 十 廿 甘 甘 其 其 其 甚 斟	To deliberate, pour from/into *jam* *jēn*	*zhēn*

		斤 Section	
斤	丿 丿 斤 斤	Catty(16oz) *gàn* *jīn*	*jīn*

斤	斤 斤	To expel, scold *chìk* *chr̀* *chì*
斧	⌒ ⌒ 八 少 父 斧	An axe, hatchet *fú* *fǔ* *fǔ*
斫	一 丆 ㄒ 石 石 斫	To chop, cut *hàm* *jwó* *zho*
斬	一 一 一 一 一 車 車 斬	To cut into two, kill *jáam* *jǎn* *zhǎn*
斯	l 十 廿 甘 甘 其 其 其 斯	This, these; such *sī* *sē* *sē*
新	丶 二 六 六 立 立 辛 辛 亲 新	New, modern *sān* *syīn* *xīn*
斷	l ㄣ 幺 幺 丝 丝 纟 纟 纟 斷	To sever; certain *téuhn, déuhn* *dwàn* *duàn*
	方	Section
方	丶 二 丆 方	Direction; square *fōng* *fāng* *fāng*
於	方 方 於 於 於	At, in, on, with, by *yū* *yú* *yú*
施	方 方 於 於 施 施	To arrange, distribute *sī* *shr̄* *shī*
旁	丶 二 六 六 丆 产 旁	Side, by side of *pòhng* *páng* *páng*

旅	方 方 汸 扵 旅 旅 旅	To travel; a trip *leui* *lyǔ* *lǔ*
族	方 方 汸 汸 汸 斿 族 族	Family, clan *juhk* *dzú* *zú*
旌	方 方 汸 扵 斿 斿 斿 旌	To show; a flag *jing* *jīng* *jīng*
旋	方 方 汸 扵 扵 斿 斿 旋	To roll around, return *syuhn* *sywán* *xuán*
旗	方 方 汸 扵 扵 斿 斿 旃 旄 旗	Flag *kèih* *chí* *qí*
	无	Section
旡	ノ ケ ケ 乍 自 良 食 飣 飦 飦 既	To finish; whereas *gei* *ji* *jì*
	日	Section
日	｜ 冂 日 日	Sun, day *yaht* *r* *rì*
旦	｜ 冂 日 日 旦	Morning, dawn *daan* *dàn* *dàn*
旭	ノ 九 旭	Dawn, rising sun *yuk* *syù* *xù*
早	日 旦 早	Early morning; soon *jóu* *dzǎu* *zǎo*

旨	一 ヒ 旨	Order, purpose ji jr　　　　　zhǐ
旬	ノ 勹 旬	Decade chèuhn syún　　　　　xún
旱	日 旦 旱 旱	Dry weather, drought hon hàn　　　　　hàn
明	日 旳 明 明 明	To understand; bright mìhng míng　　　　　míng
昂	日 严 昷 昂 昂	To rise higher and higher ngòhng áng　　　　　áng
易	日 日 月 易 易	To change; easy yihk, yih yì　　　　　yì
昆	日 日 昆 昆	Brothers; descendants kwàn kwùn　　　　　kūn
昔	㇀ 十 卄 芒 昔	Former, ancient sik syì　　　　　xí
昏	ノ ㇇ 氏 氐 昏	To faint; darkness fan hwūn　　　　　hūn
旺	日 日 肝 肝 旺	Prosperous, brilliant wohng wang　　　　　wàng
昌	日 昌	Prosperous cheung chāng　　　　　chāng
昇	日 月 旵 昇 昇	To rise; sunrise sing shēng　　　　　shēng

昨	日 日' 旷 旷 昨 昨	Yesterday, previously jok dzwó zuó
映	日 日' 旷 旳 映 映	To shine, show a movie yíng yíng yǐng
昧	日 旷 旷 时 时 昧	Obscure, dim muih mèi mèi
星	日 尸 炅 早 早 星	Star, spot sing syīng xīng
春	一 二 三 夫 夫 春	Spring season cheun chwūn chūn
是	日 旦 早 早 是 是	To be; correct; yes sih shr shì
晏	日 旦 旦 旦 晃 晏 晏	Late; afternon aan yàn yàn
時	日 旷 旷 旷 時 時 時	Time, season; always sih chŕ chí
晉	一 工 云 亞 巫 晉	To proceed, advance jeun jìn jìn
晤	日 旷 旷 昕 昕 晤 晤 晤	To meet; clear ngh wù wù
晚	日 日' 日" 旷 眇 眇 眇 晚 晚	Evening, late maáhn wǎn wǎn
晦	日 日' 旷 旷 旳 晦 晦 晦	Night, last day of a month fui hwèi hùi

Character	Stroke order	Definition
晝	｀ ｺ ｺ ｹ ⺕ ⺕ ⺕ / 書 書 書 書 晝	Daytime *jau* *jou*　　　　`zhou`
晨	日 旦 尸 戶 戶 / 晨 晨 晨	Morning, dawn *sahn* *chen*　　　　*chen*
普	｀ ｀ ﾄ 丷 ﾍ 广 / ⺦ ⺦ 並 普	General, common *pou* *pu*　　　　*pu*
景	日 旦 早 旱 景 / 暑 景 景 景	Situation, scenery *ging* *jing*　　　　*jing*
智	｀ ｰ ⺊ 午 矢 知 / 知 知 智	Wisdom *ji* *jr*　　　　`zhi`
晴	日 日⁻ 日⁺ 日⺨ 時 晴 / 晴 晴 晴 晴	To clear up (weather) *chihng* *ching*　　　　*qing*
晰	日 日⁻ 日⺨ 日材 日秝 / 晰 晰 晰 晰	Clear, bright *sik* *syi*　　　　*xi*
晾	日 日｀ 日亠 日亠 晾 / 晾 晾 晾 晾	To dry in the air *leuhng* *lyang*　　　　`liang`
晶	日 昌 晶	Crystal, bright *jing* *jing*　　　　*jing*
暑	日 旦 早 星 晏 / 暑	Summer, hot weather *syu* *shu*　　　　*shu*
暈	日 旦 昇 昌 昂 / 昂 昌 冒 暈 暈	To feel dizzy *wahn* *ywun*　　　　*yun*
暗	日 日｀ 日亠 日立 日立 / 日立 暗	Dark, secret *am* *an*　　　　`an`

暖	日 日ˊ 日ˊ 日ˊˊ 日ˊˊ 日ˊˊ 日ˊ 日ˊ 暖 暖 暖	Warm, mild *nyuhn* *nwǎn*　　*nuǎn*
暢	日 申 甲ᵖ 暘 暢 暢 暢 暢	Penetrating; delightful *cheung* *chang*　　*chàng*
暱	日 日ˊ 匙 匙 匙 匙 暱 暱 暱 暱 暱	Familiar, intimate *nik* *nìˊ*　　*nìˊ*
暮	ˋ ˊ ᵗ 甘 莒 莫 莫 暮	Dusk, evening *mouh* *muˋ*　　*muˋ*
暴	日 旦 旦 旱 異 異 異 異 暴 暴 暴	To expose; violent *bouh* *bau*　　*bàoˋ*
暫	一 亓 亓 豆 車 車ˊ 軒 軒 斬 暫	Temporary, sudden *jaahm* *janˋ*　　*zhànˋ*
曆	一 厂 厂 戸 斥 戽 戽 麻 曆	Calendar, almanac *lihk* *lìˊ*　　*lìˊ*
曉	日 日ˊ 日ᵗ 旪 旪 暁 暁 膀 曉	To understand; early morning *hiu* *syau*　　*xiǎo*
曙	日 日ˊ 日ˊˋ 日ˊˋ 日ᵖ 日ᵖ 旵 暒 暒 曙	Dawn, bright *chyu* *shuˋ*　　*shuˋ*
曠	日 日ˊ 旷 旷 旷 暱 暱 暱 暗 暗 暗 曠	To leave empty; desolate *kong* *kwang*　　*kuàng*
曝	日 日ˊ 日ˊ 暝 暍 暒 暝 暝 曝 曝 曝 曝	To dry in the sun *bouh* *buˋ*　　*buˋ*
曦	日 日ˊˋ 旷 旷 旹 暙 暙 暙 暙 暙 暙 曦 曦 曦	Light of the sun *hei* *syi*　　*xi*

日 (19)　曰 (2-8)

曬	日 日 日 日 日 日 日 日 日 日 日 日 曬 曬 曬 曬 曬 曬 曬	To dry in the sun *saai* *shāi*　　　　*shài*
	曰	Section
曰	丶 冂 日 曰	To say, speak *yeuhk* *ywē*　　　　*yue*
曳	日 曳 曳	To draw, pull *yaih* *yì*　　　　*yì*
曲	丶 冂 日 曲 曲 曲	Bent; a song *kuk* *chyū*　　　　*qū*
更	一 日 更 更	To change; moreover *gang* *gēng*　　　　*gèng*
書	𠃍 ㇋ ㇋ 書 書 書 書	To write; a book *syu* *shū*　　　　*shū*
曼	日 日 曼 曼 曼 曼 曼 曼	Fine, long *maahn* *man*　　　　*màn*
曹	一 一 冂 两 曲 曲 曹	An official *chouh* *tsáu*　　　　*cáo*
最	日 旦 旦 旱 最 最 最 最 最	The most, very *jeui* *dzwèi*　　　　*zuì*
替	一 二 ≠ 夫 扶 替	To replace, substitute *tai* *tì*　　　　*tì*
曾	丶 丷 ⼧ 兯 兯 曲 曲 曾 曾	To have been, already *chahng, jang* *tséng*　　　　*céng*

- 168 -

會	丿 人 今 合 合 侖 侖 侖 會	To be able; a club, meeting; *wúih, wuih, wúi* future tense *hwèi* *hui*
	月 Section	
月	丿 几 月 月	Moon, month *yuht* *ywè* *yùe*
有	一 ナ 十 冇 有 有	To have; also *yáuh* *yǒu* *yǒu*
朋	月 朋	Friend, companion *pàhng* *péng* *péng*
服	月 肜 肜 服 服	To dress; clothes *fuhk* *fú* *fú*
朗	丶 亠 ㄅ 宁 官 良 朗	Bright, clear *lòhng* *lǎng* *lǎng*
望	丶 亠 亡 刦 劤 刦 珨 珨 珨 望	To hope, expect *mohng* *wàng* *wàng*
期	丨 十 廿 艹 甘 其 其 其 期	To hope, expect; set time, *keih* period *chí, chī* *qí, qī*
朝	一 十 十 古 古 卤 查 卓 朝	Morning; imperial court *jiù, chiùh* *jaú, chàu* *zhào, chāo*
朦	月 肜 肜 肜 肜 胪 胪 胪 膌 膌 膌 朦	Setting moon, dim *muhng* *meng* *méng*
	木 Section	

木 (1-3)

木	一 十 才 木	Wood *muhk* *mù*　　　*mu*
未	一 未	Not yet *meih* *wei*　　　*wei*
本	木 本	A volume; the root *bún* *ben*　　　*ben*
末	一 末	The end; powder *muht* *mwo*　　　*mo*
朽	木 札 朽	Rotten *nau* *syǒu*　　　*xiu*
朱	丿 仁 朱	Red *jyu* *jū*　　　*zhū*
朵	丿 几 卫 坖 朵 朵	A flower *dó* *dwǒ*　　　*duo*
杜	木 朴 村 杜	To stop, keep out *douh* *dù*　　　*du*
李	木 杢 杢 李	A plum *leih* *li*　　　*li*
村	木 木 村 村	A small town *chyùn* *twun*　　　*tun*
材	木 朴 村 材	Materials; talent *chòih* *tsái*　　　*cai*
杉	木 札 杉 杉	Fir tree *chaam* *shan*　　　*shan*

- 170 -

杓	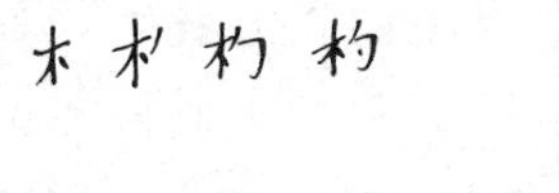	A ladle *biù* *byāu* *biāo*
杏	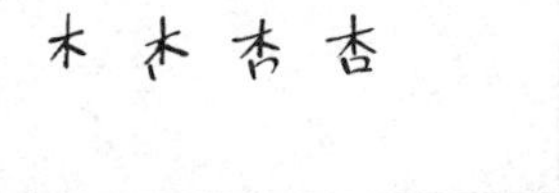	An apricot *hahng* *syìng* *xìng*
束		To restrain, tie up *chùk* *shù* *shù*
杖	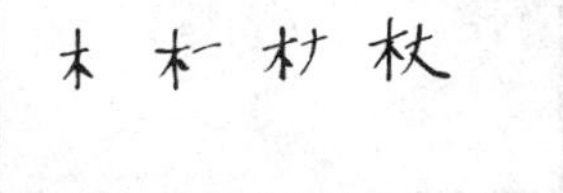	To strike; a stick *jeúng* *jàng* *zhàng*
枕	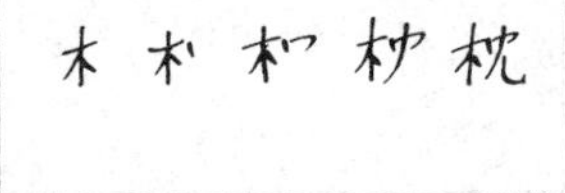	A pillow *jám* *jěn* *zhěn*
枉	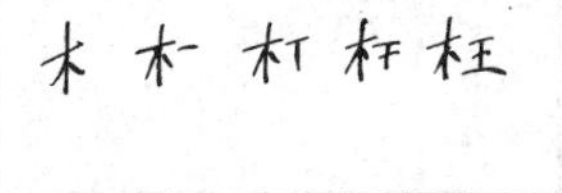	A grievance; crooked *wóng* *wǎng* *wǎng*
杳	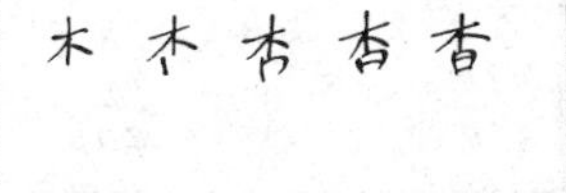	Dark obscure *míuh* *yǎu, myǎu* *yǎo, miǎo*
杷	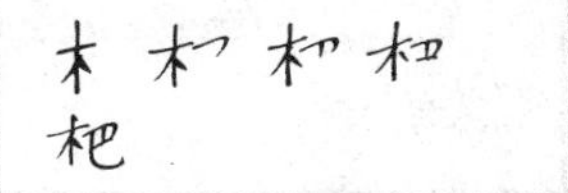	A loquat *pàh* *pā* *pā*
東	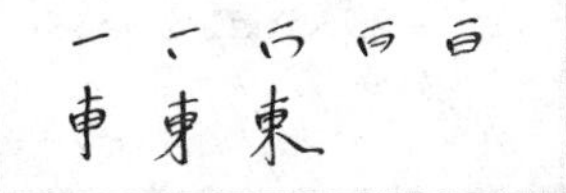	East *dūng* *dūng* *dōng*
枇	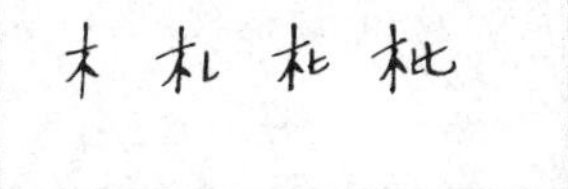	A loquat *pèih* *pí* *pí*
板	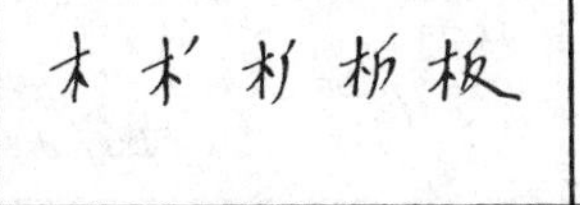	A board; stubborn *báan* *bǎn* *bǎn*
杪	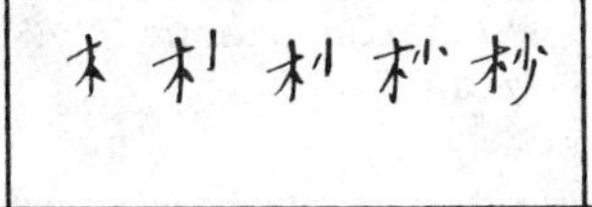	The end; a branch *míuh* *myǎu* *miǎo*

木 (4-5)

林	木 林	Woods, forest làhm lìn　　　　　lín
枚	木 朮 杚 杊 枚	A stem; a piece mùih mei　　　　　méi
松	木 朮 杕 松 松	A pine tree chùhng sung　　　　　song
析	木 朮 杤 析 析	To distinguish, analyze sīk syi　　　　　xi
果	丶 冂 日 旦 果	Fruit; results gó gwǒ　　　　　guǒ
杯	木 朮 朾 杯 杯	Cup, glass bùi bei　　　　　bei
枝	木 朮 村 杶 枝	To branch off; a branch jī jr　　　　　zhī
柩	木 朮 札 柩 柩 柩	Coffin having a corpse in it gau jyòu　　　　　jiu
柔	フ マ ヌ 予 矛 孟 孚 柔 柔	To act kindly; soft yàuh róu　　　　　róu
查	木 朮 杏 杏 查 查	To examine, investigate chàh chá　　　　　chá
柏	木 朮 村 柏 柏 柏	Cedar paak, baak bwó, bǎi　　　bó, baí
柑	木 朾 朾 柑 柑 柑	Mandarin orange gàm gan　　　　　gan

- 172 -

枯	木 朮 朴 村 枯 枯	Decayed, rotten fuh kū kū
柚	木 朮 朳 柚 柚 柚	A pomelo yau yòu yòu
某	一 十 卄 甘 甘 甘 苷 苷 某	A certain person mau móu móu
柬	一 ⺆ 币 币 币 币 申 柬 柬	An invitation, letter gaán jyǎn jiǎn
枴	木 朮 朾 柺 柺 枴	A crutch, cane gwáai gwǎi guǎi
柳	木 朮 朷 柳 柳 柳	A willow lau lyǒu liǔ
柱	木 朮 朴 柱 柱 柱	A post, pillar chyúh jù zhù
架	フ 力 加 加 加 架	A frame; to support ga jyà jià
染	一 ⺀ 氵 氿 氿 染	To dye, taint yim rǎn rǎn
柄	木 朮 朽 柄 柄 柄	A handle; power bing bǐng bìng
柵	木 朮 朷 柵 柵 柵	A palisade, fence saan jà zhà
柴	一 ⺋ 止 止 此 此 柴	Firewood chaaih chai chai

木 (6)

校	才 才 术 材 杪 杉 校	To compare; a school *gaau, haauh* *jyau, syau*　*jiao, xiao*
格	木 术 杉 格 格 格 格	A pattern; to reach *gaak* *gé*　*gé*
桅	木 术 杉 桅 桅 桅 桅	The mast of a ship *waih* *wei*　*wei*
桃	木 利 利 材 机 桃 桃	A peach *touh* *tau*　*tao*
核	术 术 杉 杉 杉 核 核	To examine; a seed *haht* *he*　*he*
框	木 木 杠 杠 框 框 框	A frame, sill *hong* *kwang*　*kuang*
栽	一 十 士 幸 栽 栽 栽	To plant, cultivate *choi* *jai*　*zhai*
桑	丁 又 叒 叒 桑	A mulberry tree *song* *sang*　*sang*
桐	木 利 杊 杊 桐 桐 桐	A type of tree *tuhng* *tung*　*tong*
株	木 利 杉 杵 杵 杵 株	A trunk of a tree *jyu* *ju*　*zhu*
案	丶 丶 宀 宁 安 安 案	A court case; a table on *an*　*an*
栗	一 厂 亩 西 西 西 栗	A chestnut tree *lyuht* *li*　*li*

桔	木 木 木 桔 桔 桔 桔	A mandarin orange *gat* *jye* *jié*
桂	木 木 木 桂 桂 桂 桂	Cassia, cinnamon *gwai* *gwèi* *guì*
根	木 木 杓 杓 根 根 根	Root, foundation *gàn* *gēn* *gēn*
桌	丶 卜 ゖ 占 占 卣 桌	A table, stand *cheuk* *dzwō* *zuō*
栩	木 杓 杓 杓 栩	Pleased; flexible *yihk* *syǔ* *xǔ*
梳	木 木 杧 栌 梳 栌 梳 梳	To comb; a comb *so* *shū* *shū*
條	ノ 亻 竹 忪 忪 忪 條 條 條 條	A strip; a law *tiùh* *tyáu* *tiáo*
梆	木 木 杧 杧 栚 栚 梆	A wooden cylinder *bong* *bāng* *bāng*
梁	丶 亠 氵 汀 汋 汋 梁	A bridge; a beam *leuhng* *lyáng* *liáng*
梅	木 木 杧 杧 栂 梅 梅 梅	A plum, prune *mùih* *méi* *méi*
梭	木 木 杧 杧 栊 栊 栊 梭	A shuttle *so* *swō* *suō*
桶	木 杓 杧 杧 杧 栯 桶 桶	A bucket, barrel, tub *tǔng* *tǔng* *tǒng*

梗	木 杧 杧 杧 栖 桓 栶 梗	The stem of a flower; thorny gang geng geng
械	木 杧 杧 杧 栃 械 械 械	Weapons, tools haaih sye xie
桿	木 杧 杧 桿 桿 桿 桿 桿	A stick, handle gon gan gan
梓	木 杧 杧 杧 杧 桲 桲 梓	A linden ji dz zi
梯	木 杧 杧 杧 档 档 梯 梯	Stairs, a ladder tai ti ti
梢	木 杧 杧 杧 杧 梢 梢 梢	The end of a branch saau shau shao
梨	ノ 二 千 禾 利 利 利 梨	A pear leih li li
棕	木 杧 杧 杧 栌 栌 棕 棕	A palm tree; brown color jung dzung zong
椅	木 杧 杧 杧 枋 枋 椅 椅 椅 椅	A chair, seat yi yi yi
棧	木 杧 杧 杧 栈 栈	A store, warehouse, inn jaan jan zhan
棟	木 杧 杧 杧 栖 桓 栋 棟 棟	A beam, pillar duhng dung dong
棋	木 杧 杧 杧 栱 栱 棋 棋 棋	Chess keih chi qi

植	木 木 木 杧 桔 植 植	To plant; plants jihk jŕ　　　zhí
椒	木 木 村 桁 栌 栌 栎 椒 椒	Pepper jiù jyāu　　　jiāo
棒	木 木 栏 枳 棒 棒 棒	To strike; a stick paahng bang　　　bàng
森	木 森 森	Lush, dense sām shēn　　　shēn
棗	一 ニ 市 市 束 棗	Dates jóu dzáu　　　zǎo
棱	木 木 杧 村 栌 栌 栌 椗 棱 棱	A beam, angle nihng leng　　　leng
棘	一 ニ ョ 中 束 棘	Brambles; troublesome gik jí　　　jí
棚	木 木 机 枂 柵 棚	An awning, booth paahng peng　　　peng
棠	｜ ｜ ｜ ｺ 尚 尚 尚 尚 棠	A begonia tòhng tang　　　táng
棍	木 木 栣 栣 栟 栟 棍 棍	A stick, club gwan gwun　　　gùn
棲	木 木 杧 栖 桓 桓 楼 棲 棲	A roost, perch; to stay at chāi chī　　　qī
棺	木 木 栌 枌 柗 柗 棺	A coffin gùn gwān　　　guān

棉	木 木' 杧 杧 棉 棉 棉 棉 棉	Cotton *mìhn* *myán* *mián*
棄	、 一 云 云 云 夳 夽 夽 棄	To give up, discard *hei* *syi* *xì*
業	丨 丨丨 丨丨丨 业 业 业 业 业 苹 学 堂 業	Business, occupation *yihp* *yè* *yè*
楷	木 札 杧 柗 柗 椊 椊 楷 楷	A model *gaai* *kai* *kǎi*
楊	木 札 杧 栶 柏 柏 枵 楊 楊 楊	A willow, aspen, poplar *yeùhng* *yang* *yáng*
椰	木 木 杧 枊 栶 栶 椰 椰	A coconut tree *yèh* *ye* *ye*
楣	木 杧 杧 栌 枔 枔 栵 楣 楣 楣	A lintel of a door *mèih* *mei* *mei*
楓	木 札 机 机 枫 枫 枫 楓 楓 楓	A maple tree *fùng* *feng* *feng*
楚	木 林 栟 梺 梺 楚 楚	Clear; painful *cho* *chu* *chu*
極	木 木 朾 柯 柯 柯 柯 极 極	End; extreme, very *gihk* *ji* *ji*
槌	木 木 朾 杧 桙 椎 椎 槌 槌	A hammer, mallet *cheùih* *chwei* *chui*
槍	木 札 朾 栓 栓 栓 栓 槍 槍 槍	Spear, gun *cheung* *chyang* *qiang*

榜	木 术 朴 栌 栌 栓 桦 桦 榜 榜	A notice; to beat *bong* *bǎng*　　　　*bǎng*
榮	⺀ ⺀ ⺣ 火 炒 炒 燚 榮	Honor, glory *wìhng* *rúng*　　　　*róng*
構	木 朹 朹 柑 榼 栉 榼 構 構 構 構	To build *kau* *chòu*　　　　*chòu*
槐	木 朮 朾 朾 柏 梖 柚 柳 槐 槐 槐	An ash-tree *waaìh* *hwai*　　　　*huai*
榴	朮 朳 朾 栁 柳 栁 栉 榴 榴 榴	A pomegranate *làuh* *lyóu*　　　　*líu*
榻	木 朮 朾 栂 栂 枵 枵 榀 榻	A couch, bed *taap* *tà*　　　　*tà*
模	木 朮 朾 柑 枱 栉 栉 楷 楂 模 模	A pattern, model *mouh* *mwó*　　　　*mó*
標	木 朮 朾 柏 柛 栖 桹 標 標 標 標	A signal, flag *biu* *byāu*　　　　*biāo*
樓	木 朮 朳 柏 柤 枏 栂 楼 樓 樓 樓	A building; floors *làuh, láu* *lóu*　　　　*lóu*
槽	木 朮 朾 栉 栉 栭 桻 槽 槽 槽 槽	A channel, trough *chòuh* *tsáu*　　　　*cáo*
椿	木 朮 朾 梣 枺 栈 桊 桊 椿 椿 椿	A stake, post *jung* *jwāng*　　　　*zhuǎng*
概	木 朮 朾 栖 栖 栖 桹 桹 榔 概	To sum up; an outline *kọi* *gài*　　　　*gài*

樣	木 杧 杧 柈 様 様 様 樣 様 様	A fashion, style *yeuhng* *yang* *yang*
樑	木 杧 杧 杒 枂 枂 樑	A beam *leuhng* *lyang* *liang*
樂	ノ イ 竹 白 白 白 纳 纳 绌 缴 樂	Happy, cheerful; music *louh, ngouh* *le, ywe* *le, yue*
樞	木 杧 杧 杧 杧 杷 椢 樞	A hinge *shyu* *shu* *shu*
槳	し 丬 斗 斗 扑 捋 捋 捋 将 将 槳	An oar, paddle *jeung* *jyang* *jiang*
機	木 木 杧 松 桜 榁 楑 樺 機 機 機	A machine, opportunity *gei* *ji* *ji*
橋	杧 杧 杧 枔 枔 枔 栝 栝 梢 橋 橋	A bridge *kiuh* *chyau* *qiao*
樽	木 术 杧 杧 杧 栌 栖 椢 椢 椢 樽 樽	A bottle, glass *jeun* *dzwun* *zun*
橙	木 村 杧 杧 杧 桃 橯 楈 橙 橙 橙	An orange *chaang* *cheng* *cheng*
橡	木 术 杧 杧 栌 梅 椈 榢 楊 楊 橡 橡	An oak tree *jeuhng* *syang* *xiang*
樹	木 术 杧 杜 杜 桔 桔 桔 桔 桓 樹 樹	To plant; a tree *syuh* *shu* *shu*
樵	木 术 杧 杧 杧 梆 桩 椎 椎 樵	To collect fire wood; fuel *chiuh* *chyau* *qiao*

橫	木 木 朾 朾 桁 横 桔 桔 横 横 横	Horizontal; unreasonable *waahng* *héng* *héng*
樸	木 木 朴 朴 朴 样 样 样 様 様 様	Plain, simple *pok* *pú* *pú*
橘	木 朾 朾 栌 柽 柽 柽 橘 橘 橘 橘 橘 橘	An orange *gwàt* *jyú* *jú*
檀	木 木 朾 朾 栢 栴 栴 栴 檀 檀 檀 檀 檀	Sandalwood *taahn* *tán* *tán*
檢	木 木 松 柃 柃 柃 柃 杦 桧 檢 檢 檢	To examine *gím* *jyán* *jiǎn*
檔	木 木 朾 朾 栫 栫 栫 桔 桔 檔 檔 檔 檔	A crosspiece *dong* *dàng* *dàng*
檸	木 木 朾 松 松 柠 柠 柠 桴 桴 橙 橙 檸	A tree with yellow leaves *nìhng* *níng* *níng*
檬	木 木 朾 朾 样 样 样 様 様 様 様 檬 檬	A lemon *mung* *méng* *méng*
櫃	木 木 朾 朾 朾 朾 柜 柜 柜 櫃 櫃 櫃	A case, closet *gwaih* *gwei* *guì*
櫈	朾 杸 杸 杸 栥 栥 栥 栥 橙 橙 櫈	A stool *dang* *dèng* *dèng*
檯	木 木 木 朾 梏 梏 橰 橰 橰 木 檯 檯 檯	A table, stage *toih* *tái* *tái*
欄	朾 朾 柙 柙 楣 楣 楣 楣 楣 楣 欄 欄 欄	A railing *laàhn* *lán* *lán*

權	木 村 村 枌 榊 榊 柑 椹 榊 榊 槲 槲 榊 權	Power, authority kyùhn chyẁan quán
	欠	Section
欠	ノ ／ ケ 欠	To owe; deficient him chyàn qiàn
次	` ; 次	A time; the next chi tsè cè
欣	ノ ／ ｆ 斤 欣	Cheerful, delighted yàn syīn xīn
欲	ノ 八 夕 父 谷 谷 谷 欲	To want, wish yuhk yù yù
款	一 十 士 吉 圭 寺 寺 素 款	Money, a style fún hwǎn huǎn
欺	l 卄 卄 廿 甘 甚 其 其 欺	To cheat, insult hèi sȳi xī
欽	ノ 人 人 合 今 余 余 金 欽	Imperial; to respect yàm chīn qīn
歇	` 冂 日 日 旦 曷 号 号 曷 歇	To rest, stop kit sȳe xiē
歉	` ` ` ソ 当 当 当 羊 兼 兼 兼 歉	To regret; insufficient hip chyàn qiàn
歌	一 丆 帀 百 可 可 可 哥 哥 歌	To sing; a song gò gē gē

歐	一 厂 厂 厂 厊 屄 屄 屄 區 歐	Europe ngàu oū oū
歎	丶 十 卄 廿 节 苎 苎 苩 莗 萛 萛 歎	To sigh, moan taan tàn tàn
歡	丶 十 艹 艹 莳 苜 苗 苗 苜 苜 苜 莊 荁 荁 歡	Joy, gladness fùn hwān huān
止	Section

止	丶 卜 止 止	To stop jí jř zhǐ
正	一 正	To correct; exact; chief jing jèng zhèng
此	止 此 此	This, the chí tsě cě
步	止 牛 芀 步	Footsteps bouh bù bù
歧	止 止 此 岐 歧	Forked, diverging kèi, kèih chí qí
武	一 二 正 武 武	Military moúh wǔ wǔ
歪	一 丆 不 不 歪 歪	Awry, slanting waai wāi wāi
歲	止 止 芦 芦 芦 芦 芦 歲 歲 歲	Age, years seui swèi sùi

| 歷 | 一 厂 厂 厂 严 斥 斥 屏 麻 歷 | To experience; in order, history
lihk
lì　　　　*lì* |
| 歸 | ´ ´ ㇇ 宀 自 自 追 歸 歸 歸 歸 歸 歸 歸 歸 | To return, belong to
gwai
gwēi　　　*gūi* |

| | 歹 | Section |

歹	一 丁 万 歹	Bad, evil *dáai* *dǎi*　　　　*dǎi*
死	一 丁 歹 歹 歼 死	To die; dead *sáy* *sé*　　　　*sé*
殊	歹 歹 歼 歼 殊 殊 殊	To distinguish *syuh* *shu*　　　　*shū*
殘	歹 歹 歼 残 残 殘	Cruel; to ruin *chaàhn* *tsán*　　　*cán*
殖	歹 歹 歼 歼 殖 殖 殖 殖 殖	To produce, grow *jihk* *jŕ*　　　　*zhí*
殞	歹 歹 歼 歼 歼 殞 殞 殞 殞 殞 殞	To die *wáhn* *ywǔn*　　　*yǔn*

| | 殳 | Section |

| 段 | ´ ´ ㇒ 斤 斤 斤 郋 郋 段 段 | A piece; a paragraph
dyuhn
dwàn　　　*duàn* |
| 殷 | ´ ㇒ 尸 尸 ㇌ 身 殷 | Abundant
yàn
yīn　　　　*yīn* |

殺	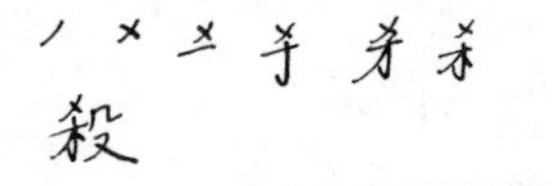	To kill *saat* *shā*	*shā*
殼	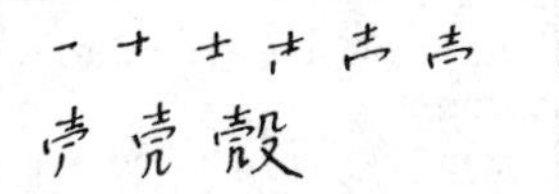	A shell *hohk* *chỳwe*	*què*
毀	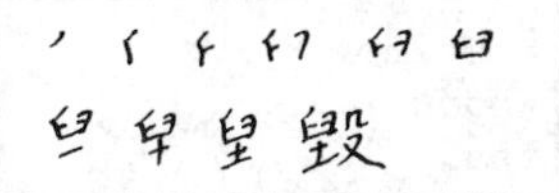	To ruin, destroy *wái* *hwěi*	*huǐ*
殿	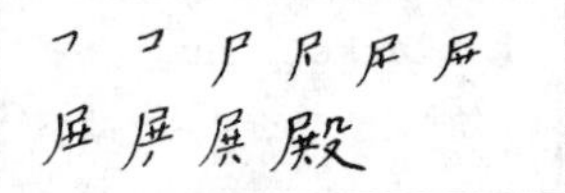	The main hall in a temple *dihn* *dyàn*	*diàn*
毆	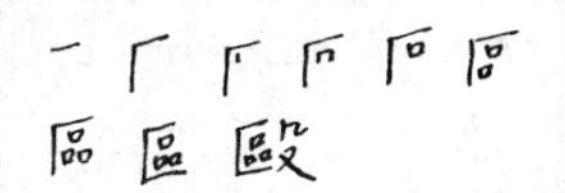	To strike, fight *ngàu* *ōu*	*ōu*
毅	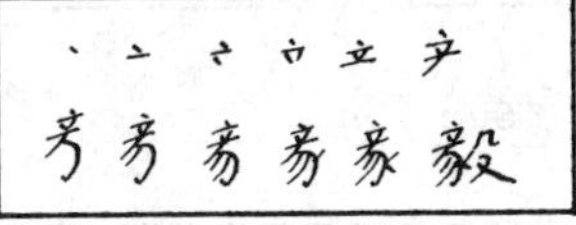	Firm *ngaih* *yì*	*yì*
	毋	Section	
母	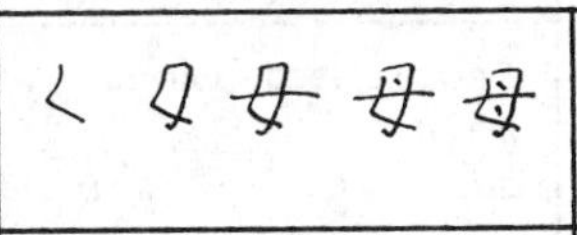	Mother *móuh* *mǔ*	*mǔ*
每		Each, every *múih* *měi*	*měi*
毒	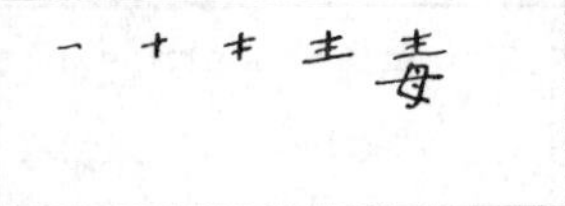	To poison; noxious *duhk* *dú*	*dú*
	比	Section	
比	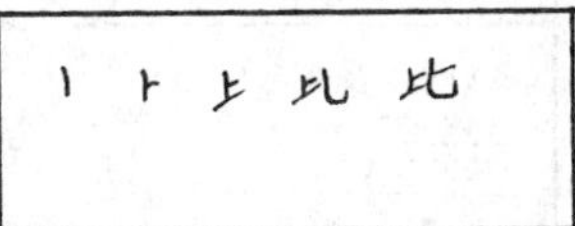	To compare, sort *béi* *bǐ*	*bǐ*

	毛	Section
毛	ﾉ ㇒ 二 毛	Hair, fur, feathers *mòuh* *máu*　　　*máo*
毫	丶 ㆒ ㇐ 宀 亠 亠 宀 高 毫	A dime *hòuh* *háu*　　　*háo*
毯	毛 毛 毛 毛 毯 毯	A blanket, rug *jìn* *tǎn*　　　*tǎn*
氈	丶 ㆒ 宀 宀 宀 宀 宀 亶 亶 亶 亶 亶 氈	A blanket, carpet *jìn* *jàn*　　　*jàn*
	氏	Section
氏	㇒ 𠂉 𠃋 氏	A person; a family name *sìh* *shr*　　　*shì*
民	㇕ ㇆ 尸 尸 民	People, citizens *màhn* *mín*　　　*mín*
	气	Section
氛	ﾉ ㇒ 𠂉 气 气 氛 氛 氛	Vapor; the atmosphere *fàn* *fēn*　　　*fēn*
氧	气 气 气 気 氧 氧 氧	Oxygen *yéuhng* *yǎng*　　　*yǎng*
氣	气 气 气 気 氣 氣 氣	Air, gas *hei* *chì*　　　*qì*

- 186 -

| 氫 | 气 气 气 氙 氫 氢 氫 氫 | Hydrogen
hiǹg
chǐng　　　*qīng* |
| 氯 | 气 气 气 氧 氯 氯 氯 氯 | Chlorine
lúk
lyū　　　*lǜ* |

	水	Section

水	⺀ ⺁ 水 水	Water *seúi* *shwěi*　　*shǔi*
永	⺀ ⺁ ⺂ 永 永	Long, everlasting *wìhng* *yǔng*　　*yǒng*
求	一 十 寸 寸 求 求 求	To beg, inquire, request *kàuh* *chýou*　　*qíu*
汁	⺀ ⺀ ⺡ ⺡ 汁	Juice *jàp* *jr*　　　*zhī*
氾	⺡ ⺡ 氾	Flooding *faahn* *faǹ*　　*faǹ*
汝	⺡ ⺡ 汝 汝	You, your *yúh* *rǔ*　　　*rǔ*
污	⺡ ⺡ ⺡ 污	To dirty; dirt *wù* *wū*　　　*wū*
汗	⺡ ⺡ ⺡ 汗	Perspiration, sweat *hohn* *haǹ*　　*haǹ*
江	⺡ ⺡ 汇 江	River *gòng* *jyāng*　　*jiāng*

池	氵 氿 沖 池	Pool, tank, pond *chìh* *chr*　　　*chí*
汞	一 丅 エ 于 牙 禾 汞	Mercury, quicksilver *hung* *huǐng*　　　*hǒng*
汽	氵 氵 氵 汽 汽	Gas *hei* *chì*　　　*qì*
沙	氵 氵 氵 沙 沙	Sand *sà* *shā*　　　*shā*
沖	氵 氵 沪 沪 沖	To rush at, rise in air, *chùng*　　　infuse *chūng*　　*chōng*
沃	氵 氵 氵 汏 沃	To water; fertile *yùk* *wò*　　　*wò*
沒	氵 氵 沪 沕 沒	To drown; not *muht* *méi, mwo*　　*méi mò*
決	氵 氵 氵 決 決	To determine, decide *kyut* *jywe*　　　*júe*
沐	氵 氵 汁 汭 沐	To bathe *muhk* *mù*　　　*mù*
汪	氵 氵 汪 汪 汪	Vast and calm as a sea *wòng* *wang*　　　*wāng*
汰	氵 氵 汁 汏 汰	Excessive; to rinse *taai* *tài*　　　*tài*
沉	氵 氵 沪 沪 沉	To sink, drown *chàhm* *chén*　　　*chén*

泉	´ ⺅ 白 白 白 皁 皁 泉 泉	A spring, fountain chuhn chwan chúan
沸	⺡ 沪 沪 冯 沸 沸	To boil fat fèi fèi
泛	⺡ ⺡ 泛 泛 泛	To float; unguided faahn fàn fàn
油	⺡ 汁 汩 汩 油 油	Oil, grease yauh yóu yóu
波	⺡ 沪 沪 沪 波 波	Waves bo bwo bō
法	⺡ ⺡ 汁 法 法 法	Laws, ways faat fǎ fǎ
沿	⺡ ⺡ 沪 沪 沿 沿	To follow along yuhn ywan yúan
治	⺡ 沁 治 治 治	To remedy, govern jih jr zhì
注	⺡ ⺡ 泸 汁 注 注	To pour into jyu ju zhù
沾	⺡ ⺡ 汁 沽 沾 沾	To stain, receive benefit from jim jan zhān
泳	⺡ ⺡ 沪 泂 泳 泳	To dive under water wihng yung yǒng
河	⺡ 沪 沪 河 河 河	A river, canal hoh hé hé

泡	氵汀汋泃泡泡	Foam *póuh* pàu pào
況	氵氵沪沪沪況	More *fong* kwàng kuàng
泥	氵氵沪沪泥泥	Soil, mud *nàih* ní ní
泰	一二三夫夫 夵泰泰泰泰	Large, extreme *taai* tài tài
沫	氵氵汒汁沐沐	Foam, bubbles *muht* mwò mò
泣	氵氵汒泣泣泣	To weep *yàp* yì yì
沽	氵氵汁汁沽沽	To sell, buy *gu* gū gū
洞	氵汩汩汩洞 洞洞	A hole, opening *duhng* duǹg dòng
活	氵氵氵汗汗 活活	To live; active *wuht* hwó huó
洒	氵氵汀洒洒 洒洒	To sprinkle, scatter *sá* sǎ sǎ
洗	氵氵汼洗洗 洗洗	To bathe, cleanse *sái* sýi xǐ
洋	氵氵汁洋洋洋	The ocean; foreign *yèuhng* yáng yáng

洽	氵 氵 洴 洽 洽 洽 洽	To be in harmony with *hàp* *sýa*　　　*xa*
津	氵 氵 汀 津 津 涅 津	Allowance; to moisten *jeùn* *jīn*　　　*jīn*
洩	氵 氵 沪 沪 泗 沖 洩	To secrete, leak *sit* *sýe*　　　*xìe*
洲	氵 氵 汋 沙 洲 洲 洲	A continent *jàu* *jōu*　　　*zhōu*
洪	氵 氵 汢 沣 洪 洪 洪	Great, vast *huhng* *huńg*　　　*hońg*
派	氵 氵 沪 沪 派 派 派	To appoint; a faction *paai* *pài*　　　*pài*
流	氵 氵 汇 汏 法 泸 流 流	To flow; a stream, class *lauh* *lyóu*　　　*líu*
消	氵 氵 氵 沙 沙 消 消 消	To dissolve, eliminate *siu* *syāu*　　　*xiāo*
涉	氵 氵 汢 沙 沚 涉 涉 涉	To wade, concern *sit* *she*　　　*shè*
海	氵 氵 汷 汱 海 海 海 海	The sea; marine *hói* *hǎi*　　　*hǎi*
浪	氵 氵 沪 沪 浔 浪 浪	Waves *lohng* *làng*　　　*làng*
浮	氵 氵 氵 沪 沪 浮 浮 浮	To float, drift *fauh* *fú*　　　*fú*

涕	シ シ ゙ シ ゙ 汁 汁 浩 涕 涕	Tears, mucous tai tì　　　　tì
涎	シ シ ゙ シ ゙ シ ゙ 涎 涎 涎 涎	Saliva yihn syán　　　xián
浸	シ シ ゙ シ ゙ シ ゙ シ ゙ 浸 浸 浸	To immerse; wet jam jìn　　　jìn
浩	シ シ ゙ シ ゙ 汁 汁 浩 浩 浩	Great, vast houh hàu　　　hào
浴	シ シ ゙ シ ゙ シ ゙ 次 浴 浴 浴	To wash, bathe yuhk yù　　　yù
凄	シ シ ゙ 汁 汁 汁 凄 凄 凄 凄	Cold, miserable chài chī　　　qī
深	シ シ ゙ シ ゙ 汃 汃 汃 浮 浮 深	Extremely; deep sam shēn　　　shēn
淡	シ シ ゙ シ ゙ 汁 汃 淡	Tasteless, dull daahm dàn　　　dàn
清	シ シ ゙ 汁 汁 汁 清 清 清 清	Pure, clear chìng chīng　　qīng
淘	シ シ ゙ 汋 汋 汋 淘 淘 淘 淘	To cleanse, sift tòuh táu　　　táo
混	シ シ ゙ 汀 汩 汩 混 混 混 混	To mix; confused wahn hwǔn　　hǔn
淨	シ シ ゙ シ ゙ 汃 汃 汋 淨 淨 淨	Pure; net amount jihng jing　　　jìng

淹	氵氵氵氵沆沐淹 淹淹淹	To immerse; to stay *yihm* *yān*　　　*yān*
淫	氵氵氵氵沪沪 沪浮淫	Obscene; to commit adultery *yàhm* *yín*　　　*yín*
液	氵氵氵沪沪 沪沪液液	Liquid, juice *yihk* *yi*　　　*yì*
淺	氵氵氵氵浅浅浅	Shallow, easy *chín* *chýan*　　　*qián*
涼	氵氵氵氵沪 沪沪涼涼	Cool *leuhng* *lýang*　　　*liáng*
淋	氵氵氵汁汁沐 淋	To flow down; to moisten *làhm* *lín*　　　*lín*
涯	氵氵氵沪沪沪 沪涯	A limit, shore *ngàaih* *yá*　　　*yá*
添	氵氵氵沪沪沐 添添添添	To increase, add to *tìm* *tyān*　　　*tiān*
淑	氵氵氵沪沪沪沪 沐沐淑	Virtuous *suhk* *shú*　　　*shú*
港	氵氵氵沪洪洪 洪港港	Port, harbor; Hong Kong *góng* *gǎng*　　　*gǎng*
淚	氵氵氵沪沪沪 沪淚淚	Tears *leuih* *lèi*　　　*lèi*
溫	氵氵沪沪沪 沪溫溫溫溫	To warm; mild, warm *wàn* *wēn*　　　*wēn*

渠	氵 氵 汇 汇 泹 渠 涥 涥 渠	A gutter, drain *keuih* *chyu*　　　　*qú*
渺	氵 氵 氵 沢 汋 泪 泪 洌 渺 渺	Vast; vague *miu* *myau*　　　*miǎo*
渡	氵 氵 氵 沪 沪 沪 沪 沪 渡 渡	To cross; a ferry *douh* *dù*　　　　*dù*
游	氵 氵 氵 汸 汸 汸 汸 游 游	To swim, travel *yauh* *you*　　　*yóu*
湖	氵 氵 汁 汁 沽 沽 湖 湖 湖 湖	A lake *wuh* *hu*　　　　*hú*
渣	氵 氵 汁 沫 沫 沫 浩 浩 渣 渣	Refuse, dregs *jà* *jā*　　　*zhā*
渦	氵 氵 氵 沢 沢 沢 沢 渦 渦 渦	A whirlpool *wo* *chwo*　　　*chūo*
湧	氵 氵 氵 沪 沪 浿 洦 涌 湧 湧	To flow rapidly, gush *yung* *yuǎng*　　*yǒng*
測	氵 氵 汎 汎 浿 浿 浿 浿 測 測	To estimate, measure *chaak* *tse*　　　*cè*
渴	氵 氵 汈 汈 泪 泪 渴 渴 渴 渴	Thirsty, very dry *hot* *hě*　　　*hě*
湯	氵 氵 沪 沪 浿 浿 湯 湯 湯 湯	Soup; hot *tong* *tāng*　　*tāng*
減	氵 氵 汇 汇 泝 泝 洉 減 減 減	To decrease, subtract *gáam* *gan*　　　*gǎn*

滙	氵汀汇汇汇 汇汇滙滙滙滙	To remit wuih hwēi huì
滋	氵氵氵浐浐滋 滋滋	To produce, increase ji dz̄ zī
滅	氵氵汇沪沪派 沥派滅滅滅	To destroy, extinguish miht mye miè
溺	氵氵汈污污污 溺	To drown, indulge in nihk nì nì
滑	氵氵汩汩汩汩 泗滑滑滑滑	Slippery; crafty waaht hwá huá
溶	氵氵氵沪沙浗 浗浗滚溶溶	To dissolve yuhng rúng róng
溜	氵氵汇沂汭汭 汭溜溜溜溜	To glide; slippery lauh lyōu līu
源	氵氵汇沪沂沉 沉沍源源源	A fountain, source yuhn ywán yuán
溝	氵氵汁沬洰洰 洪溝溝溝溝	A ditch, gutter kau kōu kōu
溢	氵氵氵氵汽洪 洪浴溢溢溢	To overflow; abundant yaht yì yì
溪	氵氵氵氵浐浑 淫溪溪溪溪	A stream kāi syī xī
準	氵氵汇沪沪沂 沂淮淮準準	Standard, accuracy jéun jwǔn zǔn

演	氵氵氵氵沪沪沪 沪沪涌涌演演	To perform, act *yin* *yǎn* *yǎn*
漠	氵氵氵氵汁汁沪 洪洪渣渣漠漠	A desert; indifferent *mok* *mwo* *mò*
滯	氵氵氵氵洲洲泄 泄泄泄滞滞滞	To detain; an obstruction *jaih* *jr* *zhì*
漬	氵氵汁沭沣津清 清清清清漬	To soak, wet thoroughly, *jik* stain *dz* *zì*
漂	氵氵氵沪沙漂 洒洒漂漂漂漂	To float, bleach *piu* *pyāu* *piāo*
漲	氵氵氵污污涁 涁涁涁涁漲漲	To expand, innundate *jeung* *jang* *zhǎng*
漁	氵氵氵沄沪泊 渔渔渔渔漁漁	To fish *yuh* *yú* *yú*
滲	氵氵沪汰淤淤 漆漆滲	To soak *sam* *shèn* *shèn*
漸	氵氵氵污污洹洹 漙漙漸漸漸	Gradually *jihm* *jyàn* *jiàn*
滴	氵氵氵沪沪沪 滴滴滴滴滴滴	To drip; drops *dihk* *dī* *dī*
漆	氵氵汁汁沭沐 涞漆漆漆漆漆	To paint *chat* *chī* *qī*
滿	氵氵氵洲洪洪滿 滿滿滿滿	Fullness; proud *múhn* *man* *mǎn*

漢	シジ汗汗沣泄泄漢 淒淒漢漢漢	Chinese; a good fellow *hon* *hàn*　　　　*hàn*
漏	シジ沪沪沪沪漏 漏漏漏漏	To leak, drip *lauh* *lòu*　　　　*lòu*
漱	シ沪江沔泪沭沭 涑涑漱漱漱	To rinse *sau* *sòu, shù*　　*sòu, shù*
漫	シジ沪沪沪沪 沪沪沪湿漫漫	Limitless; to overflow *maahn* *màn*　　　　*màn*
漿	レ니ㅋㅂ뇌米米 뵈뷔將將將將獎	A thick fluid *jeung* *jyāng*　　　*jiāng*
滾	シジ沪沪泸泸 涼涼涼滾	To boil, roll about *gwan* *gwún*　　　*gǔn*
潑	シ沪沪沪沪沙洣 潑潑潑潑潑潑	To spill water *put* *pwō*　　　　*pō*
潛	シ沪江沪沉溉 溉潛潛潛	To dive; to hide *chihm* *chyán*　　　*qián*
潤	シ沪沪沪沪沪 澗澗澗澗潤	To moisten, enrich *yuhn* *ruhn*　　　*rong*
澎	シジ汁沣汴洁洁 洁洁沪澧澎澎	Noise of rushing waters *paahng* *pēng*　　　*pēng*
澈	シジ沪法法済済 清清清潦澈澈	Clear water *chit* *chè*　　　　*chè*
潔	シジ汁沣洼潔潔 潔潔潔潔潔潔	Pure, clean *git* *jyé*　　　　*jié*

- 197 -

澄	シ 汀 汀 汀 汐 泝 泝 泝 澄 澄 澄 澄 澄	Clear; to settle chìhng chéng chéng
潮	シ 氵 汁 汁 洪 沽 沽 湖 淖 潮 潮 潮 潮	A tide; moist chyuh cháu cháo
濁	シ 氵 汛 汛 汛 汹 濁 濁 濁 濁 濁 濁	Muddy juhk jwó zhó
激	シ 氵 氵 汩 泊 泊 洎 湨 湻 滂 滂 激 激 激 激	To excite, encourage gìk jī jī
濃	シ 氵 汋 汋 汭 油 泄 泄 濃 濃 濃 濃 濃 濃	Thick, heavy nùhng núng nóng
澡	シ 氵 汀 汀 汩 澑 澑 浮 澡 澡	To bathe, wash chou dzǎu zǎo
濕	シ 氵 汩 汩 汩 汩 浬 浬 濕 濕 濕	Wet sàp shř shī
濫	シ 氵 汁 汇 沪 汹 湦 泗 濊 濊 濴 濫 濫	To overflow; superficial laàm làn làn
濟	シ 氵 汁 汴 沴 沴 沴 济 涐 涐 瀬 瀬 濟 濟	To help jai jì jì
濱	シ 氵 汋 沪 沪 汸 汸 汸 泙 淬 淬 淬 濱 濱	A shore, border bàn bīn bīn
瀉	シ 氵 氵 汧 汧 汧 沪 沪 洧 洧 涫 瀉 瀉 瀉 瀉	To purge se sye xiè
瀑	シ 氵 汩 汩 汩 汩 浬 浬 淐 淐 淏 瀑 瀑 瀑 瀑	A waterfall, cascade bou pù pù

濾	シ シ シ- シ- シア シア 泸 泸 滹 滹 滹 滹 滹 瀘 瀘 瀘	To strain, filter *leuih* *lyù*　　　　　*lǜ*
灌	シ シ シ- シ- シ- シ- 洪 洪 洪 洪 灌 灌 灌 灌 灌 灌	To pour on or into, irrigate *gun* *gwàn*　　　　*guàn*
灘	シ シ シ- シ- シ- シ- シ- 滹 灘 漢 漢 瀰 瀰 灘 灘 灘	A beach, bank *taan* *tàn*　　　　　*tān*
灑	シ シ シ- シ- シ- 涌 滷 滷 滷 灑 灑 灑 灑 灑 灑	To sprinkle *sá* *sá*　　　　　*sǎ*
灣	シ シ シ- シ- シ- 涫 涫 滷 滷 滷 灣 灣 灣 灣	A bay *wàan* *wàn*　　　　　*wān*

| | 火 | Section |

火	丶 丶 少 火	Fire *fó* *hwǒ*　　　　*huǒ*
灰	一 ナ 灰	Gray color, ashes *fùi* *hwēi*　　　　*huī*
災	く 巜 巛 災	Disaster, distress *jòi* *dzāi*　　　*zāi*
灼	火 灼 灼 灼	To burn; bright *cheuk* *jwò*　　　*zhò*
灶	火 灶 灶 灶	A stove, furnace *chòuh* *dzàu*　　　*zào*
灸	ノ ク 久 灸	Acupuncture *gau* *jyǒu*　　　*jiǔ*

火 (4-6)

炒	火 灯 灼 炒 炒	To pan fry *cháau* *cháu* chǎo
炎	火 炎	A flame; hot *yìhm* *yàn* yán
炕	火 火 灯 炉 炕	A brick bed warmed by fire *haàng* *kàng* kàng
炳	火 灯 灯 炳 炳 炳	Bright, luminous *bing* *bing* bǐng
炬	火 灯 灯 炬 炬	A torch *geuih* *jyu* jù
炮	火 火 炒 灼 灼 炮	A gun, cannon *paau* *pau* pào
炸	火 火 灶 炸 炸 炸	To explode, deep fry *ja* *ja* zhà
炭	丨 山 山 屵 岸 炭	Charcoal *taan* *tàn* tàn
烟	火 灯 炉 烟 烟 烟 烟	Smoke, cigarettes, tobacco *yin* *yàn* yān
烘	火 火 炑 炑 烘 烘 烘	To roast, dry by the fire *huhng* *hung* hōng
烤	火 灯 炑 炷 炴 烤 烤	To toast *haau* *kǎu* kǎo
烝	一 了 彐 承 承 承 烝 烝 烝	To steam *jing* *jēng* zhēng

烈	一 丁 歹 歹 列 列 烈	Fierce, fiery liht lyè ___ liè
烏	′ ′ ′ ′ 户 白 烏 烏	Black wù wū ___ wū
烹	′ 亠 亠 亠 言 言 亨 烹	To cook paang pēng ___ pēng
焦	′ ′ ′ ′ 亻 仁 什 住 住 佳 焦	Scorched; anxious jiu jyāu ___ jiāo
無	′ ′ 亠 ′ 乍 冊 無 無 無	No, none, not mòuh wú ___ wú
然	′ ′ ′ ′ 夕 ′ 匆 匆 然 然 然	However, still, but yihn rén ___ rén
焰	火 灯 灯 焰 焰 焰 焰 焰 焰	Flame yihm yàn ___ yàn
焚	一 十 才 木 林 焚	To burn, set on fire fàhn fén ___ fén
照	′ 刀 日 日 日′ 日″ 日″ 昭 昭 照	To illuminate jiu jàu ___ zhào
煮	一 十 土 耂 耂 者 者 者 煮	To cook jyú jǔ ___ zhǔ
煲	′ ′ ′ 亻 尸 伊 伊 伊 保 保 煲	To boil bōu bàu ___ bāo
煎	′ ′ ′ 亠 广 芀 首 首 前 前 煎	To fry in oil jin jyān ___ jiān

煤	火 㸌 灶 㶶 炑 炑 煤 焯 煤 煤	Coal, charcoal muìh méi méi
煩	火 灯 灯 灯 炳 炳 炳 煩 煩 煩	Troubled, annoyed faàhn fán fán
煉	火 灯 灯 炉 炳 炳 炉 煉 煉 煉	To refine, purify lihn lyàn liàn
熄	火 火 灯 炉 焰 焰 焰 焰 熄 熄	To extinguish sìk syì xí
熔	火 火 火 炉 炉 焌 炉 焌 烤 熔 熔	To smelt yuhng rúng róng
熊	ㄥ ㄥ 广 自 自 自 能 能 能 熊	A bear huhng syúng xióng
熱	一 十 土 ㆝ 夫 去 圥 坴 剗 執 執 熱	Hot, zealous yiht rè rè
熟	丶 亠 广 亠 古 亨 亨 亨 孰 孰 孰 熟	Ripe, cooked, familiar with suhk shú shú
熨	一 コ ㄓ 尸 尸 居 屈 屈 屌 尉 尉 熨	To iron tong ywùn yùn
燙	丶 丷 氵 沪 沪 沪 沪 渇 湯 湯 湯 燙	To iron, burn tong tàng tàng
燃	火 灯 灯 灯 灼 灼 焌 燃 燃 燃 燃	To light a fire yihn rán rán
燒	火 火 炒 炒 炷 烤 烤 燒 燒 燒	To burn, roast siu shāu shāo

燉	火 火` 灯 炉 炉 焙 焙 焙 焞 焞 焞 燉 燉 燉	To stew *dahn* *dwun*　　　　　*dùn*
燕	⼀ ⼗ ⾲ ⾲ ⾢ ⾢ ⾢ ⾢ ⾢ ⾢ 蔬 蔬 燕	A swallow *yin* *yan*　　　　　*yàn*
燈	火 灯 灯 灯 灯 烬 焫 熔 熔 燈 燈 燈	A lamp, light *dang* *dēng*　　　　*dēng*
燦	火 火` 灯 灯 炒 炒 炒 焖 焖 焖 焜 熤 燦 燦	Brilliant, glittering *chaan* *tsàn*　　　　*càn*
燭	火 火` 灯 灯 灯 灯 炉 炉 焐 焐 熠 熠 燭 燭	A candle *juk* *jú*　　　　　*zhu*
營	火 炊 炊 灶 灶 営 営 営 營	A camp, battalion *yihng* *yíng*　　　　*yíng*
燬	火 火 火` 灯 灯 炉 炉 炉 焊 焊 熄 熔 燦 燬	To destroy by fire *wái* *hwěi*　　　　*hǔi*
燥	火 火` 灯 灯 焐 焐 焐 焊 燥 燥	Dry *chou* *dzàu*　　　　*zào*
爆	火 火` 灯 煙 煙 煙 焊 焊 焊 燰 爆 爆 爆 爆	To explode, burst *baau* *baù*　　　　*bào*
爐	火 火` 灯 灯 炉 炉 炉 熘 熘 熘 熘 爐 爐 爐 爐 爐	A stove, fireplace *louh* *lú*　　　　　*lú*
爛	火 灯 灯 炉 炉 燗 燗 燗 燗 燗 燗 燗 爛 爛 爛	Broken, rotten *laahn* *làn*　　　　*làn*
	爪　　　　Section

- 203 -

爪	ノ ⼁ ⼂ 爪	Claws *jaau* *jau*　　　　*zhǎo*
爬	爪 爬 爬 爬 爬	To climb, crawl *pàh* *pá*　　　　*pá*
爭	ノ ⼂ ⼂ ⼂ 乛 当 当 争	To quarrel, struggle *jang* *jeng*　　　*zhēng*
為	⼂ ノ ヅ 为 为 為	To do; because of *waih, waih* *wéi, wèi*　　*wéi, wèi*
爵	ノ ⼂ ⼂ 爫 罒 罒 罒 爫 罘 罾 爵 罿 爵 爵 爵	Nobility *jeuk* *jywe*　　　　*jué*
	父　Section	
父	ノ ⼁ ⼃ 父	A father *fuh* *fù*　　　　*fù*
爸	父 奀 爸 爸 爸	Father, papa *ba* *bà*　　　　*bà*
爺	父 奀 爷 斧 斧 斧 斧 爺 爺 爺	A father, grandfather *yèh* *yé*　　　　*yé*
	爻　Section	
爽	一 ナ オ オ 豸 爽 爽 爽	Cheerful, refreshed *song* *shwang*　　*shuǎng*
爾	一 ⼌ 大 不 亦 禾 爾 爾 爾 爾	You, yours *yu* *er*　　　　*er*

	爿	Section
牀	㇄ 丬 爿 爿 爿 爿 爿 牀	A bed *chohng* *chwang*　　*chuáng*
牆	爿 爿 爿 爿 爿 牀 牀 牀 牆 牆 牆	A wall *cheuhng* *chyáng*　　*qiáng*

	片	Section
片	ノ ノ ㇓ 片 片	A piece, slice *pin* *pyàn*　　*piàn*
版	片 片 片 版 版	A board; an edition *báan* *bǎn*　　*bǎn*
牌	片 片 片 片 片 牌 牌 牌 牌 牌	A sign, permit *paaih* *pái*　　*pái*

	牙	Section
牙	一 ㇒ 工 牙 牙 牙	A tooth *ngah* *yá*　　*yá*

	牛	Section
牛	ノ ㇒ 上 牛	An ox, cow *ngàuh* *nyóu*　　*niú*
牢	丶 丷 宀 牢	A prison; firmly *louh* *láu*　　*láo*

- 205 -

牧	ノ 一 ｷ ｷ 半 牜 牜 牧	To tend *muhk* mù mù
物	牛 牜 牣 物 物	An article, substance *maht* wù wù
牲	牛 牜 牜 牪 牪 牲	Cattle *sang* shēng shēng
特	牜 牜 牜 牜 特 特 特	Special; purposely *dahk* tè tè
牽	丶 一 亠 玄 玄 玄 牵 牽	To drag, pull *hin* chyān qiān
犁	ノ 二 千 千 禾 利 利 利 犁	To plow; a plow *laih* lí lí
犢	牛 牜 牜 牪 牪 牪 牪 犕 犕 犢 犢 犢 犢 犢	A calf, heifer *suhk* dú dú
犧	牛 牜 牜 牜 牪 牪 牪 牪 牪 牪 犠 犠 犧 犧	To sacrifice *hei* syī xī
犬		Section
犬	一 ナ 大 犬	A dog *hyun* chwǎn chǔan
犯	ノ ｊ ｊ 犭 犯 犯	To violate, offend *faahn* fàn fàn
狀	乚 ㇄ ㇄ 爿 狀 狀	From *johng* jwàng zhuàng

狂	犭 犭 犭 狂 狂	Violent, crazy *kòhng* *kwàng* *kuáng*
狗	犭 犭 狗 狗 狗 狗	A dog *gáu* *góu* *gǒu*
狐	犭 犭 犭 狐 狐 狐	A fox *wùh* *hú* *hú*
狠	犭 犭 犭 狠 狠 狠 狠	Cruel, hard-hearted *hán* *hén* *hěn*
狡	犭 犭 犭 犭 狡 狡 狡	Sneaky, cunning *gaau* *jyáu* *jiǎo*
狼	犭 犭 犭 狛 狛 狼 狼 狼	A wolf, cruel *lòhng* *láng* *láng*
狹	犭 犭 犭 犭 狹 狹 狹	Narrow *hahp* *sya* *xá*
猛	犭 犭 犭 犭 狩 猛 猛 猛 猛	Fierce *máang* *méng* *měng*
猜	犭 犭 犭 狂 狂 猜 猜 猜 猜	To guess, doubt *chàai* *tsāi* *cāi*
猴	犭 犭 犭 犭 狉 狉 狉 猴 猴 猴 猴	A monkey, ape *hàuh* *hóu* *hóu*
猪	犭 犭 犭 狂 狉 狉 猪 猪 猪	A pig *jyu* *jū* *zhū*
猶	犭 犭 犭 犭 犴 猶 猶 猶 猶 猶	Undecided; a Jew *yàuh* *yóu* *yóu*

獅	犭 犭' 犭' 犭" 狮 狮 狮 狮 獅 獅	A lion *si* *shr̄*　　　　　*shī*
猾	犭 犭' 犭冂 狎 狎 猾 猾 猾 猾 猾 猾	Sneaky, cunning *waaht* *húa*　　　　*húa*
獄	犭 犭' 犭 犭' 狺 狺 猂 猂 獄	A prison, jail *yuhk* *yù*　　　　　*yù*
獨	犭 犭冂 犭冂 狎 狎 狎 猖 猖 猖 獨 獨 獨	Single, alone *duhk* *dú*　　　　　*dú*
獲	犭 犭' 犭' 犰 犰 犰 犰 犰 犴 獲 獲 獲	To obtain, catch *wohk* *hwó*　　　　*hùo*
獵	犭 犭' 狩 狩 猟 猟 猟 猟 猟 猟 獵 獵 獵	To hunt; hunting *lihp* *lỳe*　　　　*lìe*
獸	丶 冂 口 吅 吅 甲 咢 咢 咢 咢 單 嘼 獸	Beasts, wild animals *sau* *shou*　　　　*shòu*
獻	丨 卜 上 广 庐 虍 虍 虐 虍 虜 虜 虜 膚 膚 膚 獻	To offer, present *hin* *syàn*　　　　*xiàn*
	玄	Section
玄	丶 亠 亠 玄 玄	Dark, profound *yihn* *sywàn*　　　*xuán*
率	玄 玄 泫 泫 泫 泫 率	To guide, follow *syut, lyuht* *shwò, lù*　　*shùo, lù*
	玉	Section

王	一 丁 干 王	A king, ruler wòhng wáng · · · · · · wáng
玉	王 玉	Jade yuhk yù · · · · · · yù
玫	王 王' 玝 玟 玫	A rose muih méi · · · · · · méi
玩	王 玉' 玉⁻ 玗 玩	To play, amuse with wuhn wǎn, wàn · · · wǎn, wàn
玻	王 王' 玗 玻 玻 玻	Glass bò bwō · · · · · · bō
珍	王 王' 玪 珍 珍 珍	Precious jan jēn · · · · · · zhēn
珠	王 王' 玗 玤 珪 珠 珠	A pearl, bead jyu jū · · · · · · zhū
班	王 玉 玌 班	A class, grade baan bān · · · · · · bān
現	王 玌 玑 玥 珇 珇 現 現	To appear; now yihn syàn · · · · · · xiàn
球	王 玗 玗 玝 玣 球 球 球	A ball, sphere kàuh chyou · · · · · · qiú
理	王 玑 玗 玗 珇 珇 理 理	To manage; the reason leíh lǐ · · · · · · lǐ
琴	王 珏 珏 珡 琴 琴	A lute, piano kàhm chín · · · · · · qín

瑞	王 王' 玎 玗 瑞 玡 玡 瑞 瑞 瑞	A good omen, auspicious *seuih* rwèi rùi
瑰	王 王' 玎 玏 珀 瑰 珥 珢 瑰 瑰 瑰	A rose; precious *gwai* gwèi guēi
瑣	王 玎 玎' 玑 玼 玼 珰 珰 瑂 瑣 瑣	Trifling *só* swǒ suǒ
環	王 玎 珂 珂 理 理 瑈 瑈 琭 瑈 環 環 環	To surround; a ring *waahn* hwan huán
璧	一 コ ㄖ 尸 月 启 启' 启' 启' 启' 辟 辟 辟 璧 璧	A piece of jade *bik* bì bì
	瓜	Section
瓜	ノ 厂 瓜 瓜 瓜	A melon, squash *gwā* gwā guā
瓣	丶 亠 六 六 立 立 辛 辡 辡 辬 辬 辬 辧 辧 瓣 瓣	Petals of a flower *faan* bàn bàn
	瓦	Section
瓦	一 工 瓦 瓦	Tiles *ngáh* wǎ wǎ
瓷	丶 冫 冫 汐 汐 次 瓷	Porcelain, china *chìh* tsz cí
瓶	丶 ㇀ 冫 兰 羊 并 瓶	A bottle, jug *pìhng* píng píng

甘 Section		
甘	一 十 廿 甘 甘	Sweet; voluntary *gàm* *chān*　　*chān*
甚	一 十 廿 甘 甘 甚 芺 其 甚	Very, how, why *sahm* *shèn*　　*shèn*
甜	丿 一 千 千 舌 舌 甜	Sweet *tìhm* *tyán*　　*tián*
生 Section		
生	丿 一 牛 牛 生	To give birth, to be born, *sēng*　　live; raw *shēng*　　*shēng*
產	丶 亠 亠 文 立 产 產	To produce *cháan* *chǎn*　　*chǎn*
甥	生 乡 乡刀 乡刀 乡刃 乡刃 乡男 甥	A nephew, niece *sēng* *shēng*　　*shēng*
用 Section		
用	丿 冂 月 月 用	To use, spend; expense *yuhng* *yung*　　*yòng*
田 Section		
田	丶 冂 冃 用 田	A field, land *tìhn* *tyán*　　*tián*

由	丶 冂 月 由 由	To let; from, by; reason *yauh* *yóu* *you*
甲	丶 冂 月 日 甲	The fingernails; the first *gaap* *jyǎ* *jiǎ*
申	丶 冂 月 日 申	To extend; to express *san* *shēn* *shēn*
男	丶 冂 月 田 田 罗 男	A man, male *naahm* *nán* *nán*
界	田 罗 界 界 界	A boundary, frontier *gaai* *jye* *jie*
畏	田 里 畏 畏 畏	To fear, dread *wai* *wèi* *wèi*
留	丶 丿 囗 囟 卯 留	To keep, remain *lauh* *lyou* *liú*
畜	丶 亠 亠 玄 玄 畜	To raise or feed animals *chuk* *chù* *chù*
畢	田 甲 畢 畢 畢 畢 畢	To finish; entirely *bat* *bi* *bì*
畧	田 甲 罗 畧 畧 畧 畧	To summarize; briefly *leuhk* *lywe* *lüe*
番	丿 夕 丩 平 采 采 番	Barbarians; foreign *faan* *fān* *fān*
異	田 甲 罗 界 畀 異 異	Different, foreign *yih* *yi* *yi*

| 畫 | ㄱ ㄋ ㄱ ㄋ ㅌ 畫
畫 | To draw; a picture, strokes
wa
hwa   hùa |
| 當 | ㅣ ㅣ ㅐ ㅐ 当
当 尚 尚 當 | To bear, take place; when,
dong   during
dāng   dāng |

| | 疋 | Section |

疋	一 丁 下 疋 疋	A piece(for cloth) pat pi pi
疏	一 丁 下 疋 正 正 正 疏 疏 疏 疏 疏	Careless sò shu shu
疑	ㄴ ㄴ ㅏ ㅌ 乍 乍 巨 毕 疑	To doubt, suspect yìh yi yí

| | 疒 | Section |

疫	丶 一 广 广 广 疒 疒 疒 疫	A disease yihk yì yì
症	疒 疒 疒 疒 症 症	A disease, sickness jing jeng zheng
疹	疒 疒 疒 疹 疹 疹	A rash, measles chan jen zhěn
疾	疒 疒 疒 疟 疾 疾	Sickness, disease; quick jaht ji jí
病	疒 疒 疒 病 病 病	Illness, disease bihng bing bìng

疲	疒 疒 疒 疒 疲 疲	Tired, exhausted pèih pí　　　　　pí
痕	疒 疒 疒 疒 痕 痕 痕	A mark, scar hàhn hén　　　　　hén
痊	疒 疒 疒 疒 疒 痊 痊	Cured, recovered chyùhn chywán　　　quán
痛	疒 疒 疒 疒 痛 痛 痛 痛	Pain, ache tung tùng　　　　　tòng
痣	疒 疒 疒 疒 疒 痣 痣 痣	A mole chi jr　　　　　zhì
痰	疒 疒 疒 疒 痰 痰	Phlegm tàahm tán　　　　　tán
痲	疒 疒 疒 疒 痲 痲	Numbness, paralysis màh má　　　　　má
瘋	疒 疒 疒 疒 疯 疯 瘋 瘋 瘋 瘋	Leprosy; insane fùng fēng　　　　　fēng
瘤	疒 疒 疒 疒 疒 疒 瘤 瘤 瘤 瘤	A tumor làuh lyóu　　　　　liú
瘦	疒 疒 疒 疒 痟 痟 瘦 瘦 瘦	Thin, lean sau shòu　　　　shòu
療	疒 疒 疒 疒 疒 疒 疒 瘆 瘆 瘆 瘆 瘆 療	To cure, heal liuh lyàu　　　　liáo
癌	疒 疒 疒 疒 疒 癌 癌 癌 癌	Cancer ngàahm yán　　　　　yán

- 214 -

癢	疒 疒 疒 疒 疒 疒 疹 疹 疹 痒 痒 痒 痒 痒 痒	To itch *yeúhng* *yǎng*　　　*yǎng*
	癶	**Section**
登	フ ヲ ヲ ヲ ヲ 癶 癶 癶 癶 癶 癶 登 登	To go up, register *dāng* *dēng*　　　*dēng*
發	癶 癶 癶 癶 癶 發 發 發	To send out, proceed *faat* *fā*　　　*fā*
	白	**Section**
白	丿 亻 白 白 白	White, clear, bright *baahk* *bái*　　　*bái*
百	一 百	A hundred; numerous *baak* *bǎi*　　　*bǎi*
皂	白 皀 皂	Soap; black *jouh* *dzàu*　　　*zào*
的	白 白 的 的	Actual; possessive pronoun *dik* *dí, dì, de*　　*dí, dì, de*
皆	丨 匕 比 比 皆	All, altogether *gaài* *jyē*　　　*jiē*
皇	白 白 皁 皇 皇	Imperial; a ruler *wòhng* *hwǎng*　　　*huáng*
	皮	**Section**

- 215 -

皮	一 厂 广 皮 皮	Skin, leather, fur, peel peìh pí pí
	皿 Section	
皿	丶 冂 冂 皿 皿	A vessel, utensil mihng ming ming
盅	丶 冂 口 中 盅	A covered cup, bowl jùng jung zhong
盆	丿 八 分 分 盆	A basin, tub puhn pén pén
盈	乃 乃 乃 丒 盈	To overflow; excess yìhng ying yíng
益	丶 八 ㇐ 关 关 益	Benefit, advantage yik yi yì
盒	丿 入 仝 仝 合 合 盒	A box, case hahp hé hé
盛	一 厂 厉 盅 盅 盛 盛	To contain; abundant sihng shéng shèng
盗	丶 冫 氵 氵 汐 次 盗	To steal; a robber douh dau dào
盟	丨 冂 日 日 明 明 明 明 盟	To swear; an oath màhng méng méng
監	丨 厂 厂 戶 臣 臣 臣 臤 臤 臨 監	To supervise; a prison gàam jyān jiān

| 盡 | フ ユ ヨ ヨ 圭 肃 盡 | To exhaust; the extreme
jeuhn
jìn　　　　*jìn* |
| 盤 | ′ ′ 冇 凢 舟 舟 舟 舲 舩 般 盤 | A tray, plate
puhn
pán　　　　*pán* |

目　Section

目	｜ 冂 冃 月 目	To see; an eye, a leader *muhk* *mù*　　　　*mù*
盲	′ 亠 亡 盲	Blind; blindly *maahng* *máng*　　　　*máng*
直	一 十 十 古 内 肖 直 直	Straight, honest; directly *jihk* *jŕ*　　　　*zhí*
相	一 十 才 木 相	Mutual, reciprocal *seùng, seung* *syāng, syàng　xiāng, xiàng*
盼	目 目 盼 盼 盼	To hope for; to look at *paan* *pàn*　　　　*pàn*
省	｜ 小 小 少 省	To save; a province *saáng, síng* *shěng*　　　　*shěng*
看	′ 二 三 手 看	To see, **visit**, take care of *hon* *kàn*　　　　*kàn*
眉	フ ア ﾛ 尸 眉	The eyebrows *meih* *méi*　　　　*méi*
眠	目 目 目 跙 眇 眠	To sleep, lie down *mihn* *myán*　　　　*mián*

目 (5-12)

真	一 十 十 古 古 直 直 直 真 真	Real, sincere jàn jēn　　　　zhēn
眼	目 目 目 目 目 眼 眼	An eye ngáahn yan　　　　yǎn
眷	、丷丷兰半类 眷	To be fond of; relatives gyun jywàn　　　　juàn
眾	、八介甶血血 血 盯 盯 盯 盯 眾	A crowd; many jung juǹg　　　　zhòng
着	、丷丷丷羊羊 着	To put on, wear jeuk, jeuhk　　　　zhe jwó,jáu,jāu,jè zhó,zhāo,zhāo,
睛	目 盯 盯 盯 睛 睛 睛 睛 睛	The eyeball jìng jīng　　　　jīng
睡	目 目 目 目 目 睡 睡 睡 睡	To sleep seuih shwèi　　　　shùi
督	、卜上卡才未村 叔 督	To supervise, direct dùk dū　　　　dū
瞄	目 目 目 盯 盯 盱 盱 盹 瞄 瞄	To aim at miuh myáu　　　　miáo
瞎	目 盯 盯 盱 盰 盰 睯 睯 瞎 瞎	Carelessly, blindly got syā　　　　xā
瞞	目 目 盯 盯 盯 盯 睲 睲 瞞 瞞	To hide, conceal the truth mùhn mán　　　　mán
瞥	、八介价舟 甫 甫 敝 敝 瞥	To peep; a glimpse bai pyē　　　　piē

瞻	目 目ˊ 盺 盺 盺 盺 盺 盺 盺 瞻 瞻 瞻 瞻 瞻	To look up to; respect *jim* *jan*　　　　*zhan*
	矛　Section	
矛	﹁ マ ヌ 予 矛	A spear, lance *maauh* *máu*　　　　*máo*
	矢　Section	
矢	﹑ ﹅ ﹄ 午 矢	An arrow *chi* *shř*　　　　*shǐ*
知	矢 知 知 知	To know, comprehend *ji* *jr*　　　　*zhī*
短	矢 矢 知 知 短 短 短 短	Brief; to lack *dyun* *dwan*　　　　*duǎn*
矮	矢 矢ˊ 知ˊ 矦 矮 矮 矮 矮	Low, short *ngai* *ai*　　　　*ai*
矯	矢 矢ˊ 知ˊ 矦 矫 矫 矫 矫 矫 矯 矯	To pretend; strong *giu* *jyǎu*　　　　*jiǎo*
	石　Section	
石	一 丆 丆 石 石	A rock, stone *sehk* *shŕ*　　　　*shí*
砌	石 石 矵 矵 砌	To build, pave *chai* *chì*　　　　*qì*

砍	石 石 矿 矿 砍	To chop, cut down ham kan kan
破	石 石 矿 矿 砵 破	To break, destroy po pwo pò
研	石 石 矿 矼 研	To study, research yihn yán yán
硬	石 石 矿 矼 硬 硬 硬 硬	Hard, solid ngahng ying yìng
碗	石 石 矿 矿 砵 破 碗 碗 碗	A bowl wun wán wǎn
碎	石 石 石 矿 砕 砕 碎 碎	To break into pieces; broken seui swei suì
碰	石 石 石 砕 砕 砎 碰 碰 碰	To meet, collide with pung peng pèng
碟	石 石 石 砝 砝 砝 碟 碟 碟 碟 碟	A dish, saucer dihp dyé dié
確	石 石 矿 矿 砕 砕 砕 砕 碓 確 確	Certainly, actually kok chywe que
碼	石 石 石 矼 矼 码 码	A wharf, yard mah ma mǎ
磁	石 石 石 矿 砕 砕 磁 磁	Magnetic, chinaware chih tse cé
磅	石 石 石 石 石 砕 砕 砕 磅 磅 磅	A pound bohng bang bàng

| 磨 | 亠 广 广 庐 庐 床 麻 麻 磨 | To grind, rub
moh
mwo   mó |
| 碑 | 石 石 石 砂 砑 砑 砖 砗 砗 砖 磚 磚 | A brick
jyun
jwan   zhuan |

| | 示 | Section |

示	一 二 丁 亍 示	To proclaim; announcement sih shr shì
社	、 宀 礻 礻 礻 礻 社	A society, association seh she she
祈	礻 礻 礽 祈 祈	To pray, implore keih chi qí
祖	礻 礼 初 袒 袒 祖	An ancestor jou dzu zú
神	礻 礼 初 袒 袒 神	God, a spirit sàhn shen shén
祕	礻 礼 祂 祕 祕 祕	Secret, mysterious bei bì bì
祝	礻 礼 初 祁 祁 祝	To bless, pray juk dzu zù
票	一 冖 冖 两 西 覀 覀 票 票 票	A ticket, bill piu pyau piào
祥	礻 礻 礽 袢 袢 袢 祥	Luck, a good omen cheuhng syang xiáng

祭	ﾉ ク タ タ ﾀﾞ 夘 夗 夘 祭 祭 祭	To offer a sacrifice *jai* jì　　　　　jì
禁	一 十 才 木 林 林 埜 埜 禁 禁	To prohibit, prevent *gam* jìn　　　　　jìn
祿	礻 礻 礻 礻 袜 禄 禄 禄	Prosperity *luhk* lù　　　　　lù
福	礻 礻 礻 袻 袻 袻 禍 禑 福 福	Happiness, fortune, luck *fuk* fú　　　　　fú
禍	礻 礻 初 袇 袇 袇 禍 禍 禍 禍	Disaster, misfortune *woh* hwò　　　　　hùo
禮	礻 礻 初 袘 袡 神 袡 禮 禮 禮 禮 禮 禮 禮	Politeness; a ceremony *laih* lí　　　　　lí
	内	Section
禽	ﾉ 人 人 亼 今 令 令 含 含 禽 禽 禽	Birds, poultry *kàhm* chín　　　　　qín
	禾	Section
禾	ﾉ 二 千 才 禾	Crops, grain *woh* hé　　　　　hé
禿	禾 禾 禿	Bare, hairless *tuk* tū　　　　　tū
私	禾 私 私	Private, selfish *sì* sē　　　　　sē

秀	禾 季 秀	Graceful, elegant *sau* *syòu*　　　*xìu*
秋	禾 禾 利 秒 秋	Autumn *chàu* *chyōu*　　　*qiū*
秒	禾 利 利 秒 秒	A second of time *miúh* *myǎu*　　　*miǎo*
科	禾 禾 利 科 科	A class; studies *fo* *kē*　　　*kē*
租	禾 利 和 租 租 租	To rent, lease *jou* *dzū*　　　*zū*
秩	禾 利 秒 秩 秩 秩	Order, official rank *dìht* *jr*　　　*zhì*
移	禾 利 秒 移 移	To shift, remove *yih* *yí*　　　*yí*
稀	禾 利 利 秳 秳 秳 稀 稀	Thin *hèi* *syī*　　　*xī*
稅	禾 禾 利 秒 秒 稻 秒 稅	A tax *seui* *shwei*　　　*shùi*
程	禾 利 和 和 和 秆 秆 程	A journey; a measure *chìhng* *chéng*　　　*chéng*
稚	禾 禾 利 利 秒 秒 秒 稚 稚	Young, tender *jih* *jr*　　　*zhì*
種	禾 利 秒 秒 稻 稻 稻 種 種 種	To plant; a seed, a kind *jung, jung* *jùng, jǔng*　*zhòng, zhǒng*

稱	禾 禾 禾 禾 稆 秆 稆 稱 稱 稱	A title, name *ching* *chēng* *chēng*
稿	禾 禾 禾 禾 秸 梋 槁 稿 稿 稿	A sketch, original copy *góu* *gǎu* *gǎo*
穎	㇑ ㇗ ㇗ 禿 禾 穎 穎 穎 穎 穎 穎 穎 穎	Clever, eminent *wihng* *yǐng* *yǐng*
積	禾 禾 禾 禾 秸 秸 秸 秸 秸 積 積 積	To store up, accumulate *jīk* *jī* *jī*
	穴 Section	
穴	丶 丷 宀 宀 穴	A cave, hole *yuht* *sywe* *xue*
究	丶 宀 宀 宂 穷 究	To investigate, search *gau* *jyou* *jiu*
空	宀 宀 空 空	Space; empty *hung* *kūng* *kōng*
穿	宀 空 宀 空 穿 穿	To wear, go through *chyun* *chwān* *chuān*
突	宀 宀 突 突 突	Suddenly *daht* *tú* *tú*
窄	宀 空 空 空 窄 窄	Narrow, compressed *jaak* *dzé, jái* *zé, zhái*
窒	宀 宀 空 空 空 窒 窒	To stop, smother *jaht* *jr̀* *zhì*

- 224 -

窗	穴 穴 穴 穴 窈 窗 窗	A window, shutter *cheung* *chwang* *chuāng*
窩	穴 穴 穴 窎 窎 窎 窩 窩 窩 窩	A nest, den *wō* *wō* *wō*
窮	穴 穴 穴 穷 窮 穷 穷 穷 窮 窮 窮	Poor, needy *kuhng* *chyúng* *qióng*
窺	穴 穴 竺 窏 窏 窏 窺 窺 窺 窺 窺 窺	To spy, watch *kwai* *kwēi* *kuī*
竊	穴 穴 窏 窏 窎 窏 窎 窏 窊 窃 窃 竊 竊	To steal; secretly *sit* *chye* *qiè*

立   Section

立	丶 二 十 立 立	To stand, establish *lahp* *lì* *lì*
站	立 立 站 站 站 站	To stand; a station *jaahm* *jan* *zhàn*
竟	立 产 音 音 音 章 竟	Actually, finally *gíng* *jìng* *jìng*
章	立 产 音 音 音 音 章	A section; a seal *jeung* *jāng* *zhāng*
童	立 产 音 音 音 童 童 童	A child *tuhng* *túng* *tóng*
端	立 立 立 立 立 立 端 端 端	Straight up; an end *dyun* *dwān* *duān*

| 競 | 立 亠 咅 音 竟 竟
競 | To compete, strive
gihng
jing   *jing* |

| | 竹 | Section |

竹	ノ ト ケ 竹 竹 竹	Bamboo *juk* *jú* *zhú*
竿	ノ ト ⺮ ⺮ 竺 竿 竿	A pole, stick *gòn* *gān* *gān*
笑	⺮ ⺮ 竺 笑 笑	To laugh, smile *siu* *syàu* *xiào*
第	⺮ 竺 竺 笃 笃 第	A series, order *daih* *dì* *dì*
笛	⺮ ⺮ 竺 竺 笛 笛	A flute, fife *dehk* *dí* *dí*
符	⺮ ⺮ 符 符 符 符	To agree with; a charm *fuh* *fú* *fú*
笨	⺮ 竺 竿 笨 笨 笨	Stupid, clumsy *bahn* *bèn* *bèn*
答	⺮ 竺 炎 答 答 答 答	To answer, reply *daap* *dá* *dá*
筆	⺮ 竺 竺 竺 筆 筆 筆	A brush, pen *bat* *bi* *bi*
等	⺮ 竺 竿 竺 竺 等 等	To wait; equal to *dáng* *dèng* *dèng*

筋	竹 竹 竹 竹 竹 筋 筋	Muscles, tendons *gan* *jin̄*　　　　*jīn*
筒	竹 竹 竹 筒 筒 筒 筒	A pipe, tube *tuhng* *tunḡ*　　　*tong*
筍	竹 竹 笋 笋 筍 筍 筍	Bamboo shoots, sprouts *séun* *swun*　　　*sun*
策	竹 竹 笁 笁 策 策	To whip a horse; a plan *chaak* *tse*　　　　*ce*
筷	竹 竹 笊 笊 笊 筷 筷 筷	Chopsticks *faai* *kwai*　　　*kuai*
筵	竹 竹 笁 笁 笁 筵 筵 筵	A banquet; entertainment *yihn* *yan*　　　*yan*
管	竹 竹 笊 笁 笁 笁 管 管	To manage; a pipe *gwun* *gwan*　　　*guan*
算	竹 竹 笁 笁 笁 笁 算 算 算	To calculate *syun* *swan*　　　*suan*
箋	竹 竹 笺 笺 箋 箋	A note; note-paper *jaan* *jyan̄*　　　*jian*
箏	竹 竹 笁 笁 笁 笁 笁 箏 箏	A kite *jang* *jeng*　　　*zheng*
箭	竹 竹 笁 笁 笁 笁 笁 笁 笁 箭	An arrow *jin* *jyan*　　　*jian*
箱	竹 竹 笁 笁 笁 笁 笁 箱 箱 箱	A box, trunk *seung* *syang*　　　*xiang*

範	𥫗 𥫗 𥫗 𥫗 𥫗 𥫗 箮 箽 斬 斬 範	A pattern, model *faahn* fàn fàn
節	𥫗 𥫗 𥫗 𥫗 𥫗 筲 節 節 節	A festival; a knot; a chapter *jit* jyé jié
篇	𥫗 𥫗 𥫗 𥫗 笭 笭 筥 篇 篇 篇 篇	A chapter; a page *pin* pyān piàn
築	𥫗 𥫗 𥫗 𥫗 筑 筑 筑 築 築 築 築	To construct *juk* jú zhú
篤	𥫗 𥫗 笲 笲 筲 筐 篤 篤	Sincere, honest *duk* dǔ dǔ
篷	𥫗 𥫗 笁 笁 笺 䇺 篧 筆 篷 篷 篷	A sail; an awning *fùhng* péng péng
簡	𥫗 𥫗 𥫗 筲 筲 筲 簡 簡 簡 簡 簡 簡 簡	Simple; a letter *gáan* jyán jiǎn
簫	𥫗 笁 笋 筲 筆 筆 籬 籬 簫 簫 簫 簫	A flute *siu* syāu xiāo
簿	𥫗 𥫗 𥫗 𥫗 𥫗 𥫗 溥 溥 溥 溥 溥 簿 簿	An account book *bóu* bù bù
簽	𥫗 笻 笶 笶 笶 答 答 答 賛 簽	To sign; a label *chim* chyān qiān
簾	𥫗 𥫗 竺 筲 筲 管 筐 簥 簥 簥 簝 簾 簾 簾	A curtain, screen *lìhm* lyán lián
籃	𥫗 𥫗 筲 筲 筲 筲 筲 箆 箆 籃 籃 籃 籃 籃	A basket, hamper *laahm* lán lán

籌	虻 炷 竺 竺 笁 筥 笃 笺 笺 筥 篝 篝 簙 簙 籌 籌	To calculate; a ticket *chàuh* *chóu* *chóu*
籍	虻 炷 竿 笁 笁 笄 笄 笄 箖 絓 籍 籍 籍 籍	One's native town; a register *jihk* *ji* *ji*
籠	虻 竺 竺 笁 笁 筥 笞 筩 箐 箐 箐 籠 籠	To confine in a cage; a cage *lùhng* *lúng* *lóng*
籤	虻 竺 竿 笁 竿 竿 竿 蜚 蛬 籤 籤 籤	A slip of bamboo, label *chìm* *chyān* *qiān*
米		Section
米	丶 丶丶 丷 半 米 米	Uncooked rice *máih* *mǐ* *mǐ*
粉	米 米 粁 粉 粉	Powder, flour *fán* *fén* *fěn*
粒	米 米 粁 粋 粒 粒	A grain of a kernel *làp* *lì* *lì*
粗	米 粁 粁 粗 粗 粗	Rough, coarse *chóu* *tsū* *cū*
粟	一 丆 西 西 西 粟	Corn, grain *sùk* *sù* *sù*
粧	米 米 粁 粋 粉 粧 粧	To dress up, beautify *jòng* *jwāng* *zhuāng*
粵	丷 丬 向 向 甬 甬 粵 粵	Canton *yuht* *ywe* *yùe*

粥	ㄱ ㄱ 弓 䉬 粥	Rice gruel jùk jù　　　　　　zhu
精	米 米⁻ 米† 粁 粁 精 精 精 精	The essence, spirit; semen jīng jīng　　　　　jīng
粽	米 米' 米' 米'' 粅'' 粸 粺 粺 粽	A rice dumpling júng dzung　　　　zòng
糊	米 米 料 粁 粘 粘 糊 糊 糊 糊	Paste wùh hú　　　　　　hú
糕	米' 米' 米'' 粁 粁 粁 糕 糕	Cake, pastry gòu gāu　　　　　gāo
糖	米 米' 粁 粁 粁 粅 粻 糖 粻 糖 糖	Sugar, candy tòhng táng　　　　táng
糞	米 米 岩 岑 畨 畨 黄 董 畫 董 糞 糞	Manure fan fèn　　　　　fèn
糧	米 米 粔 粔 粗 米旦 糈 糧 糧 糧	Food, grain leuhng lyáng　　　　liáng
糯	米 米' 米' 粘 粘 粘 粺 粺 糯 糯 糯 糯	Glutinous rice noh nwò　　　　　nùo

	糸	Section
系	ノ ㄡ 幺 幺 幺 系 系 丶	A system; a connection haih sỳi　　　　　xì
糾	糸 糺 糾	To gather; connect dáu jyōu　　　　jiū

紅	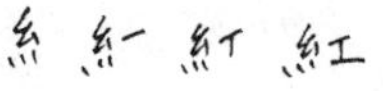	Red *hùhng* *húng* *hóng*
紀	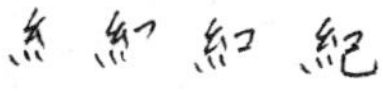	To record; annals *géi* *jì* *jì*
約		To make an appointment; about *yeuk* *ywē* *yuē*
紐		To wring, fasten, tie a knot; a knot *náu* *nyǒu* *niǔ*
納	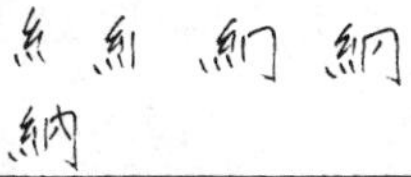	To pay; to receive *naahp* *nà* *nà*
紋		Lines, stripes *màhn* *wén* *wén*
級		A grade, step *kàp* *jí* *jí*
紡	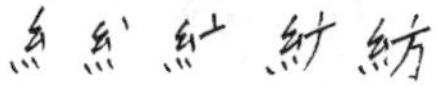	To spin cloth *fóng* *fǎng* *fǎng*
素		Plain, simple *sou* *sù* *sù*
紙	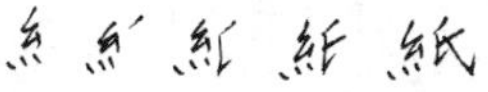	Paper *jí* *jř* *zhǐ*
純	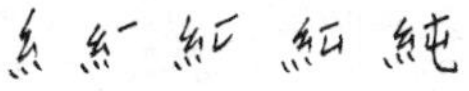	Pure, unmixed *sèuhn* *chwún* *chún*
索	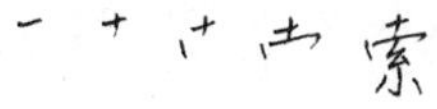	To ask for; a rope *sok* *swǒ* *suǒ*

組	糸 糹 糼 紉 絎 組	To organize; an organization *jóu* *dzŭ* *zŭ*
細	糸 糹 糼 紃 細 細	Small, fine *sai* *syi* *xì*
累	丶 冂 口 田 田 累	To involve; to accumulate; *leuih* tired *léi, lèi* *léi, lèi*
紹	糸 糹 紒 紹 紹 紹	To connect, join *siuh* *shàu* *shào*
終	糸 糹 紒 紒 終 終	To end; finally; whole *jung* *jung* *zhōng*
紫	丶 丨 卜 止 此 此 紫	Purple *jí* *dz* *zĭ*
統	糸 糹 紅 紝 紝 統 統	To rule; whole *túng* *tung* *tŏng*
給	糸 糹 紒 給 給 給 給	To give, offer *kap* *gei* *gěi*
絕	糸 糹 紒 紒 絡 絡 絕	To break off; extremely *jyuht* *jywe* *jué*
結	糸 糹 紝 紝 結 結 結	To tie; a knot *git* *jye* *jié*
絡	糸 糹 紒 紒 絡 絡 絡	To connect; blood vessels *lok* *lwò* *luò*
絲	糸 絲	Silk *si* *sē* *sē*

綁	糸 糹 糺 糹 絆 絆 綁	To tie *bong* *bǎng* *bǎng*
經	糸 糺 糽 純 紓 經 緅 經	To manage, already *gìng* *jīng* *jīng*
綿	糸 糹 糽 紵 絇 絈 絈 綿 綿	Cotton, soft *mihn* *myán* *mián*
網	糸 糹 紒 絅 絅 絅 絅 網 網	A web, net *móhng* *wǎng* *wǎng*
維	糸 糹 紒 紒 紒 紼 絓 絓 維	To maintain *wàih* *wéi* *wéi*
綱	糸 糹 紒 絅 絅 絅 絅 綱 綱	Principles, laws *gòng* *gāng* *gāng*
綢	糸 糹 紒 絅 絅 絅 綢 綢 綢	Thick silk *chàuh* *chóu* *chóu*
綠	糸 糹 絭 絲 絲 絳 絳 絳 綠	Green *luhk* *lyù* *lǜ*
緊	一 厂 厂 臣 臣 臣 臣 臤 緊	Tight; urgent *gán* *jǐn* *jǐn*
綫	糸 糹 糼 絨 綫 綫	A thread, line *sin* *syàn* *xiàn*
編	糸 糹 紒 紒 紵 紵 綗 綗 編 編	To arrange, compose *pin* *byān* *biān*
緒	糸 糹 糺 結 絣 絣 絳 緒 緒	A clue, beginning *seuih* *syù* *xù*

緩	糸 糸′ 糸″ 糸″ 緩 緩 緩 緩 緩 緩	To postpone; slowly wùhn hwǎn　　　huǎn
緝	糸 糸′ 糸″ 糸″ 絎 紆 絹 絹 絹 緝	To arrest, catch yàp chī　　　qì
練	糸 糸′ 糸″ 絎 絎 絎 綿 綞 縛 練	To practice, train lihn lyàn　　　liàn
緣	糸 糸′ 糸″ 絎 絎 綷 綷 緣 緣 緣	A relationship; a cause yùhn yán　　　yán
縛	糸 糸′ 紅 絎 絹 組 綁 綞 綿 縛	To fasten, tie up bok fu　　　fú
縣	丨 冂 冃 目 且 旦 昇 昇 県 県 縣 縣	A district, county yuhn syàn　　　xiàn
總	糸 糸′ 糸″ 紗 綷 綷 綷 總 總 總 總	All; a chief júng dzúng　　　zǒng
縱	糸 糸′ 糸″ 絎 絎 綷 縱 縱 縱 縱 縱	To allow; vertical júng júng　　　zhōng
縮	糸 糸′ 糸″ 綷 綷 綷 綷 縮 縮 縮 縮	To shrink, draw back suk sù, swò　　　sù, suō
績	糸 糸′ 糸″ 結 結 結 結 績 績 績 績	Merit jīk jī　　　jī
繁	丿 仁 乇 每 每 每 每 每 敏 敏 繁 繁	Numerous; annoying faahn fàn　　　fán
繡	糸 糸′ 糸″ 絎 綷 綷 綷 繡 繡 繡 繡 繡	To embroider sau syòu　　　xiù

織	糸 糸 糸 糸 糸 紋 結 結 綞 結 織 織 織	To weave *jik* *jr̄* *zhī*
繩	糸 糸 糸 糸 糸 紀 紀 絕 絕 絚 繩 繩 繩	A string, cord *sìhng* *shéng* *shéng*
繫	一 厂 厂 旦 旦 車 車 車 車 軎 軎 繫 繫	To fasten, bind *haih* *syì* *xì*
繳	糸 糸 糸 紒 紒 絢 絗 綢 縛 縛 繒 繳 繳	To pay *gíu* *jyáu* *jiǎo*
繪	糸 糸 糸 紒 紒 給 給 給 給 繪 繪 繪	To draw *kúi* *hwèi* *huì*
繼	糸 糸 糸 糸 糸 絲 絲 繼 繼	To continue, adopt, take *gai* place of *jì* *jì*
續	糸 糸 糸 紒 結 結 綪 綪 結 續 續 續 續	To continue *juhk* *syù* *xù*
	缶	Section
缸	丿 丿 匸 午 午 缶 缶 缸 缸	A jar, an earthen vessel *góng* *gāng* *gāng*
缺	缶 缶 缶 缸 缺 缺	To lack; a defect *kyut* *chywē* *quē*
罐	缶 缶 缶 缶 缶 缶 缶 缶 缶 缶 罐 罐 罐	A jug, jar *gwun* *gwàn* *guàn*
	网	Section

罕	丶 冖 冖 冖 罒 罕 罕	Strange, rare *hóhn* *hǎn* *hǎn*
罪	丶 冖 冖 罒 罒 罒 罪 罪 罪 罪 罪	A crime *jeuih* *dzwei* *zuì*
置	罒 罒 罒 罒 罒 罒 罒 罒 置 置	To handle, put *ji* *jr̀* *zhì*
罰	罒 罒 罒 罒 罒 罒 罰 罰 罰 罰	To punish; a penalty *faht* *fá* *fá*
署	罒 罒 罒 罒 罒 罘 罘 罘 署	To sign; a public court *chyuh* *shǔ* *shǔ*
罵	罒 罒 罒 罒 罒 罵 罵 罵 罵 罵	To scold *mah* *mà* *mà*
罷	罒 罒 罒 罒 罒 罒 罘 罷 罷 罷 罷	To cease *bah* *bà* *bà*
羅	罒 罒 罒 罒 罒 罒 羅 羅 羅 羅 羅 羅	To spread out *loh* *lwó* *luó*
	羊	Section
羊	丶 ㇏ ㇀ ㇒ 兰 羊	A sheep, goat *yeùhng* *yáng* *yáng*
美	㇙ ㇀ 羊 羊 羊 美 美 美	Beautiful, pretty *méih* *měi* *měi*
羔	羊 羊 羔	A lamb *gòu* *gāu* *gāo*

羞	羊 羊 羙 羙 羞 羞	Ashamed, disgraced sau syōu xiū
群	ㄱ ㄱ ㅋ ㅋ ㅋ 尹 君 君 群	A herd, group kwàhn chyùn qún
義	羊 羊 美 羊 羊 義 義 義	Meaning; righteousness yih yi yì
羨	羊 羊 羊 羊 羊 羊 羡 羨	To admire sihn syān xiān
羹	羊 羔 羔 羔 羔 羹 羹	Soup gāng gēng gēng

羽 Section

羽	ㄱ ㄱ ㅋ 羽	Feathers, wings, birds yúh yǔ yǔ
翁	ノ ハ ハ 公 翁	An old man, father-in-law yùng yung yōng
翅	一 十 ㄎ 支 翅	Wings, fins chi chr chì
翌	羽 羽 翌 翌 翌 翌 翌	The next day chèui yi yì
習	羽 羽 習 習 習 習	To practice; a custom jaahp syi xí
翔	丶 ㆍ ㆍ 羊 羊 羊 翔	To soar, hover chèuhng syáng xiáng

翼	羽 羽 羽 羽 習 習 習 習 習 翼 翼 翼	Wings; to aid *yihk* yì yì
翻	ノ ⺄ ⺄ ⺥ 乎 采 釆 釆 番 番 番 番 翻	To reverse, turn over *faan* fān fān
耀	l 小 小 少 少 光 耂 耂 耂 耂 耂 耀 耀	To shine on; brilliant *yiuh* yàu yào
老 Section		

老	一 十 土 耂 老 老	Old *louh* lǎu lǎo
考	耂 考 考	To examine, test *haau* kǎu kǎo
者	耂 者 者 者 者	A person *jé* je zhě

| 而 Section |||

而	一 ㄒ ㄒ 丙 而 而	Yet *yih* ér ér
耐	而 而 耐 耐	To endure; a long time *noih* nài nài
耍	而 耍 耍 耍	To play, deceive *sa* shwǎ shuǎ

| 耒 Section |||

耕	一 二 三 丰 耒 耒 耒 耒 耒 耘 耕 耕	To cultivate gaàng gēng gēng
耗	耒 耒 耒 耘 耗	To waste, spend hou haù haò
	耳 Section	
耳	一 厂 厂 厅 厅 耳	The ear; a handle yih eŕ eŕ
耿	耳 耳 耳' 耿 耿	Bright; straightforward gǎng gěng gěng
耻	耳 耶 耶 耻 耻	Shame, ashamed chǐ shř shǐ
聆	耳 耳 耺 聆 聆 聆	To hear, pay attention to lihng líng líng
聊	耳 耳' 耶 耶 聊 聊	To depend on liuh lyáu liáo
聖	耳 耵 耵 耵 耵 聖 聖 聖	Holy sing shèng shèng
聘	耳 耵 耵 耵 耵 聃 聃 聘	To employ, appoint ping pìng pìng
聚	耳 取 取 取 聚 聚 聚 聚 聚	To gather, collect jeuih jyù jù
聞	ㄱ ㄱ ㅋ 尸 尸 尸 尸ㅌ 門 聞	To smell; famous màhn wén wén

聯	耳 耵 耶 聅 聮 聮 聮 聮 聮 聮 聮	To unite; an alliance *lyùhn* *lywàn*　　　　*luán*
聲	一 十 士 吉 吉 声 声 声 声 殸 殸 聲	A sound; a reputation *sing* *shēng*　　　　*shēng*
聰	耳 耵 耵 耵 聊 聊 聊 聰 聰 聰 聰	Clever, wise *chung* *tsūng*　　　　*cōng*
職	耳 耵 耵 耵 聑 聑 聛 聛 瞉 職 職 職	Duty, position *jik* *jr*　　　　*zhí*
聽	耳 耵 耵 耵 耵 耵 聅 聇 聼 聽 聽 聽 聽	To hear, obey *ting* *tīng*　　　　*tīng*
聾	丶 亠 亠 立 产 产 育 育 育 育 育 龍 龍 聾 聾	Deaf *lùhng* *lúng*　　　　*lóng*
	聿	Section
肄	ㄴ ㄴ ㄴ ㄹ ㅌ ㅌ ㅌ ㅌ ㅌ ㅌ ㅌ 肄	To learn, practice *syu* *se*　　　　*sè*
肅	ㄱ 中 肀 肃 肃 肃 肃 肃 肃 肅	Solemn, reverential *suk* *sù*　　　　*sù*
	肉	Section
肉	丨 冂 内 内 肉 肉	Meat, flesh *yuhk* *ròu, rù*　　　*ròu, rù*
肌	丿 月 月 月 肌 肌	Flesh, muscle *gei* *jī*　　　　*jī*

肛	月 肝 肛 肛	The anus *gong* *gāng*　　　　*gāng*
肝	月 肝 肝 肝	The liver *gon* *gān*　　　　*gān*
肚	月 月 肚 肚	The belly, abdomen *touh* *dù*　　　　*dù*
股	月 股 股 股 股	The thigh *gú* *gǔ*　　　　*gǔ*
肴	ノ メ ㄨ 乡 乡 乡 肴 肴	Cooked food *ngaauh* *yáu*　　　　*yáo*
肥	月 肝 肝 肥 肥	Fat; fertile *feih* *féi*　　　　*féi*
肯	l ㅏ ㅛ ㅛ 肯	To consent to, permit *hang* *ken*　　　　*kěn*
育	丶 亠 㐅 云 育	To raise children *yuhk* *yù*　　　　*yù*
肪	月 月 肪 肪 肪	Fat, grease *fong* *fáng*　　　　*fáng*
肢	月 肝 肝 肢 肢	Limbs *ji* *jr*　　　　*zhi*
肺	月 肝 肝 肺 肺	The lungs *fai* *fèi*　　　　*fèi*
肩	丶 ㇆ ㇋ 户 肩	The shoulders *gin* *jyān*　　　　*jiān*

胎	月 肋 肞 胎 胎 胎	The womb *toi* *tāi*　　　　*tāi*
胞	月 肝 肳 肳 肳 胞	The placenta *baau* *bāu*　　　　*bāo*
背	丨 十 土 北 北 背	To turn against; the back *bui* *bei*　　　　*bèi*
胖	月 肝 肝 肚 肸 胖	Plump *buhn* *bàn*　　　　*bàn*
胃	丶 冂 日 田 田 胃	The stomach *waih* *wèi*　　　　*wèi*
能	ㄥ ㄥ 育 郎 能 能	Ability, skill *nahng* *néng*　　　　*néng*
脈	月 肝 肵 肵 肵 脈 脈	The pulse, blood vessel *muhk* *mwo*　　　　*mò*
脆	月 肝 肝 脝 胯 胯 脆	Crisp; fragile *cheui* *tswei*　　　　*cuì*
胸	月 肝 肳 肳 胸 胸	The breast, chest *hung* *syūng*　　　　*xiōng*
脂	月 肷 肷 肷 脂 脂 脂	Fat, grease *ji* *jr*　　　　*zhi*
脅	ㄱ 力 劤 劦 脅	To coerce; the ribs *hip* *sye*　　　　*xié*
脖	月 肝 肝 肚 肚 脖 脖 脖	The neck *buht* *bwo*　　　　*bó*

脫	月 月` 月´ 月´ 脬 脫 脬 脫	To undress, take off *tyut* *twō* *tuō*
腳	月 月´ 月⁺ 肬 肬 胠 胠 腳 腳	The foot *geuk* *jyǎu* *jiǎo*
脾	月 月´ 月㇆ 肥 肑 朏 脾 胂 胆 脾 脾	The temper, spleen *peih* *pí* *pí*
腑	月 月` 肝 肝 肝 肭 脏 脏 腑 腑	The bowels, viscera *fú* *fǔ* *fǔ*
腎	丨 厂 广 �尸 臣 臤 臤 臤 賢 腎	The kidneys *sahn* *shen* *shèn*
腐	` 一 广 广 疒 疒 府 府 府 腐 腐 腐	Rotten, decayed *fuh* *fǔ* *fǔ*
腕	月 月` 月´ 肑 肑 肑 脘 脘 腕	The wrist *wún* *wàn* *wàn*
腰	月 月¯ 肑 肑 肑 胛 胛 腰 腰 腰 腰	The waist, loins *yíu* *yāu* *yāo*
腦	月 肵 月ᐟᐟ 肑 脳 脳 脳 脳 腦 腦	The brain; mental *nóuh* *nǎu* *nǎo*
腹	月 月´ 肑 肑 肑 朊 朊 脂 腹 腹	The abdomen, belly *fuk* *fù* *fù*
腫	月 肵 肑 肑 脂 脂 脂 腫 腫 腫	To swell; bloated *júng* *jǔng* *zhǒng*
腸	月 月´ 月ᑭ 月ᑭ 月ᵖ 朏 朏 腸 腸 腸	The bowels, intestines *chéung* *cháng* *cháng*

腿	月 月⁷ 月⁷ 月⁷ 月⁷ 胆 胆 胆 胆 腿 腿	The leg, thigh *teúi* *twěi* *tuǐ*
膏	` 一 亠 古 古 声 亭 亭 膏	A plaster, ointment *gòu* *gāu* *gāo*
膠	月 月⁷ 月⁷ 月⁷ 肌 肌 腴 腴 膠 膠	Glue, plastic, rubber *gaàu* *jyāu* *jiāo*
膝	月 月⁻ 月⁺ 肚 肤 胩 肤 胂 胳 胳 膝	The knee, lap *sàt* *syī* *xī*
膚	` 十 上 户 庐 虍 虍 庐 庐 庸 膚 膚	The skin; superficial *fù* *fū* *fū*
膩	月 月⁻ 肝 胪 胪 脂 脂 脂 膩 膩 膩	Oily, greasy *leih* *nì* *nì*
膨	月 月⁺ 月⁺ 肚 肚 胄 脂 肺 胪 膨 膨	Fat, swollen *paàhng* *péng* *péng*
膽	月 胪 胪 脧 脧 脧 脧 膤 膽 膽 膽 膽	The gall bladder; courage *daám* *dǎn* *dǎn*
臂	` ⁻ ⁷ ⁷ 尸 尽 启 启 启 启 辟 辟 辟 臂	The fore-arm *bei* *bi* *bì*
臉	月 月⁷ 肰 肸 脸 胎 胎 脸 脸 臉	The face, cheeks *líhm* *lyǎn* *liǎn*
臘	月 胪 脬 脬 脬 脬 脬 脬 脬 膪 臘 臘	Dried meat *laahp* *là* *là*
	臣 Section	

臣	丨 厂 厂 厅 臣 臣 臣	A statesman sàhn shén　　　shén
臥	臣 卧 臥	To lie down ngoh wò　　　wò
臨	臣 臣' 臣' 臣' 臣' 臨 臨 臨	Approaching; to imitate làhm　　　writing lín　　　lín

| 自 | Section |

| 自 | 丿 亻 巾 自 自
自 | Self; since
jih
dz̀　　　zì |
| 臭 | 自 自 臭 臭 臭 | A foul smell
chau
chòu　　　chòu |

| 至 | Section |

| 至 | 一 乙 云 㐅 至
至 | To reach; until; the best
ji
jr̀　　　zhì |
| 致 | 至 到 致 致
致 | To cause, carry out
ji
jr̀　　　zhì |

| 臼 | Section |

| 舅 | 丿 亻 亻 向 向 臼 臼
臼 臼 舅 舅 舅 舅 | Uncle (mother's brother)
káuh
jyòu　　　jiù |
| 與 | 丿 亻 牛 約 約 約 綱
與 與 | With; and; to give to
yuh
yǔ　　　yǔ |

- 245 -

興	´ ㇒ ㇒ ㇒ 臼 臼 臼 臼 臼 臼 臼 臼 臼 興	To elevate, prosper, happy *hing* *syìng, syìng xing, xing*
舉	´ ㇒ ㇒ ㇒ 臼 臼 臼 臼 臼 臼 與 與 舉 舉	To elevate, lift up *géui* *jyú jǔ*
舊	` ㇒ ㇓ ㇓ ㇓ 艹 艹 艹 萑 萑 舊 舊	Old, ancient *gauh* *jyòu jiù*
	舌	Section
舌	´ ㇐ 千 千 舌 舌	The tongue *siht* *shé shé*
舍	㇒ 人 ㇒ 今 全 全 舍 舍	A cottage, residence *se* *shè shè*
舒	舍 舍 舍 舒 舒 舒	Comfortable *syu* *shū shu*
	舛	Section
舞	㇒ ㇒ ㇒ 無 無 舞 舞 舞 舞 舞 舞 舞	To dance; a dance *mouh* *wǔ wǔ*
	舟	Section
舟	㇒ ㇒ 凣 舟 舟 舟	A boat, ship *jàu* *jou zhōu*
航	舟 舟 舟 航 航	To sail, navigate *hohng* *háng háng*

- 246 -

般	舟 舟 舡 舩 般	A manner, affair *buhn* *ban*　　　　*ban*
船	舟 舟 舡 舡 船 船	A boat, junk *shyuhn* *chwan*　　　*chuan*
舵	舟 舟 舟 舟 舵 舵	A helm, rudder *toh* *dwo*　　　　*duo*
舶	舟 舟 舶 舶 舶 舶	A ship, vessel *paak* *bwo*　　　　*bo*
艇	舟 舟 舟 舟 舡 舡 艇	A boat, barge *tehng* *ting*　　　　*ting*
艙	舟 舟 舟 舟 舟 舡 舡 舡 舱 艙 艙	A cabin on a ship *chong* *tsang*　　　*cang*
艦	舟 舟 舟 舟 舺 舺 舺 舺 舺 艦 艦 艦	A battle ship *laahm* *jyan*　　　　*jian*
	艮	Section
良	丶 ㇇ ㇕ ㇕ 自 良 良	Virtuous, good *leuhng* *lyang*　　　*liang*
艱	丶 一 艹 艹 艹 艹 莒 莒 莒 莫 莫 艱	Difficult, distressing *gaan* *jyan*　　　*jian*
	色	Section
色	丿 ㇇ 勹 ⺈ 多 色	Color; beauty; lust *sik* *se*　　　　*se*

	艸	Section
芋	`丶 丶 艹 艹 艹 芊 芋`	Taro *wuh* *yu* *yù*
芒	`艹 艹 艹 芒`	A mango *mòhng* *máng* *máng*
花	`艹 艹 花 花 花`	A flower, blossom *fà* *hwa* *huā*
芬	`艹 艹 艿 芩 芬`	Fragrance *fàn* *fēn* *fēn*
芳	`艹 艹 芷 芳 芳`	Fragrant *fōng* *fāng* *fāng*
芙	`艹 艹 艿 芏 芙`	The hibiscus *fùh* *fú* *fú*
芥	`艹 艹 艿 芥` `芥`	Mustard greens *gaai* *jyè* *jìe*
芽	`艹 艹 艹 芏 芽` `芽`	A shoot, sprout *ngàh* *yá* *yá*
茄	`艹 艿 苏 茄 茄` `茄`	Tomato, eggplant *ké* *chye* *qié*
英	`艹 艹 苎 苎 英` `英`	Graceful; English *ying* *yīng* *yīng*
茂	`艹 芒 芦 芃 茂` `茂`	Exuberant, flourishing *mauh* *maù* *mào*

苗	艹 艿 苩 苗 苗 苗	Sprouts, shoots miùh myáu miáo
苔	艹 艿 艻 苔 苔 苔	Moss tòih tái tái
茅	艹 艼 艼 茅 茅 茅	Reeds maàuh máu máo
苦	艹 艼 芏 芌 苦 苦	Bitter, grievous fú kǔ kǔ
苟	艹 艹 芍 芍 苟 苟	Careless, illicit gáu gǒu gǒu
若	艹 艿 芋 若 若 若	If, as if, or yeuhk rwò, rě rùo, rě
苛	艹 艹 芢 苛 苛 苛	Cruel, harsh hò kē kē
茶	艹 艼 火 茶 茶 茶 茶	Tea chàh chá chá
荒	艹 艼 芇 芒 芒 芒 荒	Wild, barren fòng hwāng huāng
茫	艹 艼 艿 艿 艿 茫 茫	Vague, vast mòhng máng máng
兹	艹 艼 芗 兹 兹	This; now jì dz zī
荆	艹 艼 芇 芉 芉 荆 荆	A bramble, thorn gìng jīng jīng

茸	北 芒 芊 芢 芢 茸 茸	A deer's horns yùhng rung　　　　rŏng
荔	北 芀 芀 荔 荔	A lichee laih lì　　　　lì
草	北 芐 芐 芒 苫 苜 苜 草	Grass, straw; careless chóu tsáu　　　　cǎo
莊	北 芒 芓 芓 芓 芘 芘 莊	A farm; serious jŏng jwāng　　　　zhuāng
莫	北 芐 芐 苩 苩 莫 莫 莫	Not, do not mohk mwò　　　　mò
莖	北 芒 芏 苤 苤 莖 莖 莖	The stem of a plant ging jing　　　　jīng
荷	北 芐 芀 芀 芀 荷 荷 荷	The lotus, water lily hòh hé　　　　hé
華	北 芏 芢 芢 茓 蓕 蕐 華	Chinese, elegant wàh hwà　　　　húa
菇	北 芐 芐 茓 茓 菇 菇 菇 菇	A mushroom gù gū　　　　gū
萃	北 芐 芏 芏 茓 茓 莁 萃	A collection seuih tswei　　　　cùi
菊	北 芐 芀 芀 芀 芀 菊 菊 菊	The chrysanthemum guk jyu　　　　jù
菌	北 芐 芮 芮 茼 菌 菌 菌 菌	Bacteria, mold kwán jyun　　　　jùn

菜	艸 艼 芓 荘 芣 芷 荘 芽 菜	Vegetables, food *choi* tsài cài
萎	艸 艼 芏 芏 菾 菾 菾 菾 萎 萎	To wither, decay *wai* wēi wēi
萍	艸 艼 艿 泸 泸 泸 泸 泟 萍	Duck-weed; drifting *pìhng* píng píng
萬	艸 芏 芍 芍 苗 苗 萬 萬 萬 萬	Ten thousand, numerous *maahn* wàn wàn
落	艸 艼 芣 芥 落 落 茨 茨 落 落	To fall down *lohk* lwò luò
著	艸 芏 芢 芏 萝 萝 著 著 著	To write, compose *jyu* jù zhù
董	艸 芏 芏 芞 芐 莟 菅 菫 菫 董	To direct, govern *dung* dúng dǒng
葬	艸 芐 芅 芳 芳 芗 莁 莁 葬 葬	To bury *jong* dzàng zàng
葱	艸 芐 芍 芍 芴 菊 葱 葱 葱 葱	Onions *chung* tsūng cōng
葉	艸 芏 芊 芊 芖 芖 莣 菜 葉 葉	A leaf, page *yihp* yè yè
葡	艸 芐 芍 芍 荀 荀 葡 葡 葡 葡	Grapes *pòuh* pú pú
蒙	艸 芏 芏 芐 芌 荸 荸 荸 荸 蒙 蒙	To cover, conceal *mùhng* méng méng

菪	艹 艹 艹 艹 艹 艹 菪 菪 菪 菪	To arrive at; to manage *yap* *li*　　　　*li*
蓄	艹 艹 艹 荶 荶 荶 荶 蓄 蓄 蓄 蓄	To save *chuk* *syū*　　　　*xū*
蒸	艹 艹 艹 艻 芣 芣 蒸 蒸	To steam; steam *jing* *jeng*　　　*zhēng*
蒼	艹 艹 艹 芯 芩 苍 荃 荟 荟 蒼 蒼	Azure *chong* *tsāng*　　　*cāng*
蓉	艹 艹 艹 芢 芢 荬 芠 荬 荬 蓉 蓉	The hibiscus *yuhng* *rung*　　　*rong*
蓋	艹 艹 艹 芏 荃 荃 荃 荶 荶 荶 蓋	To cover; a roof *goi* *gai*　　　　*gai*
蔓	艹 艹 艻 苩 苩 苩 蒿 蒿 蒿 蔓 蔓 蔓	To creep; vines *maahn* *man*　　　　*man*
蓮	艹 艹 艹 苩 苩 苩 萱 萱 萱 蓮 蓮	A lotus, water lily *lihn* *lyan*　　　*lian*
蔭	艹 艹 芢 芢 荶 荶 陉 陉 陉 蔭 蔭	To protect; shade *yam* *yin*　　　　*yin*
蔬	艹 艹 芢 苃 茈 茈 茈 莚 蔬 蔬 蔬 蔬	Vegetables, greens *so* *shū*　　　　*shū*
蔽	艹 艹 艹 芇 芇 芇 茵 茵 蔐 蔽 蔽 蔽	To conceal, shelter *bai* *bi*　　　　*bi*
蕉	艹 艹 花 花 荏 荏 萑 萑 蕉	A banana *jiu* *jyāu*　　　*jiāo*

薄	薄 (stroke order)	Thin, weak bohk bwo, báu — bó, bǎo
薪	薪 (stroke order)	Salary; firewood sàn syīn — xīn
蕭	蕭 (stroke order)	Solemn sìu syāu — xiāo
藍	藍 (stroke order)	Blue laàhm làn — lán
藏	藏 (stroke order)	To conceal, store chòhng tsàng — cáng
薯	薯 (stroke order)	A potato, sweet potato syúh shǔ — shǔ
藐	藐 (stroke order)	To view with contempt; petty miúh myáu — miǎo
藉	藉 (stroke order)	To rely on; an excuse jihk jye — jie
藝	藝 (stroke order)	Art, skill ngaih yì — yì
藤	藤 (stroke order)	Vines tàhng téng — téng
藥	藥 (stroke order)	Medicine, drugs yeuhk yàu, ywè — yaò, yuè
藕	藕 (stroke order)	The lotus-root ngáuh oú — oú

蘋	艹 艹 艹 艹 芮 苹 莁 萍 萍 萍 蒴 蘋 蘋 蘋	An apple _pìhng_ _pín_ _pín_
蘭	艹 艹 艹 芦 芦 芮 蘭 蘭 蘭 蘭 蘭 蘭 蘭 蘭	An orchid _laàhn_ _lăn_ _lán_

	虍 Section

虎	⺊ ⺊ ⺊ 广 虍 虍 虎 虎	A tiger _fú_ _hŭ_ _hŭ_
虐	广 虍 虐 虐 虐	To torture; cruel _yeuhk_ _nywè_ _nüè_
虔	广 虍 虍 虔 虔 虔	Sincere, pious _kìhn_ _chín_ _qín_
處	广 虍 虍 虖 處 處	A place, office; to manage _chyu, chyu_ _chŭ, chu_ _chŭ, chù_
虛	广 虍 虍 虍 虚 虚 虚	Unreal, empty _heui_ _syū_ _xū_
號	⺊ 口 口 号 号 號 號 號	A mark, number; to shout _houh_ _haù, háu_ _hào, háo_
虧	广 虍 虍 虍 虍 虖 虖 虖 虖 虧 虧 虧 虧	To lose, fail _kwai_ _kwēi_ _kūi_

	虫 Section

虱	乙 乯 凡 凩 凩 乱 虱 虱	Lice _sāt_ _shr̄_ _shī_

- 254 -

虹	`丶 冂 口 中 虫 虫` `虫⁻ 虹 虹`	A rainbow *huǐhng* *huǐng, gàng hoǐng, gàng*
蚊	`虫 虫ˋ 虹⁻ 蚊 蚊`	A mosquito *màn* *wén wén*
蚌	`虫 虫ˊ 虹ˋ 虫三 蚌`	Oysters, mussels *pǒhng* *bàng, beng bàng, beng*
蚤	`ㄱ 又 叉 叉 蚤`	Fleas *jǒu* *dzǎu zǎo*
蛀	`虫 虫ˋ 虹⁻ 蚪 蚌` `蛀`	Moth-eaten *jyu* *ju zhu*
蛇	`虫 虫ˋ 虹ˋ 蚖 蛇` `蛇`	Serpent, snake *sèh* *she she*
蛋	`一 丁 下 疋 足` `蛋`	An egg *dǎan* *dan dan*
蛛	`虫 虫ˊ 虹ˋ 蚝 蚨` `蛛 蛛`	A spider *jyu* *ju zhu*
蛙	`虫 虫⁻ 蚪 蛀 蛙`	A frog *wa* *wā wa*
蜆	`虫 虬 蚓 蚏 蚏` `蚏 蜆 蜆`	A small clam *hín* *syǎn xiǎn*
蛾	`虫 虫ˊ 虹⁻ 蚪 蚳 蛾` `蛾 蛾`	A moth *ngòh* *e e*
蜂	`虫 虫ˊ 虹ˋ 蚊 蚊 蛟` `蜂 蜂`	A bee, wasp *fung* *feng feng*

蜕	虫 虫` 虫´ 虫´ 蚰 蚰 蛵 蜕	To shed skin seui shwei shui
蜢	虫 虫` 虫了 虫子 蚍子 蛃 蛃 蛃 蛃	A grasshopper maahng měng měng
蜜	` ` 宀 宀 宓 宓 宓 宓 蜜	Honey, nectar maht mì mì
蝠	虫 虫 蚅 蚅 蚅 蚅 蚅 蚅 蝠 蝠	A bat fuk fú fú
蝸	虫 虫 蚅 蚅 蚅 蚅 蝸 蝸 蝸 蝸	A snail wo gwā guā
蝶	虫 蚅 虫十 蚩 蚳 蚳 蚳 蝶 蝶 蝶	A butterfly dihp dyé die
蝟	虫 虫 蚅 蚅 蚅 蚅 蚅 蝟 蝟 蝟	A porcupine wai wèi wèi
蝦	虫 蚅 虫了 蚅 蚅 蚅 蚅 蝦 蝦 蝦	A shrimp, prawn hā syā xā
螢	` ` 少 炏 炏 炏 熒 螢	The glowworm, fire-fly yìhng yíng yíng
融	一 厂 厅 厅 鬲 鬲 鬲 鬲 鬲 融	To melt, dissolve yùhng rúng róng
螺	虫 虫` 蚅 蚅 蚅 蚅 螺 螺 螺 螺	A conch ló lwo luó
蟀	虫 虫 蚅 蚅 蚄 蚄 蚄 蚄 蚄 蟀	A cricket sùt shwo, shwai shwo, shuai

蟬	虫 虫 虫ʰ 虫ʰ 虫ʰ 蟬 蟬 蟬 蟬 蟬 蟬	A cicada *sihm* *shán* *shán*
蟲	虫 虫 蟲	An insect, worm, reptile *chuhng* *chúng* *chóng*
蟒	虫 虫ʰ 虫ʰ 虫ʰ 虫ʰ 虫ˢ 蟒 蟒 蟒 蟒 蟒 蟒	A python *móhng* *máng* *mǎng*
蟹	⁊ ⁊ ⁊ 丹 角 角 角 角 角 解 解 解 解 蟹	A crab *haaih* *syè* *xiè*
蠅	虫 虫ʰ 虫ʰ 虫ʰ 虫ʰ 虵 蠅 蠅 蠅 蠅 蠅 蠅	A fly *yihng* *yíng* *yíng*
蟻	虫 虫ʰ 虫ˢ 虫ˢ 虫ˢ 蟻 蟻 蟻 蟻 蟻 蟻 蟻 蟻	An ant *ngaih* *yi* *yǐ*
蠔	虫 虫ʰ 虫ʰ 虫ʰ 虫ʰ 虫ʰ 蠔 蠔 蠔 蠔 蠔 蠔 蠔	An oyster *hòuh* *háu* *háo*
蠟	虫 虫ˢ 虫ˢ 虫ˢ 虫ˢ 蠟 蠟 蠟 蠟 蠟 蠟 蠟 蠟	Wax *laahp* *là* *là*
蠢	一 三 声 夫 表 春 春 春 蠢 蠢	Foolish, stupid *chéun* *chwún* *chǔn*
蠶	⁺ 口 夕 旡 旡 旡 琴 琴 琴 蠶 蠶	A silkworm *chaahm* *tsán* *cán*
蠻	丶 亠 言 言 言 信 信 信 信 絲 絲 蠻	Barbarous, unreasonable *maahn* *mán* *mán*
血	Section	

血	ノ ノ 白 白 血 血	Blood *hyut* *sywě, sy̌we xuè, xuě*
行	(Section)	Section
行	ノ ノ イ ィ ̄ 仁 行	To walk; behavior; company *hàhng, hohng, hòhng hàng* *sỳing, sỳing, hang xíng, xìng,*
術	ノ ノ イ ィ 什 材 休 休 休 術二 術	A method, trick *syuht* *shù shù*
街	イ ィ 什 什 佳 街	A street, avenue *gaai* *jy̌e jiē*
衝	イ ィ 朾 行 行 徟 徊 徟 徟 徸 衝	To rush against, excite *chung* *chung chōng*
衞	イ ィ ィ 什 徉 徫 徫 徫 徫 衞 衞	To protect, guard *waih* *wèi wèi*
衣	(Section)	Section
衣	、 一 ナ オ 衣 衣	Clothes, garments *yi* *yī yī*
表	一 十 ± 主 圭 圭 表 表	To show; a list; cousins *biu* *byǎu biǎo*
衫	、 ラ ネ ネ ネ 衫	A shirt, coat *saam* *shān shān*
衰	、 一 一 亠 产 亩 衰	To decline, decay *seui* *shwāi shuāi*

衷	丶 亠 亠 亡 宁 宁 衷	Conscience *chūng* *jūng*　　　*zhōng*
被	衤 衤 衤 衤 被 被	Bedclothes; by *péih, peih* *bèi*　　　*bèi*
袖	衤 衤 衤 袖 袖 袖	Sleeves *jauh* *syou*　　　*xiu*
袍	衤 衤 衤 袍 袍 袍	A gown, robe *pouh* *páu*　　　*páo*
袋	丿 亻 仁 代 代 袋	A bag, pocket *doih* *dài*　　　*dài*
裁	一 十 土 表 裁 裁 裁	To cut(garments); to decide *choih* *tsái*　　　*cái*
裂	一 丆 歹 歹 死 列 裂	To crack, split *liht* *lyè*　　　*liè*
裝	㇄ ㇄ 爿 爿 爿 爿 爿 裝	To pack; baggage *jōng* *jwāng*　　　*zhuāng*
裔	衣 衣 斉 斉 斉 斉 斉 裔	Descendants, offspring *yeuih* *yi*　　　*yì*
裏	丶 亠 亠 亡 宁 宁 車 車 重 裏	Inside, inner *leuih* *li*　　　*lǐ*
裙	衤 衤 衤 衤 裙 衤 裙 裙	A skirt, dress *kwàhn* *chwun*　　　*chún*
補	衤 衤 衤 補 補 補 補 補	To repair, make up *bou* *bu*　　　*bu*

裕	衤 衤 衤 衿 衿 衿 裕 裕	Wealthy, abundant *yuh* *yù* *yǔ*
裘	一 十 寸 寸 求 求 求 裘	Fur garments *kauh* *chyóu* *qiú*
裸	衤 衤 衤 衤 袒 袒 裸 裸 裸	Naked, unclothed *ló* *lwǒ* *luǒ*
裹	丶 亠 亠 亩 亩 亩 亩 車 東 東 裹	To wrap, bundle up *gó* *gwo* *guǒ*
褂	衤 衤 衤 衤 衦 袿 褂 褂	A Chinese coat *gwa* *gwà* *guà*
裨	衤 衤 衤 衤 衤 袧 袧 裨 裨 裨 裨	To benefit, profit *bei* *bei* *bèi*
製	丿 亠 匕 匕 告 告 制 制 製	To make, manufacture *jai* *jr* *zhì*
裳	丨 丨 丬 丬 尚 尚 尚 尚 裳	Clothes, dresses *sèuhng* *cháng* *cháng*
複	衤 衤 衤 衤 衤 袍 袍 袍 複 複	Double *fùk* *fù* *fù*
褪	衤 衤 衤 衤 袒 袒 袒 袍 袍 褪	To fade, take off *tan* *twun* *tùn*
褲	衤 衤 衤 衤 衤 袮 袮 褌 褌 褲 褲	Pants *fu* *kù* *kù*
襖	衤 衤 衤 衤 衤 袮 袮 袮 袮 袮 禰 禰 禰 襖	A Chinese jacket *ou* *aū* *ăo*

襤	衤 衤 衦 衦 衦 衦 衵 裡 裡 襽 襤 襤 襤 襤	Ragged, torn *laàhm* *lán* *lán*
襪	衤 衦 衦 衦 衦 衦 衦 衦 裡 裡 禮 襪 襪 襪	Socks, stockings *maht* *wà* *wà*
襯	衤 衦 衦 衦 衦 裎 裑 裱 褙 襯 襯 襯 襯 襯 襯	To assist, give alms *chun* *chèn* *chèn*
襲	丶 亠 寺 立 产 产 育 育 龍 龍 龍 龍 龍 襲	To attack *jaahp* *syi* *xí*

	西	Section

西	一 「 冂 两 两 西	The west, European *sài* *syī* *xī*
要	西 罗 更 要	To want, require, claim *yiu* *yàu, yāu* *yào, yāo*
覆	西 严 严 严 严 覀 覈 覈 覈 覈 覆 覆 覆	To reply *fuk* *fù* *fù*

	見	Section

見	丨 冂 冂 月 目 貝 見	To see, visit; an opinion *gin* *jyàn* *jiàn*
規	一 二 キ 夫 規	A rule, custom *kwài* *gwēi* *guī*
覓	丿 丷 冖 冖 覓	To look for *mik* *mì* *mì*

視	`ㄱ ㄤ ㄤ 礻 視	To see, look at *sih* shr shi
親	`亠 六 古 立 立 辛 辛 亲 親	To love; relatives *chàn* chīn qīn
覺	`ㄱ 亻 ㄤ 厈 ㄈㄈ 臼𝇇 𝇇𝄐 𝇇𝄐 𝇇𝄐 𝇇𝄐 覺	To feel; aroused *gok* jywé, jyàu jué, jiao
覽	`丨 厂 厂 厇 臣 臣 臣 臣 臤 臥 臥 臨 臨 臨 覽	To look at *laáhm* lǎn lǎn
觀	`丷 爿 艹 艹 艹 艹 莊 莊 莊 莊 莊 萆 蓳 蓳 觀	To observe; a sight *gwun* gwān guān
	角	Section
角	`ㄱ ㄇ 产 户 角 角 角	A corner, angle, horn, dime *gok* jyǎu jiǎo
解	`角 角 郇 郇 解 解 解	To explain; to release *gaái* jyě jiě
觸	`角 角 角 郇 郇 觕 觕 觸 觸 觸 觸 觸	To strike, oppose *juk* chù chù
	言	Section
言	`丶 亠 二 亖 言 言 言	To speak; words, a speech *yihn* yán yán
訂	言 言 訂	To settle, order *ding* dìng dìng

計	言 言一 計	To calculate; a plan gai ji`                 ji`
訃	言 訃一 訃	An anouncement of death fuh fu`                 fu`
記	言 訂一 訂一 記	To remember; a register gei ji`                 ji`
討	言 言一 討 討	To ask for, demand tóu tau tǎo
訊	言 訓) 訊 訊	To investigate; a trial seun syun xun`
託	言 言' 訂' 託	To entrust tok two tuo
訓	言 訓) 訓 訓	To advise, instruct fan` syun` xun`
設	言 訂) 訂' 訂) 設	To set up, establish chit shyè shiè
訝	言 言一 訂一 訂一 訝 訝	Surprised ngah ya`                 ya`
許	言 訂) 訂一 訂一 許	To allow, promise heúi syu xǔ
訛	言 言' 訂一 訂' 訛	To lie; false ngòh é é
訟	言 言 訃ヽ 訟 訟	To dispute; a lawsuit juhng sung sóng

言 (4-6)

訪	言 言 計 訪 訪	To visit, inquire *fong* *fang*　　　*fang*
詞	言 訂 訂 詞 詞 詞	A compound word, phrase *chih* *tsz*　　　*ci*
評	言 言 訂 訐 評 評	To judge, criticize *pihng* *ping*　　　*ping*
詆	言 言 訂 訐 詆 詆	To defame, slander *dai* *di*　　　*di*
訴	言 言 訂 訢 訴 訴	To tell, make known *sou* *su*　　　*su*
註	言 言 訂 計 討 註	To remark; an explanation *jyu* *ju*　　　*zhu*
詐	言 言 訂 訐 訝 詐	To deceive; false *ja* *ja*　　　*zha*
詠	言 言 訂 詞 詠 詠	To sing, chant *wihng* *yung*　　　*yong*
診	言 言 診 訡 診	To cure, examine *chun* *jen*　　　*zhen*
詛	言 訂 訓 訓 詛 詛	To curse *jau* *dzu*　　　*zu*
詩	言 言 計 註 詰 詩 詩	Poetry *si* *shr*　　　*shi*
試	言 言 訂 訐 訌 試 試	To try, test, examine *si* *shr*　　　*shi*

- 264 -

詳	言 言 言 言 言 言 詳	In detail cheuhng syáng xiáng
詫	言 言 言 言 言 詫 詫	To be amazed tok chà chà
誇	言 言 言 誇 誇 誇 誇	To boast, exaggerate kwā kwā kūa
詭	言 言 言 言 言 詭 詭	To cheat; cunning gwái gwéi guǐ
話	言 言 言 話 話 話 話	To say; language, words wah hwà hùa
該	言 言 言 該 該 該 該	should; that gòi gāi gāi
詢	言 詢 詢 詢 詢 詢 詢	To inquire, interrogate seun syún xún
詣	言 詣 詣 詣 詣 詣 詣	To reach, go to jí yì yì
認	言 言 認 認 認 認 認	To recognize, confess yihng rèn rèn
誠	言 言 誠 誠 誠 誠 誠	Sincere; the truth sìhng chéng chéng
說	言 言 言 說 說 說 說	To speak, tell syut shwō shuō
語	言 言 語 語 語 語 語 語	To talk; words, language yúh yǔ yǔ

誓	一 十 才 扩 扩 扩 折 誓	To swear; an oath *saih* shř shì
誣	言 言 訂 訂 誣 誣 誣	To make a false accusation *mouh* wú wú
誡	言 言 訂 訐 誡 誡 誡 誡	To prohibit; a commandment *gaai* jye jiè
誤	言 言 訂 訶 誤 誤 誤 誤	Mistaken *mh* wù wù
誦	言 訂 訏 訏 訴 誦 誦 誦	To recite, chant *juhng* sung sòng
誨	言 訂 訐 訏 誋 誨 誨 誨	To teach; advice *fui* hwei huì
誌	言 言 計 計 誌 誌 誌 誌	To remember; a record *ji* jr zhì
誕	言 訂 訐 訐 誕 誕 誕 誕	To give birth to; to boast *daan* dàn dàn
誘	言 訂 訂 訐 誄 誄 誘 誘	To induce, allure *yauh* you yòu
誰	言 訂 訂 訂 訏 誰 誰 誰 誰	Who, whom *seuih* shéi shéi
請	言 訂 計 訏 誌 請 請 請 請	To invite; please *ching* ching qǐng
諒	言 言 訂 訐 訪 言 訪 諒 諒	To forgive; sincere *leuhng* lyang liàng

調	言 言 計 訂 訝 調 調 調 調	To mix, adjust; a tune *diuh* *tyáu, dyàu tiáo, diào*
課	言 言 訂 評 評 評 評 課 課	A lesson, exercise *fo* *kè kè*
論	言 言 訒 訟 診 診 論 論 論	To criticize; to debate *leuhn* *lwùn lùn*
談	言 言 言 訟 談 談	To chat; conversation *taahm* *tán tán*
誹	言 訂 訂 訓 訓 誹	To defame, slander *fei* *féi féi*
誼	言 言 訂 訝 訝 誼 誼 誼 誼	Friendship *yih* *yi yì*
諂	言 言 訒 訟 診 診 診 諂 諂	To flatter *chim* *chǎn chǎn*
諾	言 訂 訃 訝 詿 諾 諾 諾 諾	To promise *lok* *nwo nuò*
諜	言 言 計 討 討 諜 諜 諜 諜 諜	A spy *dihp* *dýe diè*
謂	言 訂 訒 訶 調 評 評 謂 謂 謂	To call, say *waih* *wèi wèi*
諧	言 計 訃 訛 訛 訛 諧 諧 諧 諧	To joke; harmonious *gaâi* *syè xiè*
謀	言 言 計 訃 訝 謀 謀 謀 謀 謀	To plan; a scheme *mauh* *móu móu*

諷	言 訁 訊 訊 諷 諷 諷 諷 諷 諷	To ridicule *fung* *fèng* *fèng*
諺	言 訁 訁 訞 訞 諺 誶 諺	A proverb *yihn* *yàn* *yàn*
謊	言 訁 訁 訁 訁 訁 誇 誇 誖 謊 謊	To lie; a lie *fong* *hwǎng* *huǎng*
謙	言 訁 訁 訁 訁 訁 訁 誹 誹 諌 謙 謙	Humble, modest *him* *chyān* *qiān*
謝	言 訁 訁 訠 訢 訽 諷 諷 謝 謝 謝	To thank, decline *jeh* *syè* *xiè*
講	言 訁 計 討 諆 講 諆 講 講 講 講	To tell, speak *góng* *jyǎng* *jiǎng*
謠	言 言 訁 訁 訁 訁 誒 誮 誶 謠 謠	A street song *yiuh* *yáu* *yáo*
謄	丿 刀 月 月 月 刖 肸 胖 胖 胖 謄	To copy, transcribe *tahng* *téng* *téng*
謎	言 言 訁 訁 訫 訫 諌 誅 謎 謎	A riddle, puzzle *maih* *mí* *mí*
謬	言 訁 訁 訠 諷 諷 諷 謬	False *mauh* *myòu* *miù*
謹	言 訁 訁 訲 訲 訲 訲 諯 諽 謹 謹 謹	Careful, respectful *gán* *jǐn* *jǐn*
證	言 訁 訁 訞 訞 訟 誂 誂 諮 諮 諮 證	To prove; evidence *jing* *jèng* *zhèng*

譜	言 言 言'言"言" 言" 言" 言"言"言"言"譜 譜	A register; a piece of music *póu* *pŭ*　　　*pu*
譏	言 言'言'言"言"言" 言"譏 譏 譏 譏	To ridicule, satirize *gei* *jī*　　　*jī*
識	言 言 言'言'言"言"言" 識 識 識 識 識 識	To know; knowledge *sik* *shŕ*　　　*shì*
譯	言 言 言'言"言"言" 譯 譯 譯 譯 譯 譯	To translate, interpret *yihk* *yì*　　　*yì*
議	言 言'言'言"言"言" 議 議 議 議 議	To discuss, negotiate *yih* *yì*　　　*yì*
譬	⌐ ⌐ 尸 尺 吊 君 君 君 启 启 辟 辟 譬	For instance; a comparison *pei* *pì*　　　*pì*
警	ˋ ˋ ⺌ 艹 芍 芍 苟 苟 苟'苟'敬 敬 警	To warn, caution *ging* *jǐng*　　　*jǐng*
譽	ˊ 亻 仵 卅 臼 臼 舆 舆 舆 舆 舉 譽	Reputation; to praise *yuh* *yù*　　　*yù*
護	言 言'言'言"言"言"言" 護 護 護 護 護 護	To guard, protect *wuh* *hù*　　　*hù*
讀	言 言'言'言"言"言" 讀 讀 讀 讀 讀 讀	To read, study *duhk* *dú*　　　*dú*
變	言 信 綜 綜 結 戀 戀 戀 變 變	To change, transform *bin* *byàn*　　　*bian*
讓	言 言'言'言"言"言" 讓 讓 讓 讓 讓 讓	To yield *yeuhng* *ràng*　　　*ràng*

讚	言 言 訂 計 訐 諮 諮 讚 諮 諮 諮 諮 諮 讚	To praise, eulogize *jaan* *dzàn*　　　　*zàn*
	谷	Section
谷	⌐ ⌐ ⌐ ⌐ ⌐ 谷 谷	A valley, ravine *guk* *chǔ*　　　　*chǔ*
	豆	Section
豆	⌐ ⌐ ⌐ ⌐ ⌐ ⌐ 豆	Beans, peas *dauh* *dòu*　　　　*dòu*
豉	豆 豆 計 豇 豉	Salted beans *sih* *shr, chr*　　*shì, chǐ*
豎	⌐ ⌐ ⌐ ⌐ ⌐ ⌐ 臣 臤 臤 豎	To erect; vertical *syuh* *shù*　　　　*shù*
豐	⌐ ⌐ ⌐ ⌐ 丰 丰 豊 豊 豐	Abundant, fruitful *fung* *fēng*　　　*fēng*
豔	豐 豐 豐 豐 豐 豐 豔 豔 豔 豔	Charming, pretty *yihm* *yàn*　　　　*yàn*
	豕	Section
象	⌐ ⌐ ⌐ ⌐ ⌐ 龟 龟 象 象 象 象 象	An elephant; a figure *jeuhng* *syàng*　　　*xiàng*
豪	⌐ ⌐ ⌐ ⌐ ⌐ ⌐ 高 高 亭 亭 豪 豪	Brave, superior *fouh* *háu*　　　　*háo*

	豸	Section
豹	ノ ィ ィ ク ク 豸 豸 豸 豹 豹	A leopard, panther *paau* *bau* *bao*
貂	豸 豸ᐟ 豸ᐢ 豸ᐢ 豸ᐢ 貂	A sable *diu* *dyau* *diao*
貌	豸 豸ᐟ 豸ᐢ 豸ᐢ 豸ᐢ 豸ᐟ 豸ᐢ 貌	Outlook, complexion *maauh* *mau* *mao*
貓	豸 豸ᐟ 豸ᐢ 豸ᐢ 豸ᐢ 豸ᐢ 豸ᐢ 豸ᐢ 豸ᐢ 貓	A cat *maau* *mau* *mao*
	貝	Section
貝	｜ 冂 冃 月 目 貝 貝	A shell, money *bui* *bei* *bei*
貞	｜ 卜 貞	Virtuous, pure *jing* *jen* *zhen*
負	冖 刀 負	To lose, owe *fuh* *fu* *fu*
貢	一 丅 工 貢	To pay tribute *gung* *gung* *gong*
財	貝 貝ᐟ 財 財	Property, wealth *choih* *tsai* *cai*
貧	ノ 八 分 分 貧	Poor, needy *pahn* *pin* *pin*

責	一 十 主 主 責	To blame; a duty *jaak* *dzé* *zé*
貪	丿 人 人 今 貪	To covet; greedy *taàm* *tān* *tān*
貨	丿 亻 仁 化 貨	Goods, merchandise *fo* *hwò* *huò*
販	貝 則′ 則′ 販 販	To sell, trade *fáan* *fàn* *fàn*
貶	貝 則′ 則′ 貶 貶	To dismiss, disparage *bín* *byǎn* *biǎn*
賀	コ カ か 加 加 賀	To congratulate *hoh* *hè* *hè*
貴	丶 冖 口 中 虫 貴	Expensive, valuable *gwai* *gwèi* *gui*
貼	貝 則 貼 貼 貼 貼	To paste up, stick *tip* *tyē* *tiē*
買	丶 冖 冖 皿 四 買	To buy *maáih* *mǎi* *mǎi*
費	コ ニ 弓 弗 弗 費	To spend, waste; expense *fai* *fèi* *fèi*
貿	丿 亻 丘 印 卯 貿	To trade *mauh* *màu* *mào*
貸	丿 亻 仁 代 代 貸	To lend with interest *taai* *dai* *dai*

貯	貝 貝 貝丶 貝宀 貯 貯	To store up, save *chyuh* *jǔ*　　　　*zhu*
資	丶 冫 冫 次 次 次 資	To help; wealth *ji* *dz*　　　　*zi*
賈	一 丷 亠 西 西 賈	To sell; a merchant *gá* *gu*　　　　*gu*
賊	貝 貝 貯 貯 賦 賊 賊	A thief, pickpocket *chaahk* *dzé, dzéi*　　*zé, zei*
賄	貝 貝 貯 貯 賄 賄 賄	To bribe; wealth *kui* *hwei, hwei*　*hui, hui*
賒	貝 貝 貯 貯 賒 賒 賒 賒	To buy or sell on credit *se* *she*　　　　*she*
賓	丶 丷 宀 宁 宁 宁 賓	A guest, visitor *bàn* *bin*　　　　*bin*
賦	貝 貝 貯 貯 賦 貯 賦 賦	To levy; to give *fu* *fu*　　　　*fu*
賣	一 十 士 士 赤 赤 赤 西 賣	To sell *maaih* *mài*　　　　*mài*
賠	貝 貝 貯 貯 賠 貯 貯 賠 賠	To compensate *puih* *pei*　　　　*pei*
賜	貝 貝 貯 貯 貯 貯 賜 賜 賜	To give, bestow *chi* *sz, tsz*　　*sì, cì*
賞	丨 丷 屵 屵 尚 尚 尚 尚 賞	To reward, bestow *seúng* *shǎng*　　*shǎng*

賬	貝 貝 貝 貼 貼 貼 貼 賬 賬 賬	An account, bill, debt *jeung* *jàng*　　　*zhàng*
質	´ ´ ｒ ｙ ｆ 所 質	Matter, substance *jàt* *jŕ*　　　*zhí*
賤	貝 貼 貶 賎 賎 賤	Without value, low *jihn* *jyàn*　　　*jiàn*
賭	貝 貝 貝 貯 財 財 賭 賭 賭	To gamble, bet *dou* *dŭ*　　　*dŭ*
賴	一 ｒ 币 ロ 申 束 束 朿 朿 賴	To rely on *laaih* *làai*　　　*lài*
購	貝 貝 貝 貯 購 購 購 購 購 購	To buy *kau* *kòu*　　　*kòu*
賺	貝 貝 貝 貯 貯 賺 賺 賺 賺 賺	To earn, gain *jaahn* *jwàn*　　　*zùn*
賽	´ ´ ´ 宀 宀 宀 宀 寉 寉 賽	To race; a match *choi* *sài*　　　*sài*
贈	貝 貝 貝 貯 貼 貼 贈 贈 贈 贈 贈	To give a gift, bestow *jahng* *dzèng*　　　*zèng*
贊	ノ ヒ 屮 生 生 生 兟 兟 贊	To assist, praise *jaan* *jàn*　　　*zhàn*
贍	貝 貝 貝 貯 賍 賍 賍 賎 贍 贍 贍 贍	To support, provide for *jìm* *shàn*　　　*shàn*
	赤	Section

赤	一 十 土 ヰ ヹ 赤 赤	Red, naked, barren *chek* *chr̀*　　　　*chì*
赦	赤 赤 赤 赦 赦	To pardon *se* *shè*　　　　*shè*

走		Section

走	一 十 土 ヰ ヰ 走 走	To go, run *jau* *dzŏu*　　　　*zŏu*
赴	走 赴 赴	To attend, go to *fuh* *fù*　　　　*fù*
起	走 赶 起 起	To rise, start *hei* *chǐ*　　　　*qǐ*
超	走 起 起 起 超 超	To exceed, excel *chiu* *chāu*　　　　*chāo*
越	走 起 起 越 越 越	To surpass, exceed *yuht* *ywè*　　　　*yùe*
趁	走 赶 赴 趁	To take advantage of an *chan*　　　　opportunity *chèn*　　　*chèn*
趕	走 赶 起 起 起 起 起 趕	To hurry, chase *gon* *gǎn*　　　　*gǎn*
趣	走 起 起 起 起 起 趄 趣 趣	Interesting, amusing *cheui* *chyu*　　　　*qù*
趟	走 赶 赶 赶 赺 趟 趟 趟 趟	Once, one time *tong* *tàng*　　　　*tàng*

趨	走 走 赳 赵 趨 趨 趨	To hasten *chĕui* *chyū* *qū*
	足	Section
足	丶 口 口 尸 尺 尺 足	The foot; enough *jŭk* *dzú* *zú*
趾	丶 口 尸 尺 足 足 趴 趴 趴 趾	The toes *jí* *jr* *zhǐ*
跋	足 距 趴 跀 跋 跋	To walk with difficulty *baht* *bá* *bá*
跌	足 趴 趴 跕 跕 跌	To fall, stumble *dit* *dyé* *dié*
距	足 趴 距 距 距	Distance from *kéuih* *jyu* *jù*
跑	足 趴 趵 跑 跑 跑	To run *paáu* *páu* *pǎo*
跛	足 趴 趴 跀 跛 跛	Lame, crippled *po* *bwǒ* *bǒ*
跳	足 趴 趴 趴 跳 跳 跳	To jump, leap *tiu* *tyàu* *tiào*
路	足 趴 趵 趵 路 路 路	A road, path *louh* *lù* *lù*
跟	足 趴 趴 趴 跟 跟 跟	To follow; the heel *gan* *gēn* *gēn*

跪	𧿶 𧿶 𧿶 𧿶 𧿶 跪 跪	To kneel gwaih gwèi guǐ
踪	𧿶 𧿶 𧿶 𧿶 踪 踪 踪 踪 踪	A trace, footprint jūng jūng zhōng
踢	𧿶 𧿶 𧿶 𧿶 𧿶 𧿶 𧿶 踢 踢	To kick tek tī tī
踏	𧿶 𧿶 𧿶 𧿶 𧿶 𧿶 踏 踏 踏	To step upon daahp dà dà
踱	𧿶 𧿶 𧿶 𧿶 𧿶 𧿶 𧿶 𧿶 踱 踱	To stroll dohk dwò duò
蹈	𧿶 𧿶 𧿶 𧿶 𧿶 𧿶 𧿶 𧿶 𧿶 𧿶 蹈	To trample, tread on douh daù dào
躍	𧿶 𧿶 𧿶 𧿶 躍 躍 躍 躍 躍 躍 躍	To leap, skip yeuk ywe yuè
躡	𧿶 𧿶 𧿶 𧿶 𧿶 躡 躡 躡	To walk on tiptoes sip nyè niè
	身 Section	
身	丶 亻 亇 甪 身 身 身	The body sān shēn shēn
躬	身 躬 躬 躬	To bow gūng gūng gōng
躭	身 身 躭 躭 躭	To delay, hinder daàm dān dān

躲	身 身³ 身⁵ 躬 躬 躬 躬 躲	To hide, avoid *dó* *dwo* *duo*
躺	身 躬 躬 躬 躬 躬 躺 躺 躺	To lie flat *tong* *tang* *tang*
	車	Section
車	一 ㄷ 币 百 亘 車	A car, vehicle *chē* *chē* *chē*
軌	車 軋 軌	A rail, track *gwái* *gwěi* *gǔi*
軍	一 ㄷ 冃 冃 冃 冒 冒 宣 軍	An army *gwàn* *jwūn* *zūn*
軟	車 軋 軋 軋 軟	Soft *yúhn* *rwǎn* *ruǎn*
較	車 車 軒 軒 軒 軡 較	To compare; rather *gaau* *jyàu, jyǎu* *jiào, jiǎo*
載	一 十 土 車 載 載 載	To contain; a year *joi* *dzài* *zài*
輕	車 軒 軒 輕 輕 輕 輕 輕	Light *hing* *chīng* *qīng*
輔	車 軒 軒 軒 輔 輔 輔 輔	To assist *fuh* *fǔ* *fǔ*
輪	車 軒 軩 軩 軩 輪 輪 輪 輪	To rotate; a wheel *leùhn* *lwún* *lún*

輝	⺌⺌⺌⺌⺌⺌⺌⺌ 光 ⺌ ⺌ 輝	Brightness; splendid fāi hwēi huī
輩	⺍⺍⺕彐非輩	A sort, generation bui bèi bèi
輸	車車軨軨軨 輸輸輸輸輸	To transport; to lose syu shū shū
輾	車車軒軒斬斬 斬輄輄輾輾	To roll, turn over jín jaň zhǎn
轉	車車軒軒軒軸 軘輔輔輔轉轉	To turn, roll jyún jwǎn zhuǎn
轍	車車軒軒軐軐軐 軐軐軐軐轍轍	The track of a wheel chit chě, chè chě, chè
轎	車軒軒軒軑軑 轎轎轎轎轎	A sedan chair kiú jyàu jiáo
轟	車車轟	To bomb, blow up gwang hūng hōng
	辛	Section
辛	⺀⺍⺛⺁立辛 辛	Grievous, distressing sàn syīn xīn
辣	⺀⺍⺁立辛辛 新新辢辣辣	Spicy hot laaht là là
辨	辛辛刬辨	To distinguish, indentify bihn byàn biàn

辛 (9-14) 辰 (3-6) 辵 (3-4)

辦	辛 剥 勃 辦	To arrange, manage *baahn* *bàn*　　　　*bàn*
辭	ノ ⺕ ⺕ ⺕ ⺊ 舀 舀 舀 舀 爵 辭	To resign; a statement *chìh* *tsź*　　　　*cí*
辯	辛 辛 辛 辩 辩 辩 辞 辯	To argue, dispute *bihn* *byàn*　　　　*biàn*
辰	Section
辰	一 二 三 厂 厇 辰 辰	Time of day *sàhn* *chén*　　　　*chén*
辱	辰 辰 辱 辱	To disgrace, insult *yuhk* *rù, rou*　　　*rù, ròu*
農	丶 冂 曰 甲 曲 曲 農	A farmer; agriculture *nùhng* *núng*　　　　*nóng*
辵	Section
迅	ノ 几 凡 凡 讯 迅	Quick *seun* *syùn*　　　　*xùn*
迄	ノ ⺊ 乞 迄	Until, up to *ngaht* *lì*　　　　*lì*
返	ノ 厂 丆 反 返	To return *faán* *fán*　　　　*fàn*
近	ノ 厂 斤 斤 近	To approach; near *gahn* *jìn*　　　　*jìn*

- 280 -

迎	′ ㇉ ㇉ ㇒ 卬 迎	To welcome, receive yihng yíng　　　yíng
迫	′ ㇉ ㇇ 白 白 迫	To force; imminent bik pwò　　　pò
述	一 十 才 木 术 述	To discribe, state syuht shù　　　shù
逃	) ㇒ ㇒ 扎 兆 逃	To escape, flee touh táu　　　táo
迴	丶 冂 冋 冋 回 迴	To bend; to go back wuih hwei　　　huí
退	㇇ ㇀ ㇂ 艮 艮 艮 退	To retreat, withdraw teui twei　　　tùi
迷	丶 丷 丷 半 米 米 迷	To get lost, delude maih mí　　　mí
逆	㇒ 丷 ㇒ 屵 屰 屰 逆	To rebel, oppose yihk ǹi　　　nì
追	′ ㇉ ㇉ 㠯 㠯 追	To pursue, overtake jeui jwei　　　zui
送	丶 丷 丷 兰 关 关 送	To send, deliver sung sung　　　song
通	㇇ ㇇ 尸 冎 甬 甬 通	To pass, go through tung tung　　　tong
逐	一 ㇇ 豖 豕 豕 豕 豖 逐	To expel; one by one juhk jú　　　zhu

這	丶 亠 亠 亠 言 言 言 這	This *jéh* *je, jèi* *zhe, zhèi*
途	丿 人 𠆢 亼 佘 余 余 途	A road, passage *tòuh* *tú* *tú*
逝	一 十 扌 扌 扩 扩 折 逝	To die, pass away *saih* *shr̀* *shì*
逗	一 𠃌 口 口 豆 豆 豆 逗	To remain, loiter *dauh* *dòu* *dòu*
造	丿 𠂉 牛 生 告 告 告 造	To make, create *jouh* *dzàu* *zào*
逕	一 𡿨 巛 巛 巠 巠 巠 逕	Directly, immediately *ging* *jìng* *jìng*
速	一 𠂊 巨 巨 申 束 束 速	Fast; speed *chùk* *sù* *sù*
透	丿 二 千 禾 禾 秀 秀 透	To penetrate; thoroughly *tau* *tòu* *tòu*
逛	丿 犭 犭 犭 犭 狂 狂 逛	To stroll *kwang* *kwāng* *kuāng*
逢	丿 ク 夂 夆 夆 夆 夆 逢	To meet; whenever *fùhng* *féng* *féng*
進	丿 亻 亻 亻 什 隹 隹 隹 進	To enter, proceed *jeun* *jìn* *jìn*
週	丨 冂 月 用 用 周 周 周 週	A week; to return *jàu* *jōu* *zhōu*

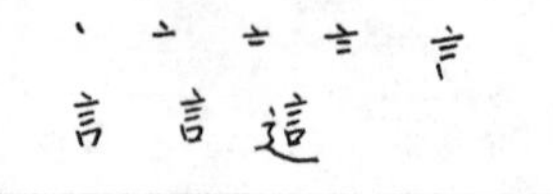

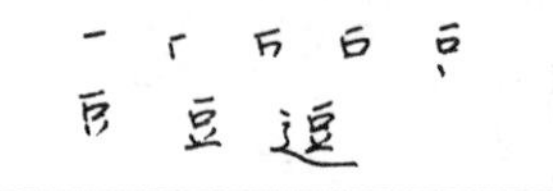

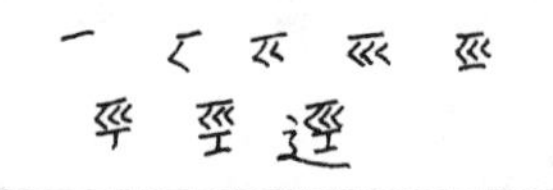

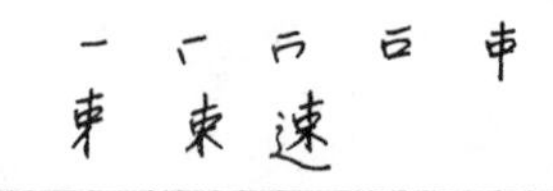

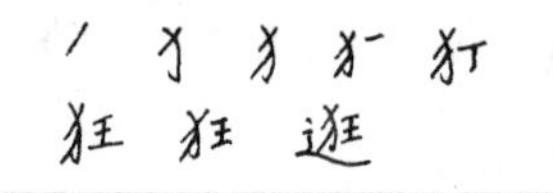

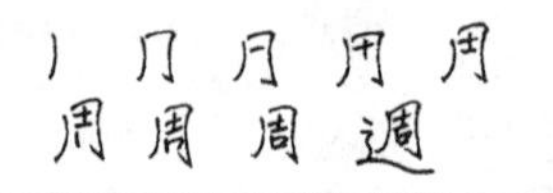

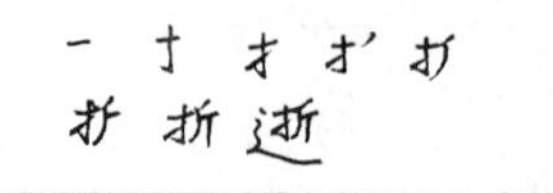

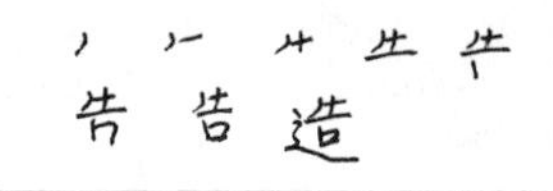

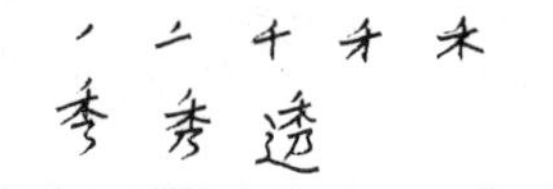

遁	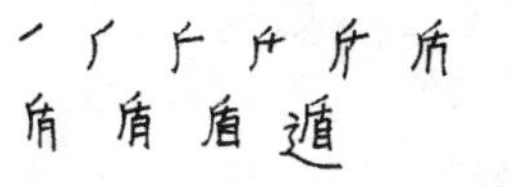	To hide, escape *chèuhn* *dwùn* *dùn*
遂		To follow; then *seuih* *swèi* *suì*
遊	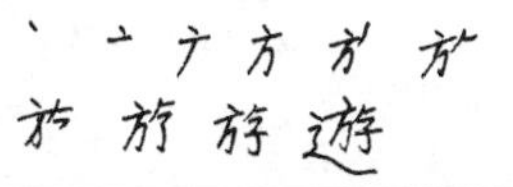	To travel, ramble *yàuh* *yóu* *yóu*
達	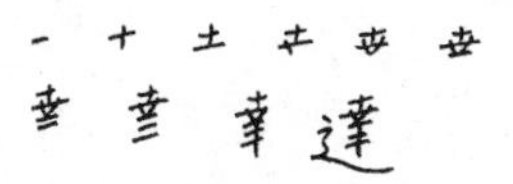	To reach, attain *daaht* *dá, dà* *dá, dà*
違	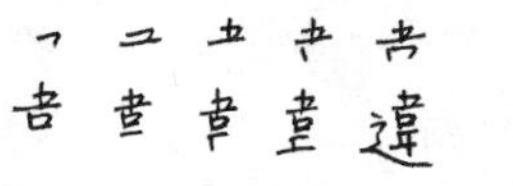	To disobey, oppose *wàih* *wèi* *wèi*
遇		To meet, to occur *yuh* *yù* *yù*
道		To say; a road *douh* *dàu* *dào*
遍	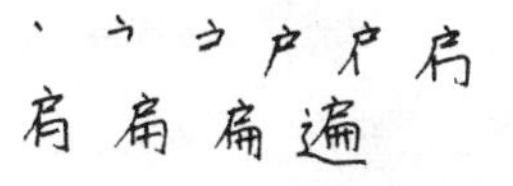	To go all over; one time *pìn* *byàn* *biàn*
過		To pass, exceed; a fault *gwo* *gwò* *guò*
運		To transport, convey *wahn* *ywùn* *yùn*
遙		Distant, remote *yìuh* *yáu* *yáo*
遞	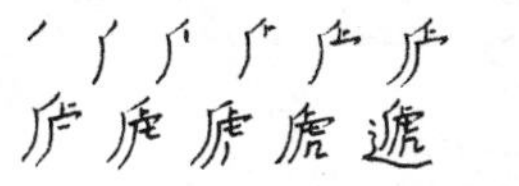	To deliver, convey *daih* *dì* *dì*

字	筆順	意義
遠	一 十 土 吉 吉 吉 声 束 表 袁 遠	Far, remote *yúhn* *ywǎn* yuǎn
遣	丶 ㅜ 口 中 虫 串 虫 虫 書 遣	To dispatch, banish *hin* *chyǎn* qiǎn
遮	丶 二 广 广 广 府 府 庶 庶 遮	To cover, protect *je* *je* zhe
遲	ㄱ コ 尸 尸 尸 尿 屖 屖 犀 犀 遲	Late *chih* *chŕ* chí
適	丶 亠 ㅗ 产 产 商 商 商 商 商 適	Suitable; just now *sik* *shr* shì
遭	一 冂 冂 西 西 曲 曲 曹 曹 曹 曹 遭	To meet; a turn *jou* *dzāu* zāo
遷	一 冂 冂 両 西 覀 覀 要 栗 卷 遷	To move *chin* *chyān* qiān
遼	一 ナ 大 太 太 交 夯 香 春 尞 尞 遼	Distant, remote *liuh* *lyáu* liáo
選	ㄱ ㄱ 己 己 己 弓 弓 巽 巽 巽 巽 選	To choose, elect *syún* *sywǎn* xuǎn
遵	丶 ㅛ 八 乂 广 首 酋 酋 酋 尊 尊 遵	To obey, follow *jeun* *jwun* zūn
遺	丶 ㅜ 口 中 虫 串 虫 眚 眚 書 貴 遺	To leave behind, forget *waih* *yí* yí
邀	丿 亻 白 白 白 白 自 身 身 躬 敫 敫 邀	To invite *giú* *yau* yāo

避	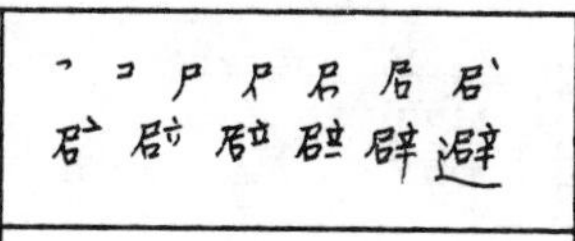	To avoid, escape *beìh* *bì* *bì*
還		To return; still *waàhn* *hwán, hái* *huán, hái*
邊	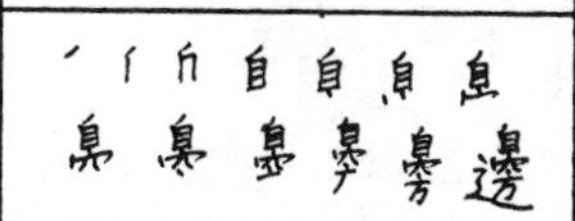	An edge, side *bìn* *byān* *biān*
	邑	Section
邑	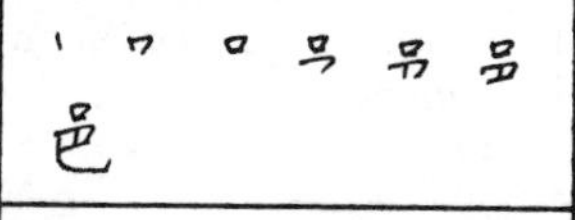	A city, district *yàp* *yí* *yí*
那	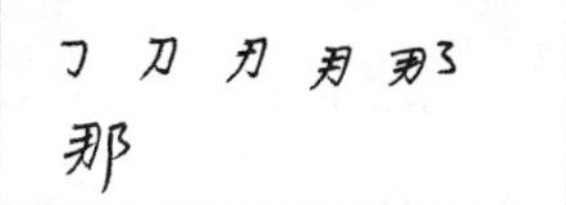	That, who *náh* *nà, ná, na, nè, nwó* *nà, ná, na, nè, nuō*
邪	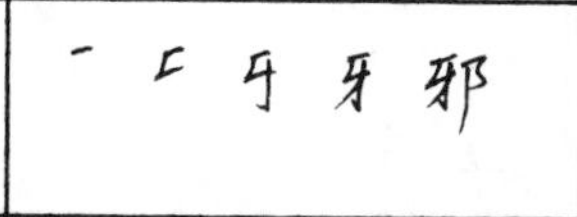	Evil, vicious *chèh* *syé* *xié*
邦	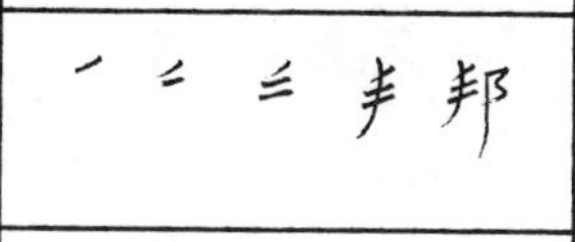	A state, country *bòng* *bāng* *bāng*
郊	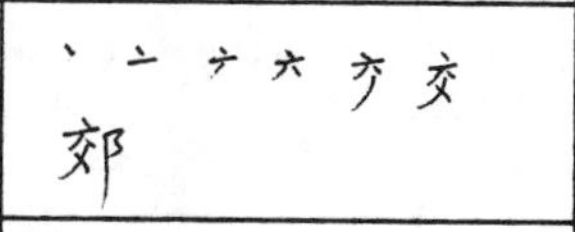	Countryside, suburbs *gaàu* *jyāu* *jiāo*
郡	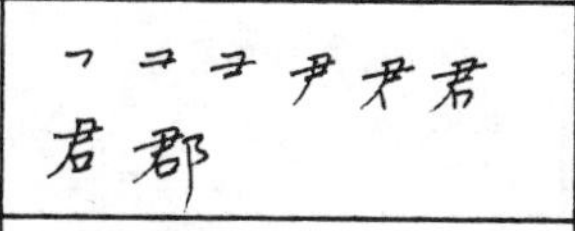	A county *gwahn* *jwùn* *zùn*
郎	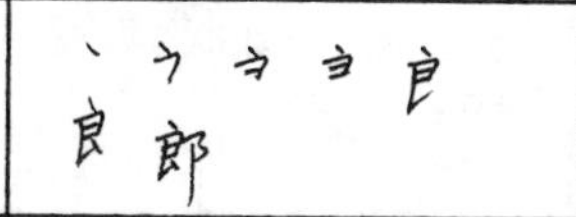	A young gentleman, bride-groom *lòhng* *láng* *láng*
部	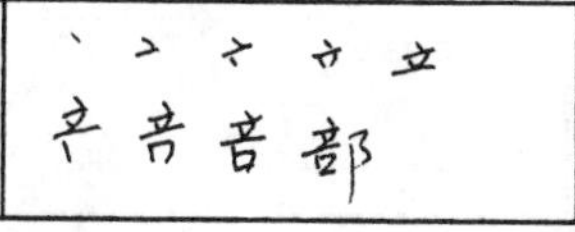	A section, department *bouh* *bù* *bù*

郵	ノ ╱ ┌ ┴ ┴ ┴ 垂 垂 郵	Mail, postal *yauh* *yóu*　　　　　*yóu*
都	一 十 土 耂 耂 者 者 者 都	A capital; also, all *dōu* *dū, dōu*　　　*dū dōu*
鄉	╰ ╯ 乡 幺′ 幺′ 幺′ 幺′ 组 纲 鄉	A village *heung* *syāng*　　　*xiāng*
鄙	╲ ╮ ┌ ┌ 冂 罒 罒 啚 啚 鄙	Low, vile *péi* *bǐ*　　　　　*bǐ*
鄰	╲ ╰ ┴ 米 米 籷 籷 籷 籷 籷 籷 鄰	A neighbor; adjacent *leuhn* *lín*　　　　*lín*
	酉	Section
酋	╲ ╯ ╰ ┴ 广 广 丙 丙 酋 酋	A chief *yauh* *chyòu*　　　*qiu*
配	一 ┌ 冂 丙 丙 酉 酉 酉′ 配	To match, unite *pui* *pèi*　　　　　*pèi*
酌	酉 酉′ 酌 酌	To pour wine; to consider; feast *cheuk* *jwo*　　　*zhó*
酒	╲ ╲ ╱ 酒	Wine, liquor *jaú* *jyǒu*　　　　*jiǔ*
酥	酉 酉′ 酉丆 酥 酥 酥	Crisp, flaky *sou* *sū*　　　　　*sū*
酪	酉 酉′ 酉夂 酪 酪 酪 酪	Cheese, fat *lok* *lwò, laù*　　*luò, laò*

酬	酉 酉ˊ 酊丿 酬 酬州	To repay; to pledge *chau* *chóu* *chóu*
酸	酉 酉ˊ 酉ˊ 酉ˇ 酸 酸 酸 酸	Sour; distressed *syun* *swān* *suān*
酵	酉 酉ˉ 酉ˇ 酉ˉ 酢 酢ˇ 酵 酵 酵	To ferment; yeast *haàu* *syàu* *xiào*
醋	酉 酉ˋ 酉ˉ 酉ˇ 酢 酢 醋 醋 醋	Vinegar *chou* *tsù* *cù*
醇	酉 酉ˊ 酉ˉ 酉ˇ 酉ˊ 酉ˊ 酉ˊ 醇 醇	Pure and good (wine) *seùhn* *chwún* *chún*
醉	酉 酉ˋ 酉ˉ 酉ˇ 酹 酉ˊ 醉 醉	Drunk *jeui* *dzwèi* *zuì*
醃	酉 酉ˉ 酉ˊ 酉大 酉大 酉大 酹 酪 酪 醃	To salt *yím* *yān* *yān*
醒	酉 酉ˋ 酉ʔ 酉ʔ 酌 酉ʔ 酉ʐ 醒 醒 醒	To wake up, be aware *sing* *sying* *xing*
醜	酉 酉ˊ 酊ˊ 酊ˊ 酹白 酊 酊 酊丿 醜 醜 醜	Ugly, shameful *cháu* *chǒu* *chǒu*
醬	㇄ 爿 爿 爿ˊ 爿ˊ 牄 牄 牄 將 將 醬	A sauce *jeung* *jyàng* *jiàng*
釀	酉ˊ 酉ˉ 酉ˊ 酹ˊ 酉ˊ 酹 酉卒 酉卒 醸 醸 醸 釀	To ferment, brew *yeùhng* *nyàng* *niàng*

采   Section

釆	ノ ヽ ヽ 丷 丷 平 平 釆	Brilliant *chói* *tsai*　　　*cai*
釋	采 釆 釈 釈 釈 釈 釈 釋 釋 釋	To explain, release *sik* *shr*　　　*shi*

	里	Section

里	ヽ 冂 口 日 甲 甲 里	Chinese mile *leih* *li*　　　*li*
重	ノ 一 白 盲 重 重	Important, weighty *chúhng, juhng* *juǹg, chúng zhoǹg, chóng*
野	里 里 野 野 野	Wilderness *yéh* *ye*　　　*ye*
量	ヽ 冂 口 日 旦 量	To measure; a quantity *leùhng, leuhng* *lyaǹg liang*

	金	Section

金	ノ 人 へ 今 全 仝 余 金	Gold, metal *gam* *jin*　　　*jin*
釜	ノ ハ 少 父 釜	A pot, pan *fú* *fu*　　　*fu*
針	金 金 一 針	A needle, pin *jam* *jen*　　　*zhen*
釘	金 金 一 釘	A nail; to nail *deng* *diǹg, diǹg diǹg, diǹg*

鈕	金 金 鈤 鈕	A buckle, button kau kou kou
釣	金 釒 釣 釣	To fish diu dyau diao
鈔	金 釓 釛 鈔 鈔	Bank notes; to copy chaau chau chao
鈕	金 釘 釦 鈕 鈕	A button, knob nau nyou niu
鉤	金 釕 釣 釣 鉤 鉤	To hook; a hook ngau gou gou
鈴	金 釒 釢 鈴 鈴 鈴	A bell lihng ling ling
鉅	金 金 釮 鉅 鉅	Huge, great geuih jyu ju
鉗	金 釕 釺 鉗 鉗 鉗	Forceps, pincers kim chyan qian
鉛	金 釕 釟 釾 鉛 鉛	Lead yuhn chyan qian
銀	金 釘 釕 釕 鈤 鈤 銀	Silver ngahn yin yin
銅	金 釕 釦 釦 銅 銅 銅	Copper, bronze, brass tuhng tung tong
銜	ノ ノ 彳 徍 徍 徍 銜	Rank, title haahm syan xian

銘	金 金 釵 釵 釵 銘 銘	To remember, carve *mihng* *míng* *míng*
銳	金 金 釒 釒 釥 釤 釣 銳	Sharp, acute *yeuih* *rwèi* *rùi*
鋁	金 釒 釗 釦 釦 鋁	Aluminium *leúih* *lyǔ* *lǔ*
銲	金 釒 釕 釦 釦 鋊 鋊 銲	To solder *hohn* *han* *hàn*
銻	金 釒 釕 釥 釥 鋊 銻 銻	Antimony *tai* *tī* *tì*
鋒	金 釒 釵 釵 釥 鋊 鋌 鋒	The sharp edge of a tool or *fung* weapon *fēng* *fēng*
鋪	金 金 針 針 鋪 鋪 鋪 鋪	To arrange; a shop *pou* *pū, pú* *pù, pu*
鋤	金 釒 釤 釧 鋤 鋥 鋤 鋤	A hoe; to cultivate *chòh* *chú* *chú*
銹	金 金 釤 針 鉥 鋷 銹 銹	Rust *sau* *syou* *xiú*
錄	金 釒 釤 鋥 鋀 鋀 鋖 錄	To record, copy *luhk* *lyu* *lù*
鋸	金 釕 釦 鋃 鋃 鋃 鋸 鋸	To saw; a saw *geui* *jyu* *jù*
錦	金 釒 釕 釦 鉤 鉑 鎬 錦 錦	Brocade; ornamental *gam* *jiň* *jǐn*

錫	金 釒 釒 釾 鈤 鈤 鍚 錫 錫	Tin, pewter *sek* *syi* *xī*
錯	金 釒 金 鉪 鉪 鈷 錯 錯 錯	A mistake; incorrect *cho* *tswo* *cuò*
錢	金 金 釒 錢 錢 錢	Money *chihn* *chyan* *qián*
鋼	金 釗 釗 釟 釟 鋼 鋼 鋼 鋼	Steel *gong* *gang* *gāng*
錶	金 釒 釒 鉪 鉪 釿 鋖 錶 錶	A watch, meter *biu* *byau* *biǎo*
鍋	金 釗 釟 鉰 鍋 釟 鍋 鍋 鍋 鍋	A sauce pan, cooking pot *wo* *gwo* *guō*
鍛	金 釒 釗 釺 鈝 鉪 鉪 鉪 鉬 鍛	To forge metal *dyun* *dwan* *duàn*
鍊	金 釒 釒 釓 鉬 鉬 鉬 鉔 鋅 鍊	To forge metal; a chain *lihn* *lyan* *liàn*
鍍	金 釒 釒 鉬 鉬 鉬 鉬 鍍 鍍	To gild *douh* *du* *dù*
錨	金 金 釗 釟 鈝 鈝 鉪 鉬 錨 錨	An anchor *miuh* *myau* *miáo*
鎗	金 釗 鈝 金 鈴 鈴 鈴 鎗 鎗 鎗	A gun *cheung* *chyang* *qiāng*
鎖	金 釗 釗 釟 鉪 鉪 鉪 鎖 鎖 鎖 鎖	To lock; a lock *so* *swo* *suǒ*

鎮	金 金 金亡 釒 鈩 鎮 鎮 鎮 鎮	A market town; trading center *jan* *jen* *zhèn*
鎚	金 金' 釒 鈩 鈤 鎚 鎚 鎚 鎚	To hammer; a hammer *cheuih* *chwei* *chui*
鎊	金 金' 金亡 釒 釒 鎊 鉣 鎊 鎊 鎊	A pound *bohng* *bang* *bàng*
鏡	金 金 金亡 釒 釒 鉢 鈝 鏡 鏡 鏡 鏡	A mirror *geng* *jing* *jìng*
鐘	金 金' 釒 釒 鈡 鈝 鉿 鐘 鐘 鐘	A clock, bell *jung* *jūng* *zhōng*
鐵	金 金 釷 釷 鈰 鈷 鋯 鐯 鐵 鐵 鐵	Iron *tit* *tyě* *tiě*
鎌	金 金 金 釕 鈷 鎊 鉣 鎌 鎌 鎌	A sickle, scythe *lihm* *lyàn* *lián*
鑑	釒 金 釒 鈩 鈩 鉬 鉬 鉬 鈭 鑑 鑑 鑑	To examine; historical events *gaam* *jyan* *jiàn*
鑄	金 釷 釷 鈷 鋯 鑄 鑄 鑄 鑄 鑄 鑄 鑄	To cast metal *jyu* *ju* *zhù*
鑰	金 金 釒 釒 釒 鈴 鉿 鎗 鑰 鑰 鑰 鑰	A key *yut, yeuk* *ywe, yau* *yuè, yào*
鑽	金 鈷 釷 釷 釷 鋯 鋨 鋨 鋨 鑽 鑽 鑽 鑽	To drill *jyun* *jwān* *zhuān*
長 Section		

長	´ ˜ F F 乒 乒 乒 長 長	Long; elder; length *cheuhng* *zhàng* *cháng,jǎng,jàng cháng,zhǎng,*
	門 Section	
門	｜ ｢ ｢ 月 月 門 門 門 門	A door, gate, entrance *muhn* *mén* *mén*
閃	門 門 閃	To flash; to avoid *sím* *shǎn* *shǎn*
閉	門 門 閉 閉	To close, shut *bai* *bì* *bì*
開	門 門 門 開 開	To open, begin *hòi* *kāi* *kāi*
間	門 門 門 間 間	Between; a space *gaan* *jyān* *jiān*
閒	門 門 開 開 閒	Idle; leisure *faàhn* *syán* *xián*
閘	門 門 閂 閘 閘 閘	A floodgate *jaahp* *já* *zhá*
閣	門 門 閂 閣 閣 閣 閣	A cabinet; mezzanine *gok* *ge* *gé*
閨	門 門 門 閏 閏 閨 閨	A boudoir *gwai* *gwēi* *gūi*
閥	門 門 門 閥 閥 閥 閥	Military *faht* *fá* *fá*

閱	門 門 門 門 閂 問 閣 閱	To read, inspect *yuht* *ywè*　　　　*yuè*
闊	門 門 門 門 閂 閂 閣 闊 闊 闊	Broad, wide *fut* *kwò*　　　　*kuo*
闖	門 門 門 門 閂 閂 閣 闖	To rush in, enter abruptly *chong* *chwǎng,chwang chuǎng,chuang*
關	門 門 閂 閂 閂 閂 閂 關 關 關	To close; a frontier *gwaan* *gwān*　　　　*guān*

阜	Section

阜	′ ＂ ｒ ｆ 自 皀 阜	A mound of earth; abundant *fauh* *fù*　　　　*fù*
防	３ ｒ ｐ` ｐ⁻ ｐｒ 防	To defend, protect *fohng* *fang*　　　　*fang*
阱	ｒ ｐ⁻ ｐ= ｐｒ 阱	A trap, pit *jehng* *jǐng*　　　　*jǐng*
阻	ｒ ｐ| ｐ冂 阝冂 阝目 阻	To hinder, obstruct *jó* *dzǔ*　　　　*zǔ*
附	ｒ ｐ′ ｐｌ ｐ⁻ 附 附	To attach; an appendix *fuh* *fù*　　　　*fù*
陋	ｒ ｐ⁻ ｐｒ 阝丂 陋 陋 陋	Vulgar, vile *lauh* *loù*　　　　*loù*
限	ｒ ｐｺ ｐ⁷ 阝彐 阝艮 阝艮 限	To limit; boundary *haahn* *syàn*　　　　*xiàn*

- 294 -

降	了 下 阝 阸 陉 陉 陉 阼 降	To descend; to surrender gong, hàhng jyàng　　jiang
陞	了 下 阝 阰 阰 阰 阰 陞	To rise, raise sing shēng　　shēng
院	了 下 阝 阝 陀 陀 陀 陀 院	A courtyard, hall yún ywàn　　yuàn
陣	了 下 阝 阝 阼 阼 阼 陌 陣	A moment; a line of troops jahn jeh　　zhèn
除	了 阝 阝 阭 阭 除 陉 除 除	To deduct, exclude cheuih chùh　　chú
陪	了 阝 阝 阝 阝 阼 陪 陪 陪	To accompany puíh peíh　　peí
陳	了 阝 阝 阿 阿 阿 陣 陳 陳	To display, state; old chàhn chéh　　chén
陶	阝 阝 阝 阹 阹 阹 陶 陶 陶	To feel happy; earthenware touh táu, táu　　tāo, táo
陷	阝 阝 阽 阽 阽 阽 陷 陷 陷	To fall; to capture hahm syàn　　xiàn
陸	阝 阝 阝 阺 阺 陸 陸 陸	Dry land; continent luhk lù　　lù
陰	阝 阝 阽 阽 阽 阽 陰 陰 陰	Shade; feminine yàm yin　　yīn
陽	阝 阝 阴 阴 阳 阳 阳 陽 陽 陽	The sun; masculine yeuhng yáng　　yáng

隊	阝 阝` 阝" 队 队 队 队` 队` 隊 隊	A group, team deuih dwei　　　dui
階	阝 阝ﾚ 阰 阰 阰 阰 阰 階 階 階	Stairs gaai jyē　　　jiē
隆	阝 阝´ 阝´ 阷 阹 队 降 降 隆	Surpassing; abundant lùhng lung　　　long
隔	阝 阝ˊ 阝" 阝" 阝" 阝" 隔 隔 隔 隔 隔	To divide, separate gaak ge　　　ge
隙	阝 阝ﺍ 阝ﾘ 阝" 阝" 阰 阰 階 階 階 隙	A crack; an opportunity gwik syi　　　xi
際	阝 阝´ 阹 队 阝" 队" 队" 队" 隊 際 際 際	A boundary; at the time jai ji　　　ji
障	阝 阝` 阝" 阝" 阝" 阰 阰 阼 階 階 障 障	To screen off; an obstruction jeung jāng　　　zhāng
隧	阝 阝" 阝" 阝" 阰 阰 阰 队 队 队 隊 隊 隧	A tunnel, subway seuih swei　　　sui
隨	阝 阝¯ 阰 阹 阹 阹 陏 陏 隋 隨 隨 隨	To follow, accompany cheuih swei　　　sui
險	阝 阝ﾘ 队 队 阶 阶 阶 阶 险 險	Dangerous him syan　　　xian
隱	阝 阝ˊ 阝" 阝" 阝" 阝" 阼 阼 隐 隐 隐 隐 隱 隱	To hide yan yin　　　yin
	隶	Section

- 296 -

隸	一 十 木 杢 李 李 奈 奈 奈 奈¹ 奈¹ 隸¹ 隸¹ 隸 隸	Attached to; subordinates *dai* *li`*          *li`*
	隹 Section	
隻	ノ イ イ 伫 伫 仹 伫 隹 隼 隻	One, single *jek* *jr* *zhi*
雀	⌄ 小 小 少 雀	Small birds *jeuk* *chye, chyau* *qie, qiao*
雄	一 十 左 左 雄	A hero; masculine *huhng* *syung* *xiong*
雅	⌐ 厂 工 于 牙 雅	Elegant, refined *ngah* *ya* *ya*
雁	一 厂 厂 厂 厥 雁	A wild goose *ngaahn* *yan* *yan*
集	佳 佳 隼 隼 集	To gather; a collection of *jaahp* essays *ji* *ji*
雌	⌐ 卜 屮 止 此 此 雌	To female of birds *chi* *tsz* *ci*
雕	ノ 几 月 用 用 用 周 周 雕	To carve, engrave *diu* *dyau* *diao*
雖	⌐ 口 口 口 号 吕 吊 虽 虽 雖	Although *seui* *swei* *sui*
雙	佳 雔 雙 雙	A pair; double *seung* *shwang* *shuang*

雛	ノ ク 勺 勾 匃 匔 匔 雛	A young bird *chō* *chu* *chu*
雜	､ ユ 广 亣 衣 亦 卒 斉 亲 雜	Mixed, assorted *jaàp* *dzá* *za*
雞	ノ ⺅ ⺌ ⺍ 幺 乡 乡 乡 乡 奚 雞	A chicken *gāi* *ji* *ji*
離	､ ユ 广 亠 亩 离 卤 离 离 离 離	To depart, separate *lèih* *lí* *li*
難	､ 一 艹 艹 芢 芢 芑 荁 荁 堇 難	Difficult; distress *nàahn* *nán, nàn* *nán, nàn*
	雨	Section
雨	一 厂 厈 雨 雨 雨 雨	Rain *yúh* *yŭ* *yu*
雪	雨 雩 雪 雪 雪	Snow *syut* *sywĕ* *xue*
雲	雨 雩 雫 雲 雲	Clouds *wàhn* *ywún* *yún*
零	雨 雫 雫 雫 零 零	Zero; fractional *lìhng* *líng* *líng*
電	雨 雫 雫 雪 雪 電	Electricity, lightning *dihn* *dyàn* *dian*
雷	雨 雫 雫 雪 雷 雷	Thunder *lèuih* *léi* *léi*

需	需 雪 雲 雲 雪 雪 雷 需	To require; necessity seui syū xū
震	雷 雲 雲 雪 霉 霉 震 震	To tremble, shake jan jeh zhèn
霉	雪 雲 雫 雫 霏 霏 霏 霏 霏 霜	Mildew, mold muih méi méi
霜	雫 雲 雫 霏 霏 霜 霜 霜 霜 霜	Frost seung shwāng shuāng
霞	雫 雲 雪 雫 霏 霏 霞 霞 霞	Vapor hah sýa xá
霧	雫 雲 雲 雲 雫 雫 霧 霧 霧 霧 霧 霧	Fog, mist mouh wù wù
露	雫 雫 雫 雪 雫 雫 霏 露 露 露 露 露 露 露	To expose; dew lquh lu lù
霸	雫 雫 雪 雫 雫 雫 雪 雫 雫 霸 霸 霸 霸	A conqueror, tyrant ba bà bà
霹	雫 雲 雪 雫 雫 雫 雫 雫 雫 霹 霹 霹 霹 霹	A thunderclap pik pī pī
靈	雫 雫 雫 雫 雫 雫 雫 雫 霏 霏 靈 靈	The soul, spirit nihng líng líng
	青	Section
青	一 十 キ 主 丰 青 青 青	Green, young ching chíng qīng

青 (8) 非 (7) 面 (4-8) 革

靜	青 青 青 青 青 青 青 青 青 青 青 靜 靜 靜 靜	Quiet, peaceful *jihng* *jìng* *jìng*
	非	Section
非	ノ ナ ヺ 非 非 非	Not; bad *fēi* *fēi* *fēi*
靠	ノ ゝ ⺊ 生 牛 告 告 靠	To rely on, lean against *kaau* *kàu* *kào*
	面	Section
面	一 丆 产 而 而 而 而 面 面	The face, front *mihn* *myàn* *miàn*
	革	Section
革	一 十 廿 廿 廿 莒 莒 革	Leather; to revolt *gaap* *gé* *gé*
靴	革 革 革 靭 靭' 靴	Boots *heu* *sywe* *xuē*
鞋	革 革 靯 靯 鞋	Shoes *haaih* *sýe* *xié*
鞏	一 丁 工 卫 巩 巩 鞏	To strengthen; secure *gúng* *gǔng* *gǒng*
鞭	革 革 靭 靭' 靭 靭 靭 鞭 鞭	A whip *bìn* *byān* *biān*

- 300 -

| | 韋 | Section |

韋	ᒻ ユ ゙ ゙ 圭 圭 吉 吉 韋 韋 韋	Soft leather *waih* *wéi*　　　　*wéi*
韌	韋 韌 韌 韌	Tough, viscous *yahn* *rèn*　　　　*rèn*
韓	ー 十 产 古 古 車 車 卓 韓	Korea *hòhn* *hán*　　　　*hàn*

| | 音 | Section |

音	丶 亠 亠 立 立 产 奇 音	A sound, tone *yàm* *yīn*　　　　*yīn*
韻	音 音 訇 音 訇 訇 韻 韻 韻 韻	Rhyme *wáhn* *ywun*　　　　*yùn*
響	' ⺩ 乡 纟 纺 纺 纺 絧 紲 縬 鄉 響	Loud, noisy *héung* *syǎng*　　　*xiǎng*

| | 頁 | Section |

頁	一 一 厂 丆 百 百 百 頁 頁	A page, sheet *yihp* *ywe*　　　　*yuè*
頂	一 丁 頂	To oppose; the top *díng* *díng*　　　　*dǐng*
項	一 丅 工 項	An item *hohng* *syàng*　　　*xiàng*

頁 (3-7)

順	ノ 川 川 順	To obey; smoothly *seuhn* *shwun*　　　*shun*
須	ノ ク 多 須	To need; necessary *seui* *syu*　　　*xu*
頌	ノ 八 公 公 頌	To praise, commend *juhng* *sung*　　　*song*
預	¬ マ マ 予 預	To prepare, be ready *yuh* *yu*　　　*yu*
頑	¯ = テ 元 頑	Noughty, obstinate *waahn* *wan*　　　*wan*
頒	ノ 八 分 分 頒	To proclaim, bestow *baan* *ban*　　　*ban*
頓	¯ 匚 屯 屯 頓	To bow (head), pause *deuhn* *dwun*　　　*dun*
領	ノ 人 人 今 令 領	To lead, receive; a collar *lihng* *ling*　　　*ling*
頗	¬ 厂 屮 皮 皮 頗	Very, somewhat *po* *pwo*　　　*po*
頭	¯ 匚 듸 豆 豆 豆 豆 頭	The first, head *tauh* *tou*　　　*tou*
頰	¯ 厂 灭 夾 夾 夾 頰	Cheek *haahp* *jya*　　　*jia*
頸	¯ 巜 죠 巠 巠 巠 巠 頸	Neck *geng* *jing*　　　*jing*

- 302 -

領	ノ 人 人 今 今 合 合 領	Chin, jaw *hahp* hàn　　　hàn
頹	ノ 二 千 千 禾 禿 頹	To descend; faded *teuih* twéi　　　túi
頻	丶 卜 止 止 步 步 頻	Frequent; hurried *pàhn* pín　　　pín
顆	丶 冂 日 日 旦 果 顆	A round thing; a lump *ló* kē　　　kē
額	丶 宀 宀 宀 宕 客 客 客 額	An amount; the forehead *ngaahk* è　　　è
題	丨 冂 日 日 旦 早 早 是 是 題	A subject, topic *taih* tí　　　tí
顏	丶 二 ㇒ 文 立 产 产 彥 彥 顏	Color; the face *ngaahn* yán　　　yán
願	一 厂 厂 厂 厉 厉 厉 原 原 原 願	To wish for; a wish; willing *yuhn* ywàn　　　yuàn
顛	一 十 ナ 古 直 直 真 真 顛	To upset; the top *dìn* dyān　　　diān
類	丶 丷 丷 半 米 米 米 类 类 類	To classify; a class *leuih* lèi　　　lèi
顧	丶 ㇇ 二 户 户 庐 庐 庐 庐 庐 雇 雇 顧	To look after, consider *gu* gù　　　gù
顫	丶 二 广 亡 向 高 亩 亩 亩 亩 亩 亩 顫	To tremble, shiver *jin* jàn　　　zhàn

顯	ヽ ㄇ 日 日 日 日 昂 㬎 㬎 顯	To appear; evident *hín* *syán* *xiǎn*
顴	ヽ ㄧ ㅛ ㅛ ㅛ ㅛ ㅛ ㅛ 节 苐 荓 葷 葷 蓶 讙 顴	Cheekbones *kyùhn* *chywan* *quan*
	風	Section
風	ノ 几 几 凡 凡 凮 凨 風 風	Wind, breeze *fùng* *fēng* *fēng*
颳	風 風 風 風 颳 颳 颳	The blowing of the wind *gwat* *gwa* *gua*
颶	風 風 風 颶 颶 颶	A typhoon, cyclone *geuih* *jyu* *jù*
飄	ヽ 一 戸 両 両 西 西 栗 栗 票 票 飄	To float *piu* *pyāu* *piāo*
	飛	Section
飛	て て て 飞 飞 飛 飛	To fly *fei* *fei* *fēi*
	食	Section
食	ノ 人 人 今 合 合 侖 食 食	To eat; food *sihk* *shŕ* *shí*
飢	食 飠 飢	Hunger; hungry *gēi* *jī* *jī*

飲	食 食 飲 飲 飲	To drink; a drink *yam* *yǐn* *yǐn*
飯	食 食 飯 飯 飯	Cooked rice, a meal *faahn* *fàn* *fàn*
飾	ノ 人 へ 今 今 令 食 食 食 食 飾 飾 飾	Ornament, decoration *sik* *shr* *shì*
飼	食 飼 飼 飼 飼 飼	To feed, nourish *jih* *sz̀* *sì*
飽	食 食 飽 飽 飽 飽	To eat to the full; satis- *baau* fied *bǎu* *bǎo*
養	⺍ ⺍ ⺶ 半 羊 養	To bring up, raise *yeuhng* *yǎng* *yǎng*
餅	食 食 食 食 食 餅 餅	Cakes, biscuits *beng* *bǐng* *bǐng*
餐	｜ ｜⺊ ⺊ ⺊ 夕 歺 歺 餐	A meal, supper *chaan* *tsān* *cān*
餓	食 食 食 飩 飩 餓 餓 餓	Hungry, starving *ngoh* *e* *è*
餘	食 食 食 餘 餘 餘 餘 餘	The remainder, surplus *yùh* *yú* *yú*
館	食 食 食 飦 飦 飦 館 館	A dwelling, restaurant *gwún* *gwǎn* *guǎn*
蝕	食 食 飩 飩 蝕 蝕 蝕	To corrode *sihk* *shr* *shí*

	首	Section
首	丶 丶 丷 丷 ソ 艹 芦 首 首 首	The head, first *sáu* *shóu* *shǒu*

	香	Section
香	丿 二 千 千 禾 禾 杢 香 香	Fragrant; incense *heùng* *syāng* *xiāng*
馨	一 十 土 吉 吉 吉 声 声 殸 殸 殸 馨	Fragrant *hìng* *syīn* *xīn*

	馬	Section
馬	一 厂 F F 馬 馬 馬	A horse *máh* *mǎ* *ma*
馳	馬 馬フ 馬ゥ 馳 馳	To gallop; fast *chìh* *chŕ* *chì*
馴	馬 馬丿 馴 馴	To tame; mild *seùhn* *syùn* *xùn*
駁	馬 馬フ 駁 駁	To argue, reject *bok* *bwó* *bó*
駐	馬 馬フ 駐 駐 駐 駐	To occupy, stay *jyu* *jù* *zhu*
駕	フ カ カ 加 加 駕	To drive, control *ga* *jyà* *jià*

駛	馬 馬ˊ 馬ㄱ 馬口 駛 駛	To drive, sail *sai* *shr* *shǐ*
駝	馬 馬ˋ 馬ˊ 馬ㄱ 馬ㄛ 駝	A camel *toh* *twó* *tuó*
駭	馬 馬ˋ 馬ㄊ 馰 駭 駭 駭	Terrified, startled *hoih* *hai* *hài*
騎	馬 馬ˊ 馬ㄌ 馬大 駝 駝ㄎ 騎 騎 騎	To ride, mount *kèh* *chí* *qí*
騙	馬 馬ˋ 馬ㄅ 馬ㄇ 騙 騙 騙 騙 騙 騙	To cheat, deceive *pin* *pyàn* *piàn*
騷	馬 馬ㄱ 馭 騷 騷 騷 騷 騷 騷 騷	To disturb *sou* *saū* *sāo*
驅	馬 馬ㄇ 馳 馳 馳 馳 駈 驅	To expel, drive away *keui* *chyū* *qū*
騾	馬 馬ˊ 馬ㄇ 馬ㄱ 駟 騏 騾 騾 騾 騾 騾 騾	A mule *leùih* *lwò* *luò*
驕	馬 馬ˊ 馬ㄇ 駝 駝 駝 騎 騎 騎 驕 驕	To be proud; arrogant *giu* *jyāu* *jiāo*
驗	馬 馬ㄇ 馭 騋 騋 騋 騋 驗 驗	To verify, prove *yihm* *yàn* *yàn*
驟	馬 馬ˊ 馬ㄇ 馬ㄇ 駟 騍ㄇ 騍 騍 騍 驟 驟 驟	Suddenly; quick steps *jaauh* *dzòu* *zòu*
驚	` ` ㄗ ㄗ 芍 芍 苟 苟 苟 苟 敬 敬 驚	To terrify, frighten *gíng* *jīng* *jīng*

| 驢 | 馬 馬′ 馬⼁ 駅 馬⼂ 馬⼃ 馬⼄ 駐 駐 騙 驢 驢 驢 馬 驢 | Donkey, ass
lòuh
lú   *lú* |

| | 骨 | Section |

骨	丶 冂 冎 冎 冎 凸 冎 骨 骨 骨	Bones *gwàt* *gŭ* *gŭ*
骼	骨 骨 骨′ 骼 骼 骼 骼	Skeleton *lok* *lé* *lé*
髒	骨 骨 骨⼁ 骨⼂ 骨⼃ 骨⼄ 骨⼅ 骨⼆ 髒 髒 髒 髒	Dirty, filthy *jòng* *dzàng* *zāng*
體	骨 骨 骨′ 骨⼁ 骨⼂ 骨⼃ 骨⼄ 骨⼅ 體 體 體 體	Body, style *tái* *tĭ* *tĭ*

| | 高 | Section |

| 高 | 丶 亠 六 亠 声 高
高 高 | Tall, high, noble
gòu
gāu   *gāo* |

| | 髟 | Section |

髮	一 厂 ㇋ 镸 镸 镸 髟 髟 髟′ 髟⼁ 髮 髮	Hair *faat* *fà* *fà*
鬆	髟 髟′ 髟⼁ 髟⼂ 髟⼃ 髟⼄ 鬆 鬆 鬆	Loose, soft, disordered *sung* *sūng* *sōng*
鬍	髟 髟′ 髟⼁ 髟⼂ 髟⼃ 髟⼄ 鬍 鬍 鬍	Mustache *wùh* *hú* *hú*

字	筆順	意味
鬚	髟 髟 髟 髟 髟 髟 鬚 鬚 鬚 鬚	Beard, whishers *sōu* *syu*　　　*xū*
	鬥	Section
鬥	一 丁 王 王 鬥 鬥 鬥 鬥 鬥 鬥	To fight, struggle *dau* *dòu*　　　*dòu*
鬧	鬥 鬥 鬧 鬧 鬧	Disturbing, noisy *naauh* *nàu*　　　*nào*
	鬯	Section
鬱	一 十 木 术 朾 杵 楛 楛 楛 楛 鬱 鬱 鬱 鬱 鬱 鬱	Grieved, sad *wat* *yu*　　　*yù*
	鬲	Section
鬻	⌐ ⌐ 弓 弓 弜 弲 粥 粥 粥 鬻 鬻 鬻 鬻 鬻 鬻	To sell; roast in a pan *yuhk* *yù*　　　*yù*
	鬼	Section
鬼	ノ イ 白 白 甶 甶 鬼 鬼 鬼	Ghost, spirit of the dead *gwāi* *gwěi*　　　*gǔi*
魁	鬼 鬼 魁 魁	Great; the highest *fūi* *kwēi*　　　*kúi*
魂	一 二 云 云 魂	The soul, spirit *wahn* *hwún*　　　*hún*

- 309 -

魄	⌒ ⺅ ⼻ 白 白 魄	The soul, spirit paak pwò pò
魅	鬼 鬼 鬼 魅 魅 魅	A demon muih mèi mèi
魔	⺊ 广 广 庐 庐 庐 麻 麻 魔	A demon, devil mò mwò mò

	魚	Section

魚	⼃ ⼓ ⼂ ⼓ 角 鱼 魚	A fish yú yú yú
鮑	魚 魚 魚⼃ 魚勹 魚勹 鮑	An abalone baàu baù baò
鮮	魚 魚⼃ 魚兰 鮮	Fresh, new sīn syān xiān
鯉	魚 魚 魚⼃ 魚⼝ 魚⽥ 鯉 鯉 鯉	A carp leíh lǐ lǐ
鯊	⼂ ⼛ ⼮ ⺲ 沙 沙 沙 鯊	A shark sà shā shā
鯨	魚 魚 魚⼃ 魚⼇ 鯨 鯨 鯨 鯨 鯨	A whale kìhng jīng, chíng jīng, qíng
鰓	魚 魚 魚⼃ 魚⼝ 魚⽥ 魚 鰓 鰓 鰓 鰓	Gills of a fish sì, soi sāi sāi
鰣	魚 魚 魚⼃ 鮖 鮖 鮖⼀ 鮖⼗ 鰣 鰣 鰣 鰣	Shad sìh shŕ shí

鰥	魚 魚 魛 魛 魛 魛 魛 魛 魛 鰥 鰥	A widower *gwaan* *gwan* *guan*
鱗	魚 魚 魛 魚 魣 鱗 鱗 鱗 鱗 鱗 鱗 鱗 鱗	Scales of a fish *leùhn* *lín* *lin*
鱷	魚 魚 魛 魚 魣 魣 魣 鱷 鱷 鱷 鱷 鱷	A crocodile, alligator *ngohk* *e* *e*
鳥	Section	
鳥	丿 亻 亣 白 白 白 鳥 鳥	A bird *liúh* *nyǎu* *niǎo*
鳳	丿 几 凡 鳳	A phonix *fuhng* *feng* *feng*
鳴	丶 口 口 鳴	To chirp; cry of a bird *mìhng* *ming* *míng*
鴉	一 厂 工 牙 鴉	A crow *ngà* *yā* *yā*
鴨	丶 口 日 日 甲 鴨	A duck *aap* *yā* *yā*
鴦	丶 口 口 央 央 鴦	A drake Mandarin duck *yeung* *yāng* *yāng*
鴛	丿 夕 夕 夘 夗 鴛	A female Mandarin duck *yun* *ywān* *yuān*
鴿	丿 人 人 今 合 合 鴿	A dove, pigeon *gap* *gē* *ge*

鵑	`丶冂口尸丹月鵑`	A cuckoo *gun* *jwān* *zhuān*
鵝	`丿一千千我我` `我鵝`	A goose *ngoh* *é* *é*
鵲	`丶十廿廿芌芌` `昔昔鵲`	A magpie *jeuk* *chywe* *què*
鶯	`丶丷丿火炒炒` `炒鶯`	A nightingale *ngāng* *yīng* *yīng*
鶴	`丶冖宀疒疒疒` `宿宿雀鶴`	A stork *hok* *he, hau* *hè, hǎo*
鷗	`一匚匸匸匸匸` `區區鷗`	A seagull *ngau* *ou* *ōu*
鷹	`丶亠广广庁府府` `庑庑雁鷹`	An eagle, hawk *ying* *ying* *yīng*
鸚	`丨刀月目貝賏賏` `賏嬰嬰鸚`	A parrot *yíng* *yíng* *yīng*
鹵		Section
鹹	`丶广卢卤卤卤卤` `卤卤卤鹹卤鹹鹹`	Salty *haahm* *syán* *xián*
鹽	`一厂厂尸尸尸臣臣` `臣臨臨臨鹽鹽`	Salt *yihm* *yán* *yán*
鹿		Section

鹿	丶 一 广 庐 庐 鹿 鹿 鹿 鹿	A deer *luhk* lù　　　　　lù
麗	一 厂 厅 厈 帀 丽 麗	Beautiful, graceful *laih* lì　　　　　lì
麟	鹿 鹿ˊ 鹿ˊ 鹿ˇ 鹿ˇ 鹿ˇ 鹿ˇ 鹿ˇ 鹿ˇ 鹿ˇ 鹿ˇ 麟	A female unicorn *leuhn* lin　　　　　lin
	麥	Section
麥	一 十 亣 亣 夾 夾 來 來 麥 麥	Wheat *muhk* mwò, mái　　mò, mái
麵	麥 麥 麥| 麥| 麵	Noodles *mihn* myàn　　　　mìan
	麻	Section
麻	丶 一 广 广 庁 庁 床 麻	Hemp, flax *màh* má　　　　　má
麼	麻 麼 麼 麼	What? an interrogative par- *mò*　　　　　　　　ticle mwò, ma, má　mò, ma, má
	黃	Section
黃	丶 十 卝 卝 世 芑 芢 芦 芦 苗 苗 黃	Yellow *wòhng* hwáng　　　　huáng
	黍	Section

黍	ノ ニ 千 禾 禾 禾 禾 季 季 黍	Millet *syu* *shŭ*　　　　　*shŭ*
黎	禾 禾 利 利 黎	Dark, dim *làih* *lí*　　　　　*lí*
黏	黍 黎 黎 黏 黏 黏	Sticky *nìm* *nyan*　　　　*nián*
	黑	Section
黑	丶 冖 冖 甲 里 黑	Black, dark *hàk* *hē, hēi*　　*hē, hēi*
默	黑 黑 黙 黙 默	Silent, quiet *mahk* *mwò*　　　　*mò*
點	黑 黑 黙 黙 點 點	To point; a dot *dím* *dyăn*　　　*diăn*
黨	丶 ⺍ ⺍ 尚 尚 尚 尚 党 堂 當 黨	A political party, league *dong* *dăng*　　　*dăng*
	鼎	Section
鼎	丨 冂 目 目 甲 甲 鼎 鼎 鼎 鼎 鼎	A caldron; firm, settled *díng* *dĭng*　　　*dĭng*
	鼓	Section
鼓	一 十 士 吉 吉 吉 吉 壴 壴 尌 鼓 鼓	To rouse; a drum *gú* *gŭ*　　　　　*gŭ*

鼠		Section
鼠	丶 宀 宀 臼 臼 臼 臼 臼 臼 鼠	A rat, a squirrel *súi* *shŭ* *shŭ*
鼻		Section
鼻	丶 宀 宀 自 自 鳥 鳥 鳥 鳥 畠 鼻	A nose *beih* *bí* *bi*
鼾	鼻 鼻 鼻 鼾	To snore *hòhn* *hàn* *hàn*
齊		Section
齊	丶 亠 𠂆 宀 齐 齐 齐 齐 齐 齐 齊	Even, orderly, level *chàih* *chí* *qí*
齋	齊 齊 齋 齋	A feast; vegeterian *jaài* *jāi* *zhāi*
齒		Section
齒	丶 ㅏ 止 止 齿 齿 齿 齿 齿 齒 齒	Teeth *chí* *chŕ* *chǐ*
齡	齒 齒 齒 齡 齡 齡	Age *lìhng* *líng* *líng*
齣	齒 齣 齣 齣 齣 齣	A scene in a play *keùi* *chū* *chū*

龍 龜 侖

	龍	Section
龍	`丶 亠 六 立 产 青 青` `青 青 剪 剪 竜 龍`	A dragon *luhng* *lung* *lóng*
	龜	Section
龜	`丿 ク 伫 产 凸 凸 龟 龟` `龟 龟 龟 龟 龟 龜 龜`	A tortoise *gwài* *gwēi* *gūi*
	侖	Section
侖	`丿 人 亽 今 合 合` `合 侖 侖 侖 侖 侖 侖`	A flute *yeuhk* *ywe* *yùe*

aunt 105 106 109
auspicious 210
authority 79 182
autumn 223
avenue 258
avoid 70 131 278 285
  293
awake 134
aware 134 287
awe 135
awning 177 228
awry 183
axe 162
azure 252
baby 106 109 110
baby sitter 106
back 129 242
bacteria 250
bad 78 135 160 184
  300
bag 94 259
baggage 259
ball 209
bamboo 226
bamboo shoots 227
banana 252
banish 284
bank 199
bank notes 289
banquet 227
barbarians 102 212
barbarous 257
bare 222
barely 67
barge 247
bark 87
barrel 175
barren 249 275
barrier 98
base on 156
bashful 137
basin 216
basket 228
bat 256
bathe 188 190 192 198
battalion 203
battle 59
battleship 247
bay 199
be 63
beach 118 199
bead 209
beam 175 176 177 180
beans 270
bear 202 213
beard 309

beasts 208
beat 150 152 160 179
beautiful 108 229
  236 247 313
because 94 204
bed 124 179 205
bedclothes 259
bee 255
before 69 76
beg 56 102 140 187
beggar 53
begin 106 293
beginning 75 97 233
begonia 177
behavior 137 258
behind 129 284
believe 64
bell 289 292
belly 241 243
belong to 117 184
belt 122
bench 73
bend 146 281
bend down 64
benefit 75 216 260
benevolent 58 133 136
bent 158 168
besides 54
best 245
bestow 149 273 274
  302
bet 274
between 293
big 102
bill 91 221 274
bind 148 235
biography 67
bird 222 237 297 298
  311
birth 211
biscuits 305
bite 89 93
bitter 249
black 201 215 314
blame 133 272
blanket 186
bleach 196
bless 221
blind 217
blindly 217 218
bloated 243
blood 258
blood vessel 232 242
blossom 248
blow 88
blow out 93

blow up 279
blowing of wind 304
blue 253
board 171 205
boast 265 266
boastful 90
boat 246 247
body 277 308
boil 189 197 201
bomb 279
bond 76
bones 308
book 168
booth 177
boots 300
border 198
bored 84 135
born 211
borrow 65
bosom 140
both 64
bothered 84
bottle 180 210
bottom 124
boudoir 293
boundary 99 212 294
  296
bow 127 152 277 302
bowels 243
bowl 216 220
box 216 227
boxing 147
boy 109
brain 243
bramble 177 249
branch 158 171 172
  176
brass 289
brave 78 270
break 143 220
break into pieces
  154 220
break off 232
break up 160
breast 56 104 242
breath 133
breeze 304
brew 287
bribe 273
brick 221
bridegroom 285
bridge 175 180
brief 219
briefly 212

bright 58 164 166
    167 169 199 200
    215 239 279
brilliant 164 203
    238 288
bring 122 147
bring together 155
bring up 305
broad 113 125 294
brocade 290
broken 100 203 220
bronze 289
broom 121 128 149
brother 69 90 127
brothers 164
brown 176
brush 76 157 226
bubbles 190
bucket 175
buckle 289
buddha 62
Buddhist 76
Buddhist monastery 114
build 126 153 179 219
building 125 142 179
bullet 127
bundle 80
bundle up 260
burn 199 201 202
burst 203
bury 97 251
business 123 178
busy 132
but 61 201
butcher 117
butterfly 256
button 289
buy 190 272 274
by 59 162 212
by side of 162
cabin on ship 247
cabinet 293
cage 229
cake 230 305
calculate 227 229 263
caldron 314
calendar 167
calf 206
call 86 89 91 92 131
    267
camel 307
camp 203
can 130
canal 189
cancer 214

candle 203
candy 230
cane 173
cannon 200
Canton 229
canvas 121
cap 122
capable 98
capital 57 286
captive 64
capture 157 295
car 278
carcass 117
careful 137 268
careless 132 213 218
    249 250
carp 310
carpet 186
carry 142 146 147
    151 156 158
carry between 2 men
    145
carry on shoulder
    143 146 150 157
carry out 245
carve 76 128 290 297
cascade 198
case 103 181 216
cassia 175
cast 145 155
cast away 155
cast metal 292
cat 271
catch 148 208 234
cattle 206
catty 161
caught between 82
cause 59 62 137 234
    245
caution 141 269
cave 224
cease 236
cedar 172
center 54 102
ceremony 68 222
certain 111 162
certainly 131 220
chain 291
chair 176
change 151 159 164
    168 269
channel 179
chant 264 266
chapter 228
character 109
charcoal 200 202

charm 226
charming 108 139 270
chase 275
chat 267
cheat 182 265 307
checks 244
cheek 302
cheekbones 304
cheerful 132 180 182
    204
cheese 286
cherish 139 140
chess 116 176
chest 242
chestnut tree 174
chew 89 94
chicken 298
chief 69 183 234 286
child 58 70 110 225
chilly 113
chin 303
china 210 220
Chinese 197 250
Chinese coat 260
Chinese foot 116
Chinese inch 114
Chinese mile 288
chirp 311
chlorine 187
choose 156 284
chop 77 162 220
chopper 74
chopsticks 227
chrysanthemum 250
cicada 257
cigarettes 200
cinnamon 175
circle 95
circular 95
citizens 186
city 97 121 285
claim 261
clamor 94
clan 111 163
class 191 209 223 303
classify 128 303
claws 204
clean 73 152 190 192
    197
clear 165 166 169
    178 192 198 215
clear throat 93
clever 159 224 240
cliff 118
climb 204

cup 172
cure 214 264
curse 264
curtain 122 228
curve 128
custom 63 138 237 261
customer 112
cut 74 77 162
cut down 220
cut garments 259
cut off 141
cyclone 304
dagger 80
dance 246
danger 83 296
dare 160
dark 100 101 123 164
    166 171 208 314
dates 177
daughter-in-law 108
dawn 163 166 167
day 102 163
daytime 166
dead 184
deaf 240
debate 267
debt 67 274
decade 164
decay 173 243 251 258
deceive 238 264 307
decide 111 188 259
decision 75
decline 258 268
decoration 305
decrease 194
deduct 143 295
deep 192
deep fry 200
deer 313
deer's horn 250
defame 264 267
defeat 159
defect 126 235
defend 97 100 148 294
deficient 182
delay 126 277
delegate 106
deliberate 161
delicate 108
delight 134 167 182
deliver 281 283
delude 281
demand 263
demon 310
den 225
dense 85 177

depart 298
department 285
depend on 239
depraved 68
depressed 135
deprive 76
descend 53 295 303
descendants 164 259
describe 151
desert 196
desire 135 138
desolate 167
destroy 146 153 185
    195 220
destroy by fire 203
detail 265
detain 196
detective 66
determination 132
determine 188
devil 310
dew 299
dictionary 71
die 57 92 160 184 282
die young 102
different 140 212
difficult 247 298
dig 147 149
dignity 106
diligent 79
dim 165 169 314
dime 186 262
direct 115 218 251
direction 87 162
directly 217 282
dirt 96 99 187 308
disaster 199 222
discard 178
disciple 130
disclose 160
discount 143
discribe 281
discuss 269
disease 213
disgrace 237 280
disguise 144
dish 220
dislike 108 133
dismiss 154 272
disobey 283
disorder 56 308
disparage 272
dispatch 284
displace 131
display 157 295
displeased 137

dispute 263 280
dissect 76
disseminate 155
dissolve 191 195 256
distance 276
distant 134 283 284·
distinguish 75 172
    184 279
distinguished 82
distorted 161
distress 135 139 199
    247 279 287 298
distribute 74 154
    155 162
district 81 234 285
disturb 155 307
disturbing 309
ditch 96 195
dive 197
dive under water 189
diverging 183
divide 74 296
dizzy 166
do 66 204
do not 75 80 250
document 121
dog 206 207
dollar 69
donkey 308
door 142 293
dot 314
double 64 260 297
doubt 136 207 213
dove 311
down 53
dozen 143
drag 144 154 206
drag out 145
dragon 316
drain 194
drake Mandarin duck
    311
draw 168 213 235
draw back 234
draw out 145 150
drawer 117
drawing 95
dread 133 140 212
dream 102
dredge 155
dregs 194
dress 144 169 229
    259 260
dried meat 244
drift 191
drifting 251

exuberant 248
eye 217 218
eyeball 218
eyebrows 217
fabric 121
face 244 303
fact 300
faction 191
factory 125
fade 73 260
faded 303
fail 254
faint 164
fake 66
fall 99 118 150 276
    295
fall down 251
fall forward 58
fall over 65
false 65 263 264 268
false accusation 266
familiar 167 202
family 112 142 163
famous 239
fan 142 153
far 284
farm 250
farmer 280
fashion 180
fast 132 282 306
fasten 142 147 231
    234 235
fat 241 242 244 286
father 204
father-in-law 237
fatigued 95
fault 283
fear 131 133 140 212
fearful 134
feast 112 286 315
feathers 186 237
feed 305
feed a child 90
feel 146 150 153 262
feelings 135
feign 72
fellow 60
female 104
female Mandarin duck
    311
female of birds 297
female unicorn 313
feminine 97 295
fence 173
ferment 287

ferry 194
fertile 188 241
festival 228
few 57 113 115
field 98 211
fierce 69 201 207
fiery 201
fife 226
fight 141 309
figure 270
filial 109
fill 69
fill up 98
filter 199
filthy 308
final article 88
finally 225 232
find 115 144
fine 168 232
finger 147
fingernails 212
finish 56 111 141
    163 212
fins 237
fir tree 170
fire 199
firefly 256
fireplace 203
firewood 173 253
firm 76 97 185 205
    314
first 69 147 212 302
    306
fish 196 289 310
five 57 60
fix 64
flag 131 163 179
flaky 286
flame 200 201
flash 293
flatter 267
flavor 89
flax 313
fleas 255
flee 281
flesh 240
flexible 175
flick 127
flight 160 185
fling 143 157
float 189 191 196 304
floodgate 293
flooding 187
floors 179
floors of building
    117

flour 229
flourishing 78 248
flow 119 191
flow down 193
flow rapidly 194
flower 170 248
flute 226 228 316
fly 257 304
foam 190
fog 299
fold up 154
follow 116 130 131
    208 276 283 284 296
follow along 189
follow as example 122
follow pattern 154
follower 130
fond 92 136 218
food 230 251 304
foolish 88 136 257
foolishly 104
foot 243 276
footprint 277
footsteps 183
for instance 269
force 127 281
force open 155
forceps 289
forearm 244
forehead 303
foreign 101 190 212
forest 172
foretell 82
forge metal 291
forget 132 284
forgive 266
fork 84
forked 183
form 126
former 76 164
formerly 129
fort 98
fortunately 134
fortune 222
fortune telling 82
foul smell 245
foundation 97 175
fountain 189 195
four 94
fox 207
fractional 298
fragile 242
fragment 117
fragrance 248
fragrant 248 306

frame 173 174
free 70
freeze 73
frequent 117 303
fresh 102 310
friend 85 169
friendship 267
frighten 94 136 137
  307
frivolous 62
frog 255
from 130 206 212 276
front 76 300
frontier 97 98 212
  294
frost 299
frugal 125
fruit 172
fruitful 270
fry by fire 200
fry in oil 201
fuel 180
fullness 196
funiture 66
fur 186 216
fur garments 260
furnace 199
furthermore 115
gain 130 274
gall bladder 244
gallop 306
gamble 82 274
gang 122
garden 95
garments 258
gas 186 188
gate 142 293
gather 149 158 159
  230 239 297
general 121 166
generation 54 279
generous 83 138
genteel 161
gentleman 58
get 85 130
get free from 150
get lost 281
get rid of 83
ghost 309
gild 291
gills of fish 310
girl 104 106
give 56 59 211 232
  245 273
give alms 261

give birth 107 266
give gift 274
give in 116
give up 149 178
gladness 183
glass 172 180 209
glide 195
glimpse 218
glittering 203
glory 179
glowworm 256
glue 244
glutinous rice 230
go 84 275
go all over 283
go back 281
go back and forth 130
go out 74
go through 131 224
  281
go to 265 275
go to bed 113
go up 215
goat 236
god 55 102 121 221
gold 72 288
good 62 91 93 104 247
good fellow 197
good luck 87
good omen 221
goods 272
goose 297 312
gorge 118
govern 189 251
government 159
government official
  87
gown 259
graceful 107 108 161
  223 248 313
grade 209 231
gradually 196
grain 222 229 230
gram 70
grandchild 110
grandfather 204
grandmother 107
grant 149
grapes 251
grasp 97 144 152 158
grass 250
grasshopper 256
grave 99 100
gray 199
grease 189 241 242
greasy 244

great 66 120 125 134
  191 192 289 309
greedy 107 272
green 233 299
greens 252
greet 138
grievance 171
grieve 135 137 138 309
grievous 249 279
grind 156 221
groan 89
grope 153
ground 95 96
group 95 237 296
grow 184
guarantee 64
guard 90 111 148 258
  269
guard frontier 141
guess 60 207
guest 112 273
guide 127 208
gun 178 200 291
gush 194
gutter 194 195
habitual 138
hair 186 308
hairless 222
half 82
hall 97 126 295
hammer 178 292
hamper 228
hand 142
hand over 57
handle 143 154 173
  176 236 239
handsome 63
hang 96 127 140
hang up 149
happily 123
happy 91 136 180 222
  246 295
harbor 193
hard 220
hard-hearted 207
harmony 89 191 267
harness 79
harsh 249
hasten 67 276
hasty 132
hat 122
hatch 110
hatchet 162
hate 58 133 139
hatred 140

haughty 67
have 169
have been 168
hawk 312
he 59 129
head 302 306
heal 214
healthy 66 125
heap 97
hear 239 240
heart 131
heavy 198
heel 276
heifer 206
hello 92
helm 247
helmet 70
help 78 122 152 154
    198 273
hemp 313
herd 237
hero 64 67 297
hesitating 130
hibiscus 248 252
hide 60 81 97 197
    218 278 283 296
high 119 308
highest 309
hill 118
hillock 54
hinder 105 151 277
    294
hinge 180
history 86 184 292
hit 143 146
hobby 92
hoe 290
hold 85 87 97 109
    143 147 151
hold under arm 148
hold up 149
hole 190 224
holiday 65
holy 239
home 112
honest 125 160 217
    228
honey 256
Hong Kong 193
honor 115 179
honorable 160
hook 80 289
hope 71 121 169 217
horizontal 181
horn 262
horse 306

hot 194 200 202
hot weather 166
house 99 111 116 125
    142
household 112
hover 237
how 133 211
however 61 103 201
howl 90
huge 120 125 289
humble 82 268
hundred 215
hundred million 68
hungry 304 305
hunt 208
hurry 63 80 103 132
    275 303
hurt 112
husband 101 102 108
hydrogen 187
hypocritical 66
I 88 141
ice 72
identical 87
identify 279
idle 140 293
idol 66
if 65 104 249
illicit 249
illness 213
illuminate 201
image 68
imaginary 123
imitate 65 154 159
imitate writing 245
immediately 83 282
immerse 192 193
imminent 281
immortal 59
impart 149
impeach 150
imperial 182 215
imperial concubine
    104
imperial court 126
    269
implore 221
important 288
imprison 94
in 96 162
in addition 71
in order 184
incense 306
include 80 147
incorrect 291

increase 64 78 99
    193 195
indentation 74
indifferent 196
induce 266
indulge in 195
infant 109
inferior 78 82
influence 136
inform 61 98
infuse 188
ingenious 120
inhale 88
injure 67 112 153
injustice 112
ink 100
inn 176
inner 259
innundate 196
inquire 187 264 265
insane 214
insect 257
insert 151
inside 70 259
inspect 66 294
instant 76
instruct 94 147 263
instrument 68
insufficient 182
insult 63 182 280
intelligent 139
intend 157
intercept 141
interest 75
interesting 275
interfere 123
interpret 269
interrogate 265
interrogative
    particle 313
interrupt 151
intestines 243
intimate 167
introduce 58 127
invade 63
inverted 65
investigate 114 172
    224 263
invitation 121 173
invite 145 266 284
involve 232
iron 202 292
irrigate 199
irritated 137 140
island 118 119
it 110

maid 107
mail 286
main hall in temple 185
maintain 233
make 62 66 126 260 282
make appointment 231
make flexible 152
make known 264
make up 259
male 212
mallet 178
man 58 212
manage 86 123 130 149 156 209 227 233 252 254 280
Mandarin orange 172 175
mango 248
manner 106 112 247
manners 68
manufacture 260
manure 230
many 81 101 102 218
maple tree 178
marine 191
mark 77 214 254
market 100 121
market town 292
marquis 63
marriage 106 107
married couple 60
marry 107
marry a husband 108
masculine 295 297
mass 95
mast of ship 174
master 55
mat 122
match 274 286
match-maker 108
mate 66
materials 161 170
matter 274
matters 56
may 130
me 141
meal 305
mean 135
meaning 237
means 103
measles 213
measure 124 194 223 288

measure for picture 122
meat 240
medicine 253
meet 165 220 282 283 284
meeting 169
melon 210
melt 72 256
member of profession 90
mental 243
mention 151
merchandise 272
merchant 91 273
mercury 188
merit 78 79 234
messenger 62 120
metal 288
meter 291
method 258
metropolis 57
mezzanine 293
middle 54 59
mild 167 193 306
mildew 299
military 183 293
military officer 114
milk 56 104
millet 314
million 69
mind 131
minute 74
mirror 292
miserable 192
miserly 87
misery 134
misfortune 222
miss 102
mist 299
mistake 120 291
mistaken 266
mix 145 154 158 192 267
mixed 298
moan 93 183
model 178 179 228
modern 162
modest 268
moist 198
moisten 191 193 197
mold 97 250 299
mole 214
moment 295
monastery 76
money 122 182 271 291

monk 68
monkey 207
monopolize 158
month 169
moon 169
morality 131
more 190
moreover 54 168
morning 163 166 167 169
mortgage 145
mosquito 255
moss 249
most 168
moth 255
moth-eaten 255
mother 106 108 185
mother-in-law 107
motherly 137
motion 78
motive 131
mound 118
mound of earth 294
mount 307
mountain 118
mountain pass 118
mountain range 119
mourn 92
mournful 137
mouth 85 89 93
move 130 150 153 284
much 101
mucous 192
mud 98 190
muddy 198
mulberry tree 174
mule 307
multiply 55
murder a superior 126
muscle 227 240
mushroom 250
music 180
mussels 255
must 131
mustache 308
mustard greens 248
mute 92
mutual 217
my 88
mysterious 103 123 221
nail 288
naked 260 275
name 77 86 186 224
napkin 121
narrow 207 224

native town 229
naughty 302
navigate 246
near 148 280
necessary 302
necessity 299
neck 242 302
nectar 256
need 302
needle 288
needy 225 271
neglect 132
negligent 138
negotiate 269
neighbor 286
nephew 106 211
nervous 136 137
nest 119 225
net 233
net amount 192
nevetheless 83
new 162 310
newspaper 98
next 182
next day 237
niece 106 211
night 101 165
nightingale 312
nine 55
no 53 88 201
nobility 204
noble 138 308
noisy 92 301 309
none 53 201
noodles 313
noon 81
north 80
nose 315
not 53 188 201 250
  300
not yet 170
note 74 227
note-paper 227
notice 179
nourish 97 305
now 209 249
noxious 185
number 160
numbness 214
numerous 215 234 251
nun 116
oak tree 180
oar 180
oath 216 266
obedient 55
obey 130 240 284 302

object 144
obliging 107
obscene 193
obscure 165
observe 262
obstinate 302
obstruct 98 151 156
  158 294
obstruction 196 296
obtain 208
obtain again 130
occupy 132 156 178
  306
occur 283
ocean 190
of 55
offend 206
offer 88 149 208 232
office 112 116 254
officer 100 111
official 61 168
official rank 223
offspring 259
often 117
oil 189
oily 244
ointment 244
old 71 85 159 238
  246 295
old man 237
old woman 106 107
omen 69 210
on 96 162
on duty 65
once 275
one 53 101 297
one by one 281
one time 275 283
oneself 120
onions 251
only 85 91 109 135
open 91 293
opening 85 190
opera 77
opinion 136 261
opportunity 180 296
oppose 84 123 156
  262 281 283 301
opposite 84
oppress 148
or 141 249
orange 180 181
orchid 254
order 94 124 164
  223 226 262
orderly 315

organization 232
organize 232
origin 83 106
original copy 224
originate 65 110
ornament 305
ornamental 128 290
orphan 110
other 59 85
ounce 70
outline 179
outlook 271
outpost 90
outside 101
overcome 70
overflow 195 197 198
  216
overseas Chinese 68
overtake 281
owe 182 271
owner 55
ox 205
oxygen 186
oyster 255 257
pack 259
paddle 180
page 228 251 301
pagoda 99
pain 214
painful 178
paint 196
pair 115 297
palace 112
palisade 173
palm 149
palm tree 176
pan 288
pan fry 200
panther 271
pants 260
para 204
paper 231
paragraph 184
paralysis 214
pardon 133 275
pare 75
park 95
parrot 312
part 60 75
participate 84
party 314
pass 124 129 281 283
pass away 282
pass the night 112
passage 282

profound 208
prohibit 222 266
promise 69 263 267
prompt 151
pronounce 146
prop up 155
property 271
prosper 246
prosperity 222
prosperous 164
prostitute 105 107
protect 64 123 252
  258 269 284 294
protrude 74
proud 67 196
  307
prove 268 307
proverb 268
provide 62
provide for 89 274
province 217
prune 175
public 71
publication 75
publish 75
puff 88
pull 144 146 148 149
  151 168 206
pull down 146
pull up 145
pulse 242
punish 236
punishment 75
pure 192 197 231 271
pure and good (wine)
  287
purge 198
purify 202
purple 232
purpose 164
purposely 206
purse 94
pursue 281
push 149
put 236
put aside 157
put in order 159
put on 145 218
puzzle 268
python 257
quantity 288
quarrel 87 204
queen 87
question mark 93
quick 159 213 280
quick steps 307

quicksilver 188
quiet 113 300 314
rabbit 70
race 274
ragged 261
rail 278
railing 181
rain 298
rainbow 255
raise 79 145 151 295
  305
raise animals 212
raise children 241
ramble 283
rampart 100
range 118
rank 89 289
rape 106
rare 103 121 236
rash 213
rat 315
rather 113 278
ration 75
ravine 270
raw 211
reach 75 116 128 174
  245 265 283
read 269 294
ready 67 302
real 218
reason 94 159 209 212
rebel 85 281
receive 85 103 144
  151 159 231 281 302
receive benefit 189
recently 76
reciprocal 217
recite 266
recognize 265
record 231 266 290
recover 130 137
recovered 214
red 54 170 231 275
reeds 249
refine 202
refined 108 128 297
reflect 139
refrain from speaking
  93
refreshed 204
refuse 83 88 145 194
region 97 99 119
register 149 215 229
  263 269
regret 134 136 140
  182

regulate 75 156
regualtion 62
reiterate 86
reject 306
related to 141
relation 63
relationship 234
relatives 218 262
relax 127
release 159 262 288
religion 159
rely on 59 63 65 139
  253 274 300
remain 212 282
remainder 305
remaining 77
remark 264
remarkable 103
remedy 189
remember 139 263 266
  290
remit 195
remote 283 284
remove 153 154 223
rent 223
repair 259
repay 287
repent 134 140
replace 168
reply 226 261
report 98
represent 59
repress 100
reptile 257
reputation 240 269
request 187
require 261 299
rescue 152 159
research 220
resemble 68 129
resentment 132 133
residence 111 116
  124 246
resign 280
resist 144 145
respect 59 62 119 134
  135 144 160 182 219
respectful 268
rest 60 113 133 182
restaurant 305
restrain 144 171
results 172
retain 77
retreat 281
return 94 163 184
  280 282 285

reverential 240
reverse 238
revolt 85 300
reward 273
rhyme 301
ribs 154 242
rice 305
rice dumpling 230
rice gruel 230
rich 113
rich earth 100
riddle 268
ride 153 307
ridge 119
ridge of hill 118
ridicule 151 268 269
right side 86
righteousness 237
ring 210
rinse 188 197
ripe 202
rise 81 164 275 295
rise in air 188
risk 72
river 187 189
road 276 282 283
roar 88 90
roast 200 202
roast in pan 309
rob 78 150 153 157
robber 81 113 216
robe 259
rock 219
roll 83 279
roll about 197
roll around 163
roll between hands
    152
roll of map 122
roll of pictures 122
roll up 150
roof 252
room 112 116 126 142
roost 177
root 170 175
rope 231
rose 209 210
rotate 278
rotten 170 173 203
    243
rough 229
round 95 303
rouse 314
row a boat 75
rub 146 147 152 157
    221

rub on 153
rubber 244
rudder 247
rug 186
rugged 119
ruin 159 184 185
ruined 100 125
rule 76 122 126 129
    232 261
ruler 88 116 209 215
run 103 275 276
rush against 258
rush at 188
rush in 294
rust 290
sable 271
sacrifice 206 222
sad 73 134 135 137
    138 309
sail 121 228 246 307
salary 253
saliva 192
salt 287 312
salted beans 270
salty 312
salute 152
sand 188
sandalwood 181
satisfied 305
satrize 269
sauce 287
sauce pan 291
saucer 220
save 69 159 217 252
    273
saw 290
say 56 168 265 267
    283
scales of fish 311
scar 214
scare 133
scatter 160 190
scene in play 315
scenery 166
scheme 267
scholar 58 68 128
school 99 174
scissors 77
scold 94 162 236
scorched 201
scrape 75
scratch 143 153
screen 117 122 228
screen off 296
scythe 292

sea 191
seagull 312
seal 83 114 145 225
search 115 150 224
search for 152
season 110 165
seat 61 124 176
secluded 68
second 57
second of time 223
secret 81 112 166 221
secrete 191
secretly 225
section 225 285
secure 105 111 300
sedan chair 279
see 217 261 262
seed 109 174 223
seek 131 144
seize 103 143 145 153
seize by force 61
select 146 148
self 245
selfish 222
sell 91 190 272 273
    309
sell wholesale 143
semen 230
send 112 120 148 281
send out 215
senior 60 110
sentence 85
separate 296 298
series 124 128 226
serious 250
serpent 255
servant 53 67 102 129
serve 62 129
service 124
set on fire 201
set time 116 169
set up 126 263
setting moon 169
settle 198 262
settled 314
seven 53
sever 162
several 123 160
severe 94 118 131
sex 132
shad 310
shade 252 295
shadow 129
shake 144 151 152
    156 299
shake off 146

shallow 193
shame 239
shameful 287
shape 128
shark 310
sharp edge of weapon 290
shave 76
she 60 104 129
shed skin 256
sheep 236
sheet 127 301
shell 185 271
shelter 117 252
shift 130 147 223
shine 165
shine on 238
ship 246 247
shirt 258
shiver 303
shivering 73
shoes 117 300
shoot 114 248
shoots 249
shop 124 290
shore 118 193 198
short 219
should 111 139 265
shoulders 241
shout 86 92 94 254
show 129 163 258
show movie 165
shrimp 256
shrink 234
shut 293
shutter 225
shuttle 175
sickle 292
sickness 133 213
side 162 285
side by side 54
side room 125
sift 192
sigh 92 93 183 236
sight 262
sign 92 205 228
signal 179
silent 92 113 314
silk 121 232 233
silkworm 257
sill 174
silly 68 88
silver 289
similar 61
simple 181 228 231

simply 67 85
since 245
sincere 132 218 228 254 265 266
sincerely 140
sing 91 182 264
single 91 109 208 297
sink 99 188
sip 89
sister 105 106
sister-in-law 105
sit 96
situation 166
six 71
skeleton 308
sketch 151 224
skill 143 242 253
skillful 91 120
skin 216 244
skip 277
skirt 259
sky 102
slander 264 267
slanting 161 183
slap 154
slaughter 77 117
slave 104
slave girl 107
sleep 217 218
sleeves 259
slice 74 205
slight 131
slip of bamboo 229
slippery 195
slope 96 118
slow 130 138 140
slowly 234
sluggish 136 140
small 115 131 232 297
small child 110
small clam 255
small town 170
smear 98
smell 89 92 239
smelt 202
smile 226
smoke 200
smooth 96
smoothly 302
smother 224
snail 256
snake 255
snatch 153
sneaky 74 207 208
snore 315
snow 298

soak 196
soap
soar 237
soicety 221
socks 261
sofa 124
soft 172 233 278 308
soft leather 301
soil 100 190
soldier 60 71 78 82 100 141 290
solemn 106 240 253
solid 113 220
some 123
somewhat 302
son 58 70 109
son-in-law 101 108
song 168 182
soon 114 163
soothe 138 155
sorrow 90 138
sorrowful 135 137
sort 185 279
soul 299 309 310
sound 77 240 301
soup 194 237
sour 287
source 195
south 82
space 224 293
spade 76
speak 168 262 265 268
spear 178 219
special 114 206
specious 160
speech 88 262
speed 282
spend 211 239 272
sphere 209
spicy hot 279
spider 255
spill water 197
spin 157
spin cloth 231
spirit 221 230 299 309 310
spirit of dead 309
spit 87
spleen 243
splendid 129 279
split 77 259
spoon 80
spot 165
spread 61 67 117 155 158

- 332 -

spread out 145 236
spring 165 189
sprinkle 190 199
sprout 248
sprouts 227 249
spy 225 267
square 162
squash 210
squeeze 103 151 153
  157
squirrel 315
squirt 114
stab 76
stable 105
stage 86 181
stain 189 196
stairs 176 296
stake 179
stall 158
stamp 83
stand 59 124 175 225
standard 195
star 165
start 77 275
startled 137 307
starving 305
state 119 281 285 295
state freely 144
statement 280
statesman 245
station 225
stay 96 193 306
stay at 112 177
steal 66 216 225
steam 200 252
steel 291
steep 118 119
stem 172
stem of flower 176
stem of plant 250
step 231 277
stern 118
stew 203
stick 171 176 177
  226 272
sticky 314
still 56 58 115 128
  201 285
sting 76 86
stir 158
stir up 104 155
stockings 261
stomach 242
stone 219
stool 73 181

stoop 116
stop 61 66 120 146
  158 170 182 183 224
store 69 124 176 253
store up 224 273
storehouse 124
stork 312
stove 199 203
straight 124 217
straight up 225
straighten 148
straightforward 130
  239
strain 199
strange 133 236
strap up 147
straw 250
stream 119 191 195
street 96 258
street song 268
strength 78
strengthen 300
stretch 61 127 157
strict 84 94
strike 150 152 153
  155 157 171 177
  185 262
string 54 235
string of instrument
  127
strip 77 175
striped 161
stripes 231
strive 78 226
strokes 213
stroll 277 282
strong 66 95 97 101
  127 219
struggle 204 309
stubborn 95 136 171
studies 223
study 64 110 220 269
stumble 276
stupid 68 226 257
style 106 180 182 308
subject 303
subject to 117
subordinates 297
subscribe 148
substance 206 274
substitute 151 168
subtract 194
suburbs 285
subway 296
succeed 141

such 162
sudden 167
suddenly 55 78 132
  224 307
suffer 134 148
sufficient 160
sugar 230
suitable 111 284
sum up 179
summarize 212
summer 101 166
sun 163 295
Sung dynasty 111
sunrise 164
sunset 101
superficial 198 244
superintendant 86
superior 270
supervise 216 218
supper 305
supply 62
support 144 147 155
  156 158 173 274
support with hand 143
suppose 65
surely 131
surname 106
surpass 275
surpassing 296
surplus 305
surprise 91 135
surprised 263
surrender 295
surround 89 95 210
suspect 213
suspicion 136
swallow 88 203
swear 216 266
sweat 187
sweep 128 149
sweet 211
sweet potato 253
swell 243
swim 194
swindle 146
swing 157
swollen 244
sword 74 77
sympathize 134 139
system 230
table 73 122 174 175
  181
tael 70
tail 116
taint 173
take 85 114

uncle 60 85 245
unclothed 260
uncooked rice 229
uncover 152
undecided 207
understand 139 164
  167
undress 243
uneven 119
unguided 189
uniform 101
unite 240 286
universe 111
unload 83
unmixed 231
unreal 123 254
unreasonable 181 257
unskillful 146
until 245 280
up 53
up to 280
upon 277
upright 148
upset 303
urge 63 67 160
urgent 132 233
urine 116
use 211
utensil 216
vague 194 249
valley 270
valuable 272
value 68
vapor 186 299
various 124
vast 111 191 192 194
  249
vegetables 251 252
vegeterian 315
vehicle 278
venture 160
verify 307
vertical 234 270
very 102 104 109 129
  168 178 211 302
very few 113
vessel 216 235 247
vexed 135
vicious 285
victory 73
view with contempt
  253
vigorous 104
vile 286 294
village 286
vinegar 287

vines 252 253
violate 206
violent 167 207
virtue 131
virtuous 193 247 271
viscera 243
viscous 301
visit 150 217 261 264
visitor 112 273
voice 92
volume 170
volume of book 71 83
voluntary 211
vomit 87 93
vulgar 294
wade 191
waist 243
wait 62 64 65 103
  129 226
wake up 287
walk 117 258
walk aimlessly 130
walk by side 131
walk on tiptoes 277
walk with difficulty
  276
wall 97 100 205
want 136 182 261
war 141
war prisoner 64
warehouse 64 176
warm 167 193
warm-hearted 138
warn 269
wash 192 198
wasp 255
waste 96 239 272
wasteful 103
wasteland 100
watch 225 291
water 187 188
water lily 250 252
waterfall 198
wave 151
waves 189 191
wax 257
ways 189
we 88
weak 127 140 253
wealth 122 271 273
wealthy 113 260
weapons 141 176
wear 142 218 224
weave 235
web 233
wedding 107

week 282
weep 90 190
weight in hand 149
weighty 288
welcome 281
well 57
west 261
wet 192 198
wet thoroughly 196
whale 310
wharf 98 220
what 61 313
wheat 313
wheel 278
when 213
whenever 282
whereas 163
which 61 110
whip 156 300
whip a horse 227
whirlpool 194
whiskers 309
white 215
who 110 266 285
whole 232
whom 266
why 133 211
wicked 104
wide 111 113 294
widow 109
widower 311
widowhood 113
wife 105 106 107 108
wife of elder brother
  108
wife of father's
  brother 109
wife's parents 118
wild 249 297
wilderness 288
will 132
willing 86 303
willow 173 178
win 79 151
wind 304
window 225
windy and rainy 73
wine 286
wings 237 238
winter 72
wipe 146 147
wipe off 146
wisdom 139 166
wise 90 240
wish 182
wish for 303

witch 120
with 162 245 303
withdraw 154 281
wither 73 251
within 70
without 101
without value 274
wizard 120
wolf 207
woman 104 107 110
womb 242
wonderful 104
wood 170
wooden bow 127
wooden cylinder 175
wooden shoes 117
woods 172

words 262 265
wordy 72
work 120
work at 159
work hard 79
work-shop 125
workman 80
worm 257
worry 138
worship 144
worth 65
wound 67
wrap 80 260
wring 231
wrist 243
write 62 114 168 251
yard 95 98 220

year 123 278
years 183
yeast 287
yellow 313
yes 165
yesterday 165
yet 115 238
yield 269
you 60 61 134 187
    204
young 110 115 127
    228 298 299
young gentleman 285
your 59 187 204
zeal 140
zealous 202
zero 298